THE PROBLEMS AND PROMISE OF COMMERCIAL SOCIETY

D1714709

The Problems and Promise of Commercial Society

Adam Smith's Response to Rousseau

Dennis C. Rasmussen

THE PENNSYLVANIA STATE UNIVERSITY PRESS

UNIVERSITY PARK, PENNSYLVANIA

Library of Congress Cataloging-in-Publication Data

Rasmussen, Dennis Carl, 1978–
The problems and promise of commercial
society : Adam Smith's response to
Rousseau / Dennis C. Rasmussen.
p.   cm.
Includes bibliographical references and index.
ISBN-13: 978-0-271-03349-5 (pbk : alk. paper)
1. Smith, Adam, 1723–1790.
2. Rousseau, Jean-Jacques, 1712–1778.
3. Capitalism.
I. Title.

HB103.S6R38 2008
330.15′3—dc22
2007034911

Copyright © 2008
The Pennsylvania State University
All rights reserved
Printed in the United States of America
Published by The Pennsylvania State University
Press,
University Park, PA 16802-1003

The Pennsylvania State University Press is a member
of the Association of American University Presses.

It is the policy of The Pennsylvania State University
Press to use acid-free paper. This book is printed on
paper that meets the minimum requirements of
American National Standard for Information
Sciences—Permanence of Paper for Printed Library
Material, ANSI Z39.48–1992.

CONTENTS

ACKNOWLEDGMENTS

The joys of finishing a first book are many, but chief among them, for me, is the opportunity it presents to express my gratitude to those who have supported me along the way. Given that this book grew out of my dissertation, I must begin by thanking my teachers, who showed me through their example what it means to be a devoted teacher and scholar. During my time as an undergraduate at Michigan State's James Madison College, Louis Hunt, David Leibowitz, Folke Lindahl, Arthur Melzer, and particularly Richard Zinman taught me both to take political theory seriously and to appreciate its charms. At Duke, I benefited from continual insight and encouragement from my dissertation committee, including Neil De Marchi, Michael Gillespie, Tom Spragens, and above all my adviser, Ruth Grant. I have also benefited greatly, both during that time and since, from the advice, conversation, and friendship of my fellow graduate students, especially Bill Curtis and Ari Kohen. My colleagues during two years in a visiting position at Bowdoin College, Gerry DiGiusto and Paul Franco, have been a constant source of support and guidance as well.

For valuable comments on the manuscript, either in whole or in part, I would especially like to thank Bill Curtis, Sam Fleischacker, Michael Gillespie, Ruth Grant, Charles Griswold, Ari Kohen, and John Scott. Several parts of the book were presented as papers at various conferences; I am grateful to Ryan Hanley, Ted Harpham, Sharon Krause, Iain McLean, Tom Merrill, Jerry Muller, Patricia Nordeen, and Joseph Reisert for their helpful observations on these papers. Portions of Chapters 2 and 4 have appeared previously as "Rousseau's 'Philosophical Chemistry' and the Foundations of Adam Smith's Thought," *History of Political Thought* 27, no. 4 (2006): 620–41; and "Does 'Bettering Our Condition' Really Make Us Better Off? Adam Smith on Progress and Happiness," *American Political Science Review* 100, no. 3 (2006): 309–18. I thank these journals for permission to reprint these materials.

Finally, it is not only out of custom that I say that my greatest debt is the one I owe to my family and friends. I could not hope to describe or repay the unstinting love and support that my parents, Richard and Jeanette Rasmussen, have given me over the years; this book is, of course, dedicated to them. I am also indebted to my friends for their encouragement, good humor, and much else besides; I would like to make special mention of Ian Boyko and Dan Eschtruth, whose friendships have been lifelong sources of fun, companionship, and intellectual stimulation. I met my fiancée, Emily Wiemers, fairly late in the writing of this book, but not too late to confirm that Smith was onto something in supposing that "the chief part of human happiness arises from the consciousness of being beloved" (*TMS* I.ii.5.1, 41).

ABBREVIATIONS

When referring to works by Adam Smith and Jean-Jacques Rousseau, I have used the abbreviations and editions listed below. All translations from French texts are my own. Where appropriate, I have included references to volume, book, part, chapter, and/or paragraph numbers in addition to the page number.

WORKS OF ADAM SMITH

Astronomy	"The History of Astronomy." In *Essays on Philosophical Subjects*. Edited by W. P. D. Wightman and J. C. Bryce. Indianapolis: Liberty Fund, 1982.
CAS	*Correspondence of Adam Smith*. Edited by E. C. Mossner and I. S. Ross. Indianapolis: Liberty Fund, 1987.
ED	"Early Draft" of Part of the *Wealth of Nations*. In *Lectures on Jurisprudence*. Edited by R. L. Meek, D. D. Raphael, and P. G. Stein. Indianapolis: Liberty Fund, 1982.
EPS	*Essays on Philosophical Subjects*. Edited by W. P. D. Wightman and J. C. Bryce. Indianapolis: Liberty Fund, 1982.
Letter	"A Letter to the Authors of the *Edinburgh Review*." In *Essays on Philosophical Subjects*. Edited by W. P. D. Wightman and J. C. Bryce. Indianapolis: Liberty Fund, 1982.
LJ	*Lectures on Jurisprudence*. Edited by R. L. Meek, D. D. Raphael, and P. G. Stein. Indianapolis: Liberty Fund, 1982.
LRBL	*Lectures on Rhetoric and Belles Lettres*. Edited by J. C. Bryce. Indianapolis: Liberty Fund, 1985.
TMS	*The Theory of Moral Sentiments*. Edited by A. L. Macfie and D. D. Raphael. Indianapolis: Liberty Fund, 1982.
WN	*An Inquiry into the Nature and Causes of the Wealth of Nations*. Edited by R. H. Campbell and A. S. Skinner. Two volumes. Indianapolis: Liberty Fund, 1981.

WORKS OF JEAN-JACQUES ROUSSEAU

d'Alembert *Letter to M. d'Alembert on the Theater.* Translated by Allan Bloom. In *Collected Writings of Rousseau,* volume 10. Hanover: University Press of New England, 2004.

CJJR *Correspondance complete de Jean-Jacques Rousseau.* Edited by R. A. Leigh. Fifty-two volumes. Geneva, Banbury, Oxford: The Voltaire Foundation, 1965–98.

Confessions *The Confessions of Jean-Jacques Rousseau.* Translated by Christopher Kelly. In *Collected Writings of Rousseau,* volume 5. Hanover: University Press of New England, 1995.

Corsica *Plan for a Constitution for Corsica.* Translated by Christopher Kelly. In *Collected Writings of Rousseau,* volume 11. Hanover: University Press of New England, 2005.

CW *Collected Writings of Rousseau.* Edited by Roger D. Masters and Christopher Kelly. Eleven volumes to date. Hanover: University Press of New England, 1990–.

Dialogues *Rousseau, Judge of Jean-Jacques: Dialogues.* Translated by Judith R. Bush, Christopher Kelley, and Roger D. Masters. In *Collected Writings of Rousseau,* volume 1. Hanover: University Press of New England, 1990.

Emile *Emile, or On Education.* Translated by Allan Bloom. New York: Basic Books, 1979.

FD *Discourse on the Sciences and Arts (First Discourse).* Translated by Judith R. Bush, Roger D. Masters, and Christopher Kelly. In *Collected Writings of Rousseau,* volume 2. Hanover: University Press of New England, 1992.

Final Reply *Final Reply.* Translated by Judith R. Bush. In *Collected Writings of Rousseau,* volume 2. Hanover: University Press of New England, 1992.

Fragments *Political Fragments.* Translated by Judith R. Bush, Roger D. Masters, and Christopher Kelly. In *Collected Writings of Rousseau,* volume 4. Hanover: University Press of New England, 1994.

GM *Geneva Manuscript.* Translated by Judith R. Bush, Roger D. Masters, and Christopher Kelly. In *Collected Writings of Rousseau,* volume 4. Hanover: University Press of New England, 1994.

Julie	*Julie, or the New Heloise.* Translated by Philip Stewart and Jean Vaché. In *Collected Writings of Rousseau,* volume 6. Hanover: University Press of New England, 1997.
Languages	*Essay on the Origin of Languages.* Translated by John T. Scott. In *Collected Writings of Rousseau,* volume 5. Hanover: University Press of New England, 1998.
Mountain	*Letters Written from the Mountain.* Translated by Judith R. Bush and Christopher Kelly. In *Collected Writings of Rousseau,* volume 9. Hanover: University Press of New England, 2001.
Narcissus	*Preface to Narcissus: Or the Lover of Himself.* Translated by Christopher Kelly. In *Collected Writings of Rousseau,* volume 2. Hanover: University Press of New England, 1992.
OC	*Oeuvres complètes.* Edited by Bernard Gagnebin and Marcel Raymond. Five volumes. Paris: Gallimard, Bibliothèque de la Pléiade, 1959–95.
PE	*Discourse on Political Economy.* Translated by Judith R. Bush, Roger D. Masters, Christopher Kelly, and Terence Marshall. In *Collected Writings of Rousseau,* volume 3. Hanover: University Press of New England, 1992.
Poland	*Considerations on the Government of Poland and Its Planned Reformation.* Translated by Christopher Kelly. In *Collected Writings of Rousseau,* volume 11. Hanover: University Press of New England, 2005.
Reveries	*The Reveries of a Solitary Walker.* Translated by Charles E. Butterworth. In *Collected Writings of Rousseau,* volume 8. Hanover: University Press of New England, 2000.
SC	*On the Social Contract.* Translated by Judith R. Bush, Roger D. Masters, and Christopher Kelly. In *Collected Writings of Rousseau,* volume 4. Hanover: University Press of New England, 1994.
SD	*Discourse on the Origins and Foundations of Inequality in Men (Second Discourse).* Translated by Judith R. Bush, Roger D. Masters, Christopher Kelly, and Terence Marshall. In *Collected Writings of Rousseau,* volume 3. Hanover: University Press of New England, 1992.

INTRODUCTION

Liberal democracy and market capitalism would seem to be the great success stories of our age—indeed, of any age. While troubling levels of deprivation and oppression still blot large regions of the globe, people living in today's liberal capitalist societies enjoy unprecedented levels of prosperity as well as a greater degree of civil, political, and economic freedom than has been attained by any other society in history.[1] Those who belong to these societies live longer and healthier lives, achieve higher levels of education, and enjoy more leisure time than almost anyone would have thought possible even a relatively short time ago.[2] And in large part because of the spread of liberal capitalism, the number of armed conflicts worldwide and the numbers of people who die as a result of those conflicts have been—against almost all expectations—in steady decline.[3] Moreover, these advances have contributed to a historically unrivaled degree of global consensus on the broadest political and economic questions: throughout the West and much of the non-Western world, there are virtually no serious alternatives to liberal democracy or to market capitalism of one stripe or another. In practice, of course, many Western nations and *most* nations outside the West fall short of fully embodying the ideals of liberal democracy and market capitalism. Yet in the wake of the discrediting of fascism after World War II and of communism after the events of 1989 to 1991, there seems to be little serious competition regarding the ideals themselves; indeed, these ideals are so dominant that one prominent scholar has famously asserted that we live at the end of history.[4]

1. On civil rights and political liberties, see Freedom House's *Freedom in the World 2006*, available online at www.freedomhouse.org (see references for a fuller citation); on economic freedom, see Gwartney and Lawson, *Economic Freedom of the World*.

2. On increases in life span and educational levels and decreases in disease and sickness, see United Nations Development Programme, *Human Development Report 2005*; on increases in leisure time, see Robinson and Godbey, *Time for Life*.

3. See Marshall and Gurr, *Peace and Conflict 2005*; Mueller, *The Remnants of War*; and Mueller, *Retreat from Doomsday*.

4. This is of course the argument of Fukuyama, *The End of History and the Last Man*. For

Yet triumphalist statements of this sort are bound to ring hollow for many readers. All but the most ardent supporters of today's liberal capitalist societies judge them to be at best a mixed blessing, and a great many people on both sides of the political spectrum offer considerably harsher assessments. Numerous antiglobalizationists, environmentalists, socialists, poststructuralists, and multiculturalists, as well as communitarians, nationalists, virtue ethicists, cultural declinists, and religious fundamentalists of all denominations—taken together, perhaps most of today's Western intellectuals—commonly blame liberal capitalism for exploiting the developing world, creating gross inequalities, harming the environment, promoting atomistic individualism, spreading conformity, and/or making people materialistic, selfish, immoral, and shallow. Of course, few of these thinkers or groups have an alternative vision for the world that is both truly different *and* truly realistic, but it is precisely the lack of alternative visions that makes these criticisms so important and pressing. The debate over the virtues and vices of liberal capitalism is, then, one of the broadest debates of our time; it shapes not only how we understand our world but also how we seek to improve it and how we approach the problems of the developing world. A uniquely valuable approach to shedding light on this debate, I believe, is to return to the thought of one of commercial society's first and greatest defenders, Adam Smith, and one of its first and greatest critics, Jean-Jacques Rousseau.

Before turning to Smith and Rousseau, however, a word on terminology is in order. Throughout this book I will be using the term "commercial society" rather than the currently more familiar "liberalism" or "capitalism." These latter two were not widely used until the nineteenth century and so are anachronistic when applied to the eighteenth-century world of Smith and Rousseau; they are also laden with unfortunate associations in a way that "commercial society" is not. Early in *The Wealth of Nations*, Smith explains what he means by this term:

Fukuyama's most recent reflections on these issues, see the new afterword in the second paperback edition of this work. Fukuyama has often been accused of prematurely proclaiming victory for liberal capitalism, especially in light of the persistence of Islamic fundamentalism in some parts of the world, but there does seem to be a degree of truth to his argument that even Islamic fundamentalism does not pose a serious intellectual challenge to liberal capitalism, given that (unlike communism and even fascism at times in the twentieth century) it holds very little appeal to most people in today's liberal capitalist societies and therefore seems extraordinarily unlikely to prevail in any ultimate sense.

> When the division of labor has been once thoroughly established, it is but a small part of a man's wants which the produce of his own labour can supply. He supplies the far greater part of them by exchanging that surplus part of the produce of his own labour, which is over and above his own consumption, for such parts of the produce of other's men's labour as he has occasion for. Every man thus lives by exchanging, or becomes in some measure a merchant, and the society itself grows to be what is properly a commercial society. (*WN* I.iv.1, 37)

Building on Smith's description here, we can say that a commercial society is one in which we find an extensive division of labor and hence a high degree of interdependence, the protection of property rights and the rule of law, and a good deal of social, economic, geographic, and occupational mobility. Smith contrasted this kind of society with less developed societies ranging from hunter-gatherer peoples to feudal European states, and today we can also contrast it with societies that have relatively developed but authoritarian or planned economies, such as the fascist and communist nations of the twentieth century. This is not to say that these other forms of society have no commerce—some form of exchange is likely inherent in all human societies—but rather that commerce in these societies is constrained by tradition or command, resulting in less mobility, less interdependence, and often a less extensive division of labor than is found in commercial societies in the sense that we will be using the term. No sharp line divides commercial societies from other forms of society, but the nations that today conform most closely to the loose definition just offered are the member states of the European Union, the United States, Canada, Australia, New Zealand, and Japan, with many others around the world now developing quickly in this direction. This type of society began to develop in the seventeenth and eighteenth centuries, first in Britain and the Netherlands and soon afterwards in other parts of Western Europe and North America.

Smith and Rousseau were two of the most thoughtful and most renowned observers of the emerging commercial societies of the eighteenth century, and their attitudes toward these societies differed dramatically. Rousseau (1712–78) was almost certainly the most famous critic of the European world of his time. Born in the Calvinist republic of Geneva, he left his native city at the age of fifteen and, after a series of youthful escapades in Savoy (famously recounted in his *Confessions*), arrived in Paris in 1742. He lived in and around this city for most of the next twenty years during the heady days of the Enlightenment, a time when intellectuals from all over the Western world were gathering in the Parisian literary salons and the *philosophes* were beginning to mount their fierce attack on the throne and altar of the *ancien régime*. Rousseau attacked the attackers, taking on the "enlightened" principles and ideals of the *philosophes* in his first major work, the *Discourse on the Sciences and Arts,* which took the European world by storm when it was published in 1751 and made Rousseau a philosophical celebrity to an extent almost unimaginable today. (Diderot's report on its reception gushed, "It is succeeding beyond the skies; there is no precedent for such a success" [*Confessions* VIII, 304].) After an even more blistering attack on their principles and ideals in the *Discourse on Inequality* (1755), Rousseau began to clash with a number of his erstwhile friends and colleagues, and he eventually became an exceptionally bitter adversary of many of the *philosophes* (most famously Voltaire). He ran afoul of the censors as a result of the heterodox religious ideas in *Emile* and *The Social Contract* (both published in 1762) and was forced to flee France, first to Neuchâtel and later, with the help of David Hume, to England. After nearly seventeen months in London and the English countryside, Rousseau's paranoia led to a much-publicized break with Hume. He returned to France, where he spent most of the rest of his life in relative seclusion with his longtime mistress and eventual wife, Thérèse Levasseur. He died suddenly in 1778 while working on his autobiographical *The Reveries of a Solitary Walker*.[5]

In sharp contrast to the famed "citizen of Geneva," Adam Smith (1723–90) was celebrated as perhaps the greatest proponent of Europe's emerging commercial order. He, too, lived in an "enlightened" society; Scotland had long been largely dismissed in European literary circles as a relative backwater, but by the late eighteenth century the thinkers of Edinburgh, Glasgow, and Aberdeen were every bit the equals of their French counterparts. Indeed, no less an authority on the matter than Voltaire acknowledged that "it is to Scotland that we look for our idea of civilization."[6] Smith was (and still is) generally regarded as one of the two leading figures of the Scottish Enlightenment, along with Hume, his closest and lifelong friend. Smith was born in the small port town of Kirkcaldy, and unlike Rousseau

5. The authoritative biography of Rousseau is Maurice Cranston's three-volume study. See Cranston, *Jean-Jacques; The Noble Savage;* and *The Solitary Self.*
6. Quoted in Herman, *How the Scots Invented the Modern World,* 120.

he received a first-rate formal education. He studied at the University of Glasgow under the eminent moral philosopher Francis Hutcheson, and then went on to spend six years at Oxford, where he found his teachers rather uninspiring and spent much of his time in self-instruction. After delivering a series of public lectures in Edinburgh, he obtained a position teaching logic at the University of Glasgow in 1751. A year later he was appointed Chair of Moral Philosophy (taking over Hutcheson's old position). Smith's first book, *The Theory of Moral Sentiments* (1759), was enthusiastically received throughout Europe. In 1763, as a result of his newfound prominence, he was offered a generous salary and lifelong pension to leave Glasgow and become the tutor of the young Duke of Buccleuch. The pair spent two-and-a-half years traveling on the Continent, where Smith met a number of prominent *philosophes* and *économistes* in Paris and Geneva. Upon their return to Britain in 1766, Smith, a lifelong bachelor, went to Kirkcaldy to stay with his elderly mother. He had been working intermittently on the material that was to become *The Wealth of Nations* at least since the early 1760s, and he began to delve into it in earnest there. He moved to London in 1773 and added to his already considerable reputation when *The Wealth of Nations* (1776) was finally published and became a resounding success. Soon afterward he was appointed Commissioner of Customs for Scotland, a job that he held during the last decade of his life, in Edinburgh.[7]

Rousseau's critique of commercial society was one of the earliest philosophic critiques of this kind of society, and even today it remains among the most comprehensive such critiques ever offered. Indeed, we will see that most of the serious arguments made today against commercial society were anticipated to some degree by Rousseau. Thus, in many ways Rousseau presents the greatest challenge to commercial society; anyone who hopes to make a persuasive defense of this kind of society will have to take all of the many different aspects of Rousseau's critique into account. And Smith, we will see, attempted to do precisely that. Smith's writings contain not only one of the earliest philosophic defenses of commercial society but also—I would venture to say—the *first* defense that takes Rousseau's critique into account and that attempts to respond to its concerns. Many of today's proponents of commercial society tend to ignore or dismiss critics of this kind

---

7. The authoritative modern biography of Smith is Ross, *The Life of Adam Smith.* Other important accounts of Smith's life include Dugald Stewart's "Account of the Life and Writings of Adam Smith, LL.D." (1793), which is reprinted in *EPS;* and John Rae, *Life of Adam Smith* (1895).

of society; by contrast, Smith took the most serious critic of his day extremely seriously and was himself deeply concerned about many of the problems that Rousseau identified.

While Smith and Rousseau never corresponded and probably never met each other, they did have a number of mutual acquaintances among Europe's "republic of letters," including Hume and several of the *philosophes,* so Smith was unquestionably well aware of Rousseau's immense intellectual influence. Smith never explicitly mentions Rousseau in either of his major works, but he does directly discuss him in a number of shorter writings and letters. In fact, one of Smith's earliest published writings, a letter to the editors of the *Edinburgh Review* (1756), includes a substantial review of Rousseau's *Discourse on Inequality.* In this review, Smith translates three lengthy passages from the *Discourse* that point to some of Rousseau's most profound critiques of commercial society. As we will see, Smith continued to grapple with Rousseau's arguments later in life, and *The Theory of Moral Sentiments* and *The Wealth of Nations* contain his answers to the tremendous challenges that Rousseau posed for him. I do not mean to claim that Smith's books were written *primarily* as a response to Rousseau or that Rousseau was the thinker who had the greatest impact on Smith—that title undoubtedly belongs to Hume, with Hutcheson and the Stoics as probable runners-up—but I will be arguing that Rousseau's critique of commercial society presented Smith with a challenge that shaped the development of his thought in a decisive way.[8]

A deeper, more thoughtful Smith emerges when he is seen in the light of the challenge posed by Rousseau. Other scholars have recognized, of course, that Smith was not the crude champion of laissez-faire capitalism

---

8. The historical and intellectual relationship between Smith and Rousseau will be treated in much greater detail in Chapter 2, as will Smith's review of the *Discourse on Inequality.* Given that Smith reviewed Rousseau's *Discourse* and that there are so many interesting parallels and contrasts between these two philosophers, surprisingly few scholars have addressed their relationship or systematically compared their arguments; there is at present no book-length work on Smith and Rousseau, and there are only a handful of articles and book chapters. The most insightful of these shorter works include Berry, "Adam Smith: Commerce, Liberty and Modernity," in *Philosophy of the Enlightenment;* Hanley, "Commerce and Corruption: Rousseau's Diagnosis and Adam Smith's Cure"; and Ignatieff, "Smith, Rousseau, and the Republic of Needs," in *Scotland and Europe.* I thank Hanley for allowing me to read an earlier version of his forthcoming article. Other works that have given some sustained attention to the Smith–Rousseau connection include Barry, "Hume, Smith and Rousseau on Freedom"; Colletti, "Mandeville, Rousseau and Smith," in *From Rousseau to Lenin;* Force, *Self-Interest Before Adam Smith;* Hanley, "From Geneva to Glasgow"; Hurtado, "Bernard Mandeville's Heir"; Pack, "The Rousseau–Smith Connection"; Schliesser, "Adam Smith's Benevolent and Self-Interested Conception of Philosophy"; West, "Adam Smith and Rousseau's *Discourse on Inequality*"; and Winch, *Riches and Poverty,* chap. 3.

and unbridled acquisitiveness that he is sometimes taken to be—Walter Bagehot noted more than a century ago that "free-trade has become in the popular mind almost as much [Smith's] subject as the war of Troy was Homer's,"[9] but this view of Smith has long been seen as a caricature among Smith scholars, even if it remains the dominant one in "the popular mind." Especially in the outpouring of work on Smith since the bicentenary of *The Wealth of Nations* in 1976, many scholars have painted a much more sub- tle picture of Smith's outlook, one that recognizes that his analysis of com- mercial society is anything but crude or naive.[10] We will see in Chapter 2, however, that even these more subtle accounts of Smith generally do not appreciate the full range and extent of his sympathy for the arguments *against* commercial society. Comparing Smith with Rousseau helps bring out these aspects of his thought, revealing the depth and complexity of his position as a social critic rather than as an apologist for commercial society.

Far from being an unabashed champion of commercial society, Smith actually shared a number of Rousseau's severe misgivings about the type of society that was emerging in their time. For instance, both he and Rousseau acknowledged that commercial society necessarily produces great inequal- ities; that an extensive division of labor can exact an immense cost in human dignity by rendering people feeble and ignorant; that an emphasis on wealth and material goods can encourage moral corruption; and that the desire for wealth often leads people to submit to endless toil and anxiety in the pursuit of frivolous material goods. This is not to say that Smith is as harsh a critic of commercial society as Rousseau, or that he does not ulti- mately defend it. In fact, I think it is even too strong to say that Smith is "ambivalent" about commercial society, as many recent scholars have con- tended. Smith does unreservedly advocate commercial society, but he also accepts—indeed, insists—that many problems are associated with it. Why he advocates commercial society despite these problems is, I believe, the central puzzle of his thought.

For many decades, Smith scholars concentrated on a different puzzle in Smith's thought, a puzzle that became known as the "Adam Smith Prob- lem." This problem was formulated in the nineteenth century by a num- ber of German scholars who argued that Smith's emphasis on sympathy

9. Bagehot, "Adam Smith as a Person," 303.
10. For only a few of the best recent examples, see Fleischacker, *On Adam Smith's Wealth of Nations*; Griswold, *Adam Smith and the Virtues of Enlightenment*; Muller, *Adam Smith in His Time and Ours*; Otteson, *Adam Smith's Marketplace of Life*; and Rothschild, *Economic Sentiments*.

in *The Theory of Moral Sentiments* was irreconcilable with the emphasis on self-interest in *The Wealth of Nations*.[11] This apparent contradiction was the central focus of Smith scholarship for many decades. Contemporary scholars, though, have generally rejected this problem (at least in its original formulation), and for good reason: it is based on the mistaken view that "sympathy" for Smith means benevolence and that "self-interest" means selfishness.[12] There are certainly differences in emphasis between Smith's two major works—as might be expected, since they deal with different subjects (moral philosophy and political economy)—but in the end I concur with the majority of recent scholars, who believe there is no fundamental contradiction between the two. Yet there *are* numerous tensions in Smith's writings—witness here his agreement with many aspects of Rousseau's critique of commercial society even though he defends this kind of society. Smith's defense of commercial society and his acknowledgment of the ills associated with it are not simply split between *The Wealth of Nations* and *The Theory of Moral Sentiments*: some of his deepest criticisms, such as his harsh denunciation of the debilitating effects of the division of labor, are found in the former work, and important parts of his defense are found in the latter work. The tensions in his thought are, rather, found in both of his works. These tensions are real, but as we will see, they are not impossible to resolve.

All of that said, the question on which I am focusing—Why does Smith defend commercial society despite his full awareness of its possible drawbacks?—does not immediately present itself as basic to Smith's thought. The main polemical thrust of his writings, after all, is the need to *reform* the commercial society of his day rather than to justify or defend that society. As its full title suggests, *An Inquiry into the Nature and Causes of the Wealth of Nations* was written above all to promote and facilitate "the wealth of nations" or economic growth, and Smith argues that the most effective way to attain this end would be to eliminate the mercantilist policies of the eighteenth century and replace them with free enterprise or "the obvious

11. For a useful summary of the original formulations of this problem, as well as of some of the responses to these formulations by twentieth-century scholars, see Teichgraeber, "Rethinking Das Adam Smith Problem." More recent works that address this "problem" include Montes, *Adam Smith in Context*; and Otteson, *Adam Smith's Marketplace of Life*.

12. The editors of the Glasgow edition of *The Theory of Moral Sentiments* go so far as to say that "the so-called 'Adam Smith problem' was a pseudo-problem based on ignorance and misunderstanding." See the "Introduction" in *TMS*, 20.

and simple system of natural liberty" (*WN* IV.ix.51, 687). Adopting "the wealth of nations" as one's end only makes sense, however, if wealth and growth are ultimately desirable or beneficial. Smith probably did not feel the need to give the justification of these things a prominent place in his writings, since most of his readers would likely have *assumed* that they were desirable, but it is also clear—given his awareness of and sympathy with Rousseau's critique—that he knew that the goodness of wealth and of commercial society itself could not be simply taken for granted, regardless of what most people thought.

Thus, throughout his works Smith offers a number of counterarguments and countermeasures for each element of Rousseau's critique of commercial society. We will examine Smith's responses to Rousseau's critique in detail in Chapters 3 and 4, but let us note at the outset the key line of reasoning running through each of these responses: his argument that commercial society's faults, though real and important, are not as numerous or as great as those of other forms of society. Smith provides a kind of cost–benefit analysis and concludes that, despite its very real problems, commercial society's overall balance sheet remains preferable to those of other societies, for it constitutes a definite improvement over the poverty, insecurity, and dependence that dominated almost all precommercial ages. In other words, commercial society *is* unequivocally preferable, for Smith, even if it is preferable only *on balance*. This defense of commercial society was in some ways in the background of Smith writings, but it is necessary to foreground it if we are to understand the foundations of his thought. And it is through a comparison with Rousseau, I believe, that this underlying basis of Smith's defense of commercial society becomes clearest and that the puzzle in his thought is brought out most starkly.

A study of Smith and Rousseau is also useful because their ideas have proven so influential and enduring. Few have had as profound (or profoundly different) effects on subsequent thought and history as these two thinkers. Smith is often hailed as the founder of economics and of capitalism itself, while Rousseau is frequently credited (or saddled) with inspiring the French Revolution, Romanticism, Idealism, nationalism, and even socialism and totalitarianism. It is difficult to overstate the impact these two thinkers have had (although many scholars have tried). Extravagant statements on this theme are too many to count, so a few representative examples will have to suffice: "After Smith . . . displayed the first true tableau of modern society, all the Western world became the world of Adam Smith: his vision became the prescription for the spectacles of generations" (Robert Heilbroner).[13] "Alfred North Whitehead stated that the history of Western philosophy can be characterized as consisting of a series of footnotes to Plato. It can be said with even greater accuracy that the history of economics over the past two hundred years can be adequately characterized as a series of footnotes to Adam Smith" (Nathan Rosenberg).[14] "The world has not seen more than once or twice in all the course of history . . . a literature which has exercised such prodigious influence over the minds of men, over every cast and shade of intellect, as that which emanated from Rousseau between 1749 and 1762" (Henry Sumner Maine).[15] "There is hardly a respect in which [Rousseau] does not appear to have had his finger on the pulse of modernity, or in which his thought and its seismic impact did not serve to quicken that pulse" (Clifford Orwin and Nathan Tarcov).[16] These may all be overstatements to one degree or another, but the prevalence of such assertions testifies to just how great the impact of Smith and Rousseau has been. Their ideas and arguments have helped form the framework within which present debates about commercial society take place.

As a result of their great intellectual and historical impact, as well as their sheer prescience and depth of insight, the questions Smith and Rousseau addressed remain our own as well, and to an astonishing degree. Given that the origins of many aspects of today's society can be traced back to their era, Emma Rothschild rightly argues that "some of the disputes of the late eighteenth century are important, in the twenty-first century, because they are also our own disputes. They are not disputes which are repeated over time, or which can illuminate our times. They *are* our disputes."[17] The world has, of course, changed enormously since Smith and Rousseau's time: in the eighteenth century, commercial society was based mainly on agriculture and small industry and was found only in one small corner of the world; that same society is now based largely on services, information, and technology and has spread throughout much of the planet. But because the defining features of today's commercial societies—the extensive division of labor, the high degree of interdependence, the prevalence of mobility of all kinds—began to arise around this time, Smith and Rousseau's assessments

13. Heilbroner, *The Worldly Philosophers*, 41.
14. Rosenberg, "Adam Smith and Laissez-Faire Revisited," 19.
15. Maine, *Ancient Law*, 84.
16. Orwin and Tarcov, "Introduction," in *The Legacy of Rousseau*, xiv.
17. Rothschild, *Economic Sentiments*, 47–48.

of commercial society's moral, intellectual, social, and political impacts remain profoundly relevant. Indeed, the fact that commercial societies in the fullest sense were first emerging in their time makes their thought in some ways *more* valuable for us today, because this means they were observing commercial society as something essentially new and groundbreaking and so were in a better position than we are to see what is truly different about it, to see what is at stake in the arguments about it. A study of their writings can remind us of the alternatives to, and presuppositions of, ideas we now take for granted; thus they can help us gain a critical distance from our own situation without requiring that we abandon our own questions and concerns.

For all of these reasons, then, a return to the thought of Smith and Rousseau is timely in an era when commercial society seems to have triumphed—in reality in most of the West and at least in principle in many other parts of the world—but when the questions and problems surrounding this kind of society loom as large as ever. Hence, this book not only provides a much-needed comparison of the thought of Smith and Rousseau and uses this comparison to highlight and resolve the fundamental puzzle of Smith's thought, but also seeks to use their deliberations to clarify and enrich the contemporary debate over the problems and promise of commercial society.

Chapter 1 of this book examines what I claim are Rousseau's three main arguments against commercial society. The first, which I call the "division of laborers" critique, holds that it is not only labor that is divided in commercial society but also the laborers themselves: people living in this kind of society can have little social or personal unity, according to Rousseau, because of the prevalence of great inequalities and because of the weakness and ignorance produced by reliance on commodities and technology. In the second argument, the "empire of opinion" critique, Rousseau contends that in commercial society people are invariably dependent on the opinions of others and that this necessarily produces a great deal of ostentation, deception, and immorality. In his third and final argument against commercial society, the "pursuit of unhappiness" critique, Rousseau posits that the acquisitiveness encouraged by commerce expands people's desires almost beyond measure, thereby ensuring that they spend their entire lives striving and toiling to attain a happiness that will always elude them. These three broad critiques encompass the most significant arguments against commercial society on both sides of the political spectrum, making Rousseau's critique of commercial society one of the most comprehensive ever offered.

The rest of the book examines Smith's response to Rousseau's powerful critique. Chapter 2 argues that Smith in fact showed a surprising degree of sympathy with each element of Rousseau's critique of commercial society. It begins by exploring the historical and intellectual relationship between these two thinkers and then examining Smith's review of Rousseau's *Discourse on Inequality*. Almost half this review is devoted to translations of three lengthy passages from the *Discourse* that (surely not coincidentally, given Smith's intellectual concerns) point to Rousseau's three main critiques of commercial society as discussed in Chapter 1. In the remainder of the chapter I show that Smith was deeply engaged with the problems articulated by Rousseau and that he struggled with them in his later writings: he, too, acknowledged that the division of labor produces great inequalities and can exact an immense cost in human dignity by rendering people feeble and ignorant; that people's great concern about the opinions of others can lead to problems such as ostentation and moral corruption; and that people tend to submit themselves to nearly endless toil and anxiety in the pursuit of "trinkets and baubles," which in the end provide at best only fleeting satisfaction. The fact that Smith agrees with so many aspects of Rousseau's critique of commercial society helps highlight the fundamental puzzle of his thought: Why did he defend commercial society, given his full awareness of the problems associated with it? Several answers to this question are offered in Chapters 3 and 4.

Chapter 3 outlines Smith's response to the "division of laborers" and "empire of opinion" critiques. Smith acknowledges that the division of labor can produce harmful side effects, yet he defends it because it generates astronomical increases in productivity, thereby opening up the possibility of raising the living standards of the poor. The inequalities produced by the division of labor are more than justified, for Smith, not only because *everyone* is materially better off in commercial society than they are in precommercial societies, but also because the worst *effect* of inequality—personal dependence—is significantly diminished by the interdependence of the market. Furthermore, he argues that the deleterious effects of the division of labor on laborers can be ameliorated through a comprehensive system of state-supported education. As for the "empire of opinion" critique, Smith concedes that people tend to be greatly concerned with the opinions of others; unlike Rousseau, however, he contends that this is actually a *good* thing, for this concern can act as the very basis of moral conduct. He maintains that the fact that people see themselves through others' eyes gives rise to social standards of propriety and leads people to (more or less) follow those standards. Smith further argues that commercial society encourages virtues such as reliability, decency, cooperativeness, and strict adherence to society's norms of justice by ensuring that these virtues are the surest path to success: the frequency of interaction in the market imposes restraints on people and obliges them to adapt their behavior to meet the expectations of others. In short, Smith argues that the overall economic and moral balance sheets favor commercial over precommercial societies, even if the former remain far from perfect.

Chapter 4 turns to Rousseau's third and in some ways decisive critique of commercial society, the "pursuit of unhappiness" critique, and shows that Smith finds an answer to this critique in the positive political effects of commerce. Smith argues that *the* most important benefit of commercial society is that it helps provide people with a greater degree of liberty and security than they enjoy in other societies; extensive commerce does not guarantee an ideal political order, but according to Smith it does tend to lead to advances such as a decrease in personal dependence, the development of the rule of law, and more effective administration of justice. And since, on Smith's account, dependence and insecurity are the chief obstacles to happiness, commercial society's alleviation of these ills—ills that have dominated most of human history—helps promote people's happiness in comparison to earlier societies. People in commercial society may not enjoy complete happiness, especially since they tend to toil constantly for meaningless luxuries, but neither do they face the degree of dependence and fear that characterized nearly all previous societies. Smith's view of commercial society, then, is far from a triumphal one: there is simply a different mixture of benefits and drawbacks in commercial society, and on the whole it seems to him to offer the preferable mixture, for it provides the best chance for the most people to lead a decent life.

This book's conclusion offers some reflections on the overall character of Smith's outlook and on what his thought can teach us today. Smith's approach, I maintain, is pragmatic rather than principled or foundationalist; his defense of commercial society rests on a kind of cost–benefit analysis rather than abstractions or ideologies. He is largely correct to suggest that commercial society is on the whole preferable to the historical alternatives; at the same time, however, his sober insistence that there are important drawbacks to commercial society helps call our attention to the need to address its very real problems. An examination of Smith's thought, then, offers a salutary reminder to those contemporary critics of commercial society who mischaracterize him (and through him, commercial society) as indifferent to economic inequalities and to issues of character and morality, but it also serves as a wake-up call for those contemporary defenders of commercial society who mischaracterize him as arguing that we *ought* to be indifferent to these things. A return to Smith's balanced, pragmatic approach seems worthwhile in an age that abounds with both dogmatic critics and doctrinaire champions of commercial society. Before exploring this approach more fully, however, we will turn, in Chapter 1, to a detailed examination of Rousseau's critique of commercial society.

O N E | ROUSSEAU'S UNHAPPY VISION OF COMMERCIAL SOCIETY

On receiving a copy of the *Discourse on Inequality* in 1755, Voltaire wrote to Rousseau: "I have received, Sir, your new book against the human race. . . . One acquires the desire to walk on all fours when one reads your work. Nevertheless, since I lost this habit more than sixty years ago, I unfortunately feel that it is impossible for me to take it up again" (*CW* III, 102). This is a common view of Rousseau's position, even if it is articulated in an uncommonly sardonic manner: Rousseau is often portrayed as a critic of society or civilization as such because of his famous argument that in the state of nature people were self-sufficient, equal, innocent, and happy, while in most societies they are dependent, unequal, corrupt, and miserable. Yet Rousseau outlines what a healthy society would look like in *The Social Contract* and even praises a number of real-life societies throughout his works—Sparta, Rome, and Geneva come immediately to mind. When scholars seek a more specific target of Rousseau's ire, most often they point to France's *ancien régime,* largely because he is so often depicted as having prepared the ground for the French Revolution.[1] This chapter will show, however, that Rousseau's main attack was directed not so much against the *ancien régime* as against the commercial societies that were beginning to emerge in his time. Indeed, we will see that Rousseau repudiated nearly every aspect of commercial society and that his critique of it is one of the most comprehensive ever offered.

We will begin by exploring the relationship between Rousseau and the other leading thinkers of eighteenth-century France. Most of the *philosophes* had tremendous hopes for commercial society, and we will briefly consider their views and Rousseau's reaction to them. The next section will examine Rousseau's description of humanity's goodness in the state of nature and his account of the degeneration from this state to the depravity of civilized society; this examination will provide a useful background for distinguishing

---

1. On Rousseau's relationship to the French Revolution, see Blum, *Rousseau and the Republic of Virtue;* Furet, "Rousseau and the French Revolution"; and Miller, *Rousseau,* chap. 6.

between Rousseau's critique of society in general and his critique of commercial society in particular. The following three sections—the heart of the chapter—outline Rousseau's three main critiques of commercial society: first, he argues that people living in this kind of society can have little social or personal unity because of the prevalence of inequality, weakness, and ignorance and the consequent decline of citizenship; second, he maintains that they will necessarily be dependent on the opinions of others in a way that produces a great deal of role playing, ostentation, deception, and immorality; and finally, he contends that their endless desires will lead them to spend their entire lives toiling in a vain attempt to attain a happiness that will always elude them. We will conclude with a short assessment of Rousseau's proposed "escape routes" from the problems of commercial society and their viability.

I. THE ENLIGHTENMENT AND ITS ENEMY

Easily the most striking feature of the milieu in which Rousseau thought and wrote was the presence, in eighteenth-century France and its environs, of a fairly tightly knit group of thinkers who dominated the intellectual scene as few groups have before or since: the *philosophes*. There were a number of differences among these thinkers, of course, but by and large they shared a similar vision. As Peter Gay has famously commented in his seminal work on the Enlightenment, "the philosophes made up a clamorous chorus, and there were some discordant voices among them, but what is striking is their general harmony, not their occasional discord. . . . the philosophes did not have a party line, but they were a party."[2] This party—which called itself the "party of humanity"—was united in its aspiration to create a more civilized, more prosperous, and more peaceful world, and above all a freer one. As we will see, the *philosophes* sought to attain these goals not only by opposing the throne and altar of the *ancien régime,* which they saw as the key impediments to nearly all progress, but also by encouraging the commercial societies that were beginning to emerge in their time. And we will also see that it was precisely this confidence in the advantages of commercial society that set them at direct odds with Rousseau.

Not all of the *philosophes* were, strictly speaking, egalitarian in outlook.

2. Gay, *The Enlightenment*, vol. 1, 3, 6.

In terms of their politics, they varied from advocates of popular government to supporters of "enlightened despotism," and some of them were at times extraordinarily disdainful of the ignorant masses. Even so, almost all of them were opposed to the hereditary aristocracy and to the entrenched inequalities of the *ancien régime*. They saw these inequalities as fetters of tradition and prejudice that held back their project of improving society by opening its opportunities to all. They believed that a society in which any individual could gain wealth and influence through ability and industry would be not only more just but also more stable and more prosperous. In their eyes, however, an even greater set of shackles was the Church: they saw organized religion as the chief source of fanaticism, intolerance, superstition, and dogma—hence Voltaire's famous battle cry to crush it in the name of humanity: *écraser l'infâme!* The religious beliefs of the *philosophes* varied; generally, though, they all agreed that a secular world would be a better and more enlightened world.

The *philosophes* sought to enlighten society through education and critical inquiry—hence their nearly universal support for Diderot's *Encyclopédie*, which served as a tool for disseminating knowledge in the arts, economics, history, medicine, philosophy, politics, and especially the sciences to a broader public. Progress in the sciences and advances in technology and medicine, the *philosophes* thought, would enable people to take steps toward making themselves, in the famous words of Descartes, the "lords and masters of nature."[3] They argued that it was not prayer and renunciation but science and technology that could make the world safer, healthier, and more comfortable by giving people power over their environment and by putting a halt to the seemingly constant cycle of disease, famine, suffering, uncertain life, and early death. The *philosophes* hoped that the spread of enlightenment would help people see their true self-interest—that security, liberty, and prosperity are the most important and most pressing needs in life— and that this enlightened self-interest could be channeled to serve the common good. In particular, they thought that the emancipation and the encouragement of people's acquisitiveness could help fuel commerce and thereby produce prosperity. Following Locke, they argued that what is needed is less a citizenry that practices the ancient or Christian virtues than industrious individuals who help increase their society's standard of living through the productivity of their self-interested labor.

---

3. Descartes, *Discourse on Method*, in *The Philosophical Writings of Descartes*, vol. 1, 142–43.

The type of society most capable of capitalizing on people's acquisitiveness, the *philosophes* argued, was one characterized by a large territory and population, an extensive division of labor, a high degree of interdependence, and a good deal of mobility. Despite their diverse political preferences, then, nearly all of the *philosophes* favored a modern commercial society similar to the one that in the mid-eighteenth century was beginning to take root in England—a country that many of them greatly admired for this very reason. They believed that freedom and commerce went hand in hand and reinforced each other; as Voltaire wrote, "commerce, which has brought wealth to the citizenry of England, has helped to make them free, and freedom has developed commerce in its turn."[4] In addition, many of the *philosophes* accepted what became known as the doctrine of *doux commerce*. This doctrine, whose most influential exponent was almost certainly Montesquieu,[5] held that commerce—meaning social interaction generally, but economic trade in particular—leads to *douceur,* or gentleness, mildness, softness, and peacefulness.[6] The idea was that by establishing bonds among people and by rendering life more comfortable, commerce softens and refines people's manners and promotes humaneness and civility. The *philosophes* believed that the spread of commerce would have beneficial economic, social, political, and even moral effects and that human well-being would be best promoted in and through commercial society, so they sought to push their own society in that direction. The party of humanity, in short, "promoted commerce and commerce-friendly virtues and so produced a new world."[7]

Rousseau's relationship to this new world and to the people who encouraged it has long been a matter of debate; indeed, it was hotly contested by Rousseau and the *philosophes* themselves. Surprisingly, however, there have been only two book-length treatments of Rousseau and the Enlightenment, and they take rather dissimilar views of the relationship between them. Mark Hulliung's *The Autocritique of Enlightenment* contends that even when Rousseau criticized the Enlightenment, he remained squarely within its bounds and thus that his critique of some Enlightenment ideals was an

---

4. Voltaire, *Philosophical Letters,* 39.

5. See, for instance, Montesquieu, *The Spirit of the Laws,* 338: "It is an almost general rule that everywhere there are gentle [*doux*] mores, there is commerce and that everywhere there is commerce, there are gentle [*doux*] mores."

6. See Hirschman, *The Passions and the Interests,* 56–63.

7. Cooper, *Rousseau, Nature, and the Problem of the Good Life,* xiii.

"autocritique." He writes of Rousseau's "entire agreement with the goals of the Enlightenment" and summarizes his "basic finding" with the statement that "as Rousseau evolved from philosophe to exphilosophe to antiphilosophe he never for a moment left the Enlightenment."[8] Graeme Garrard's *Rousseau's Counter-Enlightenment*, by contrast, insists that Rousseau's critique of the Enlightenment ran deep enough to put him entirely in opposition to it and thus that he should be regarded as a counter-Enlightenment figure.[9] Garrard argues that Rousseau "was an enemy rather than merely a critic of the Enlightenment"; in contrast to Hulliung, he maintains that Rousseau aimed at "deliberately undermining rather than correcting—and thereby strengthening—the Enlightenment."[10] He concludes that Rousseau "was the first enemy of the Enlightenment, a status that both Rousseau and the *philosophes* would have thought self-evident."[11]

In the examination of Rousseau's thought that follows we will see that while Hulliung's claim about Rousseau's place in the Enlightenment has a modicum of validity, Garrard's is much closer to the mark. As Hulliung notes, Rousseau *did* pen nearly four hundred entries for the *Encyclopédie*, befriend many of the most important *philosophes* early in his career, lead them in the quarrel over French and Italian music, and accept their scientific approach to the study of nature.[12] He also, perhaps most fundamentally, shared their opposition to the throne and altar of the *ancien régime*. Yet he deliberately distanced himself from Paris and its "high culture," and he became an exceptionally bitter enemy of the vast majority of the leading *philosophes*. Even more decisively, he rejected root and branch most of their fundamental aims and ideals: he saw the popular dissemination of the arts and sciences, the reliance on technology and medicine, the emphasis on

8. Hulliung, *The Autocritique of Enlightenment*, 35, 242; for similar statements see 213, 243. For a similar view of Rousseau's relationship to the Enlightenment, see Gay, *The Enlightenment*, vol. 2, 529–30, 552; and *The Party of Humanity*, 255, where it is claimed that Rousseau "fits into this age with ease" and in fact is "one of its representative thinkers."

9. The term "counter-Enlightenment" is often reserved for the conservative (especially Catholic) opponents of the Enlightenment in the eighteenth and early nineteenth centuries; see McMahon, *Enemies of the Enlightenment*. Garrard's argument, however, is *not* that Rousseau opposed the Enlightenment from the conservative right, but rather that he presents a civic republican critique of the Enlightenment, that he rejected the "republic of letters" in favor of a "republic of virtue." As will become clear over the course of this chapter, I feel that Rousseau's critique is too comprehensive to be easily categorized.

10. Garrard, *Rousseau's Counter-Enlightenment*, 5; for similar statements see x, 6. For a slightly different but related argument, see Melzer, "The Origin of the Counter-Enlightenment."

11. Garrard, *Rousseau's Counter-Enlightenment*, 120.

12. Hulliung, *Autocritique of Enlightenment*, 3.

self-interest and prosperity rather than virtue, the emancipation and encouragement of acquisitiveness, the enjoyment of luxury and refinement, and the trend toward large nations and cosmopolitanism as utterly incompatible with a healthy politics or a free and happy way of life. It was this opposition to everything they held dear that prompted Diderot to describe the gulf between the *philosophes* and Rousseau as a "vast chasm between heaven and hell."[13]

Rousseau stood in opposition, then, not only to the pre-revolutionary political and religious establishment, but also to the intellectual "progressives" who understood themselves to be the proper critics of that society. The emerging commercial societies no less than the *ancien régime* provoked his ire. In fact, his concern about the old order was tempered by the fact that he (correctly) thought it would soon come to an end. "I hold it impossible that the great monarchies of Europe still have long to last," he bluntly stated. "All have shined, and every state which shines is on the decline. I have reasons more particular than this maxim for my opinion, but it is unseasonable to tell them, and everyone sees them only too well" (*Emile* III, 194n).[14] If a revolution was going to sweep away the *ancien régime*, the real issue was what kind of society would replace it. Because Rousseau (again, correctly) thought that the future belonged to the emerging commercial societies, they became his central target.

Thus, while it is certainly true that Rousseau was no friend of monarchy, rigid inequalities, or an established Church, the chief thrust of his writings seems in fact to have been directed against the principles of the *philosophes*— the dissemination of the arts and sciences, the emancipation of acquisitiveness, and the rest. The *Discourse on the Sciences and Arts* and the *Discourse on Inequality*, in particular—two of his earliest works, the ones that established his reputation—presented a blistering attack on everything that the *philosophes* thought of as "progress." Rousseau recognized that his critique of the arts and sciences, refinement, and commerce constituted a condemnation of the most universally admired aspects of eighteenth-century Europe; as he wrote in the preface to the *Discourse on the Sciences and Arts*,

13. Diderot, *Essai sur les règnes de Claude et Néron*, quoted in Garrard, *Rousseau's Counter-Enlightenment*, 2.

14. For an analysis of this prediction—including both the general maxim and the "more particular" reasons, which have to do with the political consequences of Christianity—see Kelly and Masters, "Rousseau's Prediction of the European Revolution," in *Jean-Jacques Rousseau et la Révolution*. For slightly different forecasts about a European revolution, see *SC* II-8, 158; and *Poland*, 170.

"running counter to everything that men admire today, I can expect only universal blame" (FD, 3). And many if not most of the things the *philosophes* admired, we have seen, were associated with commercial society.

2. NATURAL GOODNESS, CIVILIZED BADNESS

To see why Rousseau criticized the "civilized" European societies of his time so harshly, it will be helpful to take a brief look at what he saw civilization as a departure *from*—the state of nature—and how that departure occurred. He believed that people had been so fundamentally altered by life in society that human beings in their original state would today be virtually unrecognizable to us. As depicted in the *Discourse on Inequality*, the inhabitants of the state of nature were essentially animals; nearly all of the distinctive traits of humanity—reason, language, foresight, memory, imagination, love, morality, vanity—were absent.[15] Wandering in the forests without any fixed place of residence, family, or property of any kind, people were completely solitary; the inhabitants of the state of nature had no need of or care for one another, so they would "perhaps meet hardly twice in their lives, without knowing each other and without talking to each other" (SD, 29).

The dominant motivating force in people living in the state of nature, Rousseau argues, was a healthy love of self: "The love of oneself [*amour de soi*] is always good and always in conformity with order" (*Emile* IV, 213; see also II, 92; CW IX, 28). This love of self is not to be confused with *amour-propre*, which is a relative or comparative form of self-love that is "artificial and born in Society" (SD, 91). *Amour-propre*, too, is a desire for one's own good, but it involves the opinions of others in a way that *amour de soi* does not; in Laurence Cooper's careful formulation, *amour-propre* is "the self-love of a being whose estimate of his own worth is contingent, whose self-esteem is neither absolute nor assured by nature."[16] *Amour de soi* seeks only absolute goods such as security, health, and pleasure—goods that do not involve comparing oneself to others—whereas *amour-propre* seeks comparative

15. There has been a good deal of scholarly controversy over the historical status of Rousseau's state of nature. For an argument that Rousseau understands this state more or less as a historical reality, see Plattner, *Rousseau's State of Nature*, 17–25. For an argument that the existence of this state is conjectural and that it was developed principally as a way of examining human nature and its limits, see Gourevitch, "Rousseau's Pure State of Nature."

16. Cooper, *Rousseau, Nature, and the Problem of the Good Life*, 137; see also the extensive discussion of both forms of self-love in Chapter 4 of this work.

goods and so is the source of vanity, pride, resentment, anger, envy, jealousy, and in fact all of the hostile passions (see *Dialogues*, 100).[17] *Amour-propre* did not even exist in the state of nature, Rousseau argues, because people in this state were not intellectually capable of comparing themselves to others, because inequalities hardly manifested themselves in this state and so there was little basis for comparison, and because people were not dependent on others in any way and so their opinions did not really *count* for anything (see *Dialogues*, 113; *SD*, 91–92).

Given that the artificial passions associated with *amour-propre*—along with faculties such as imagination and foresight that people in the state of nature did not yet have—are the ultimate source of most human desires, Rousseau argues, people's desires in this state were extremely limited. Indeed, he claims that their desires were restricted to their needs and that their needs were few: he envisions a person in this state "satisfying his hunger under an oak, quenching his thirst at the first Stream, finding his bed at the foot of the same tree that furnished his meal; and therewith his needs are satisfied" (*SD*, 20; see also 27–28; *CW* XI, 63). Most of people's modest needs were found close at hand, and since they were accustomed to the harshness of the seasons and life in the wild, they developed "all the vigor of which the human species is capable" and so were able to bear these hardships with ease (*SD*, 21). For the most part, life for people in the state of nature was not one of strenuous labor but rather one of leisure and inner repose (see *Languages*, 310n; *SD*, 28). Above all, their needs and their powers were perfectly matched—they were self-sufficient—and so they rarely had frustrated desires or restless strivings. Although people in the state of nature were brutes—or, more precisely, *because* they were brutes—they were robust and vigorous, independent and self-sufficient, unified and tranquil. Their desires were limited to their needs, and their needs were easily satisfied, and thus they were happy (see *Emile* II, 80; III, 177; *SD*, 28, 86).

Rousseau argues, in short, that people in the state of nature were good for themselves in the sense that their bodies and minds were well ordered and hence that they were nearly always content. He further claims that they had

17. For Rousseau, it is possible (though rare) for *amour-propre* to take a positive form: it can manifest itself as pride (*orgueil*), the desire to *deserve* praise; or as vanity (*vanité*), the desire to be praised whether one is praiseworthy or not. Pride *can* be a beneficial passion—when it is not too excessive and when it serves a larger purpose, as in the pride of a true citizen—although it can be harmful as well, whereas vanity is always harmful. See Cooper, *Rousseau, Nature, and the Problem of the Good Life*, 162–70; Kelly, *Rousseau's Exemplary Life*, 24, 98–100, 192–93; and Reisert, *Jean-Jacques Rousseau*, 19–20.

little inclination or reason to harm others (because of their self-sufficiency and lack of *amour-propre*) and had an aversion to seeing others suffer (because of their natural pity) and so were also relatively good for others (see *SD*, 36–38).[18] The idea that humanity is naturally good in these two senses is, Rousseau says repeatedly, the fundamental principle of his thought (see, for example, *CW* V, 575; *CW* IX, 28; *Dialogues*, 212–13), yet he harbored no illusions about the goodness of human beings as he knew them. As Arthur Melzer writes, "Rousseau speaks of civilized humanity with a disgust and contempt that yield nothing to Saint Augustine."[19] Rousseau claims that nearly all civilized people—and, as we will see, especially people living in commercial society—are corrupt, materialistic, weak, hypocritical, vain, deceitful, acquisitive, and hence miserable. "Men are wicked; sad and continual experience spares the need for proof," he writes. "However, man is naturally good; I believe I have demonstrated it" (*SD*, 74). As Cooper has noted, few thinkers have argued for humanity's natural goodness *or* for its present badness as forcefully as Rousseau does, much less both sides at the same time.[20] Yet in a way, the former argument reinforces the latter: Rousseau condemns civilized people so vehemently precisely *because* they have strayed so far from their natural goodness; an account of how good human beings once were only serves to highlight how bad they are now.

In Part Two of the *Discourse on Inequality*, Rousseau describes how humanity evolved from its essentially subhuman state to its present civilized state.[21] According to Rousseau's account, the presocial, "pure" state of nature described above lasted for a long time with no progress whatsoever (see *SD*,

---

18. It should be noted that the goodness of people in the state of nature is a kind of premoral goodness; they are good rather than virtuous. For Rousseau, goodness (*bonté*) is a matter of inclination or spontaneous feeling, whereas virtue (*vertu*) is the product of self-discipline and so is more dependable: virtuous people will do their duty even if it conflicts with their inclinations (see *Emile* V, 444; *Reveries*, 51). People in the state of nature were not virtuous in this sense because they were governed entirely by their passions rather than by reason or law (see *SD*, 34–35); they were naturally good only because they were so primitive. Hence, there is nothing in his depiction of the inhabitants of the state of nature that would merit the term "noble savage"—a term that has become associated with Rousseau but that he never uses himself.

19. Melzer, *The Natural Goodness of Man*, 15.

20. See Cooper, *Rousseau, Natural, and the Problem of the Good Life*, x.

21. The evolution that Rousseau describes is that of how extremely primitive human beings evolved into civilized human beings, *not* how human beings evolved from a nonhuman ancestor. Nevertheless, the idea that human beings were at one time essentially brutes was extremely controversial in Rousseau's time, especially because this idea seemed to contradict the Biblical account of Creation.

40), but eventually people began to develop language and other faculties as natural calamities forced them to communicate in order to survive (see *SD*, 43–46). These developments led to "savage" or "hut" society, which was characterized by families living together and by "a sort of property" in huts, but without private ownership of land (*SD*, 46). In savage society there was a division of labor between men and women—with the men hunting and the women gathering—but people were still largely self-sufficient. As people had more interaction with one another, *amour-propre* started to develop; this led to occasional conflicts, but since people were still largely able to provide for themselves it also brought with it "the sweetness [*douceurs*] of independent commerce" (*SD*, 49). (Rousseau here links *douceur* with independence and self-sufficiency, whereas the *philosophes* linked it with interdependence and exchange.) This period was, Rousseau says, one of "a golden mean between the indolence of the primitive state and the petulant activity of our amour-propre," and so it constituted "the happiest and most durable epoch" (*SD*, 48; see also *Languages*, 306). Rousseau's story is not, we see here, *simply* one of decline: the first movements toward society were in fact beneficial on the whole, and it was only with further developments that humanity experienced its deepest miseries.

Savage society lasted a very long time, according to Rousseau, until "some fatal accident" forced people to leave this happy state (*SD*, 48). Through some "extraordinary circumstance" such as a volcano, people learned to use metal to make tools, and this in turn made possible the development of farming (*SD*, 49–51). These two arts, metallurgy and agriculture, brought about both a want of land, which resulted in the institution of private property, and a much greater division of labor, which resulted in inequality and dependence. From this point on, Rousseau contends, the rest of humanity's path was more or less inevitable. These economic and social developments brought with them cognitive developments such as the full flowering of *amour-propre*, imagination, and foresight, and these developments in turn expanded people's desires well beyond their capacities—by making them care about what others think, by depicting new possibilities to them, and by leading them to always look to the future, respectively—and thereby kept them from enjoying tranquility or self-sufficiency (see *SD*, 51–52). Ever since human beings left savage society, Rousseau says, "all subsequent progress has been in appearance so many steps toward the perfection of the individual, and in fact toward the decrepitude of the species" (*SD*, 49).

It is evident, then, that nearly all of humanity's ills arose long ago, according to Rousseau's account—even before the formation of the first political societies. He reserves his harshest criticism, however, for what he often calls "modern" or "bourgeois" society, by which he plainly means the commercial societies that were emerging in his time. Commercial society clearly is not the sole cause of humanity's problems, for Rousseau—natural goodness ended well before commercial society emerged—but it does exacerbate them to a great degree; developed faculties and moral corruption are both a cause and a consequence of commercial society and its attendant division of labor, superfluous commodities, technology, acquisitiveness, interdependence, mobility, and cosmopolitanism. Thus, as we will see in the next three sections, most of Rousseau's attacks on society in general should also be read as attacks on commercial society in particular.

I will now turn to Rousseau's critique of commercial society and the question of why he attacks this form of society above all others. His critique, I will show, consists of three related arguments.[22] The first, which I call the "division of laborers" critique, holds that it is not only labor that is divided in commercial society but also the laborers themselves: because of the prevalence of great inequalities and the widespread dependence on commodities and technology in commercial society, people living in this kind of society can have little social or personal unity. The second argument, the "empire of opinion" critique, posits that in commercial society people invariably depend on the opinions of others and that this other-directedness produces a great deal of role playing, ostentation, deception, and immorality. The final argument, the "pursuit of unhappiness" critique, has it that the acquisitiveness encouraged by commerce expands people's desires well beyond their capacities, thereby ensuring that people spend their entire lives toiling and striving in a vain attempt to attain a happiness that will always elude them. We will explore each of these critiques in some depth.

3. THE DIVISION OF LABORERS

According to Rousseau's narrative in the *Discourse on Inequality*, we have seen, the increased division of labor that arose immediately after the invention of metallurgy and agriculture is what initially started humanity on its

---

22. As we will see in Chapter 2, these three arguments correspond to the three lengthy quotations from the *Discourse on Inequality* that Adam Smith translates in his review of this work. See *Letter*, 251–54.

inexorable downward path. "As long as men . . . applied themselves only to tasks that a single person could do and to arts that did not require the cooperation of several hands," he writes, "they lived free, healthy, good, and happy insofar as they could be according to their Nature" (*SD*, 49). But the rise of the division of labor led to an enormous set of changes, the only step in humanity's development that Rousseau calls a "great revolution": "from the moment one man needed the help of another, as soon as they observed that it was useful for a single person to have provisions for two, equality disappeared, property was introduced, labor became necessary; and vast forests were changed into smiling Fields which had to be watered with the sweat of men, and in which slavery and misery were soon seen to germinate and grow with the crops" (*SD*, 49). As we will see in this section, Rousseau believes that the problems introduced by this rudimentary division of labor are compounded almost immeasurably by the much more extensive division of labor of commercial society. For Rousseau, the division of labor results not only in the division of work and responsibility among the members of society but also in the division of the laborers themselves: it both divides their souls and divides them against one another. He argues that it divides people in these ways for two broad reasons: First, it generates great wealth, which is always accompanied by great inequalities. Second, it produces superfluous commodities and promotes the arts and sciences, and these combine to make people weak and ignorant and thereby to undermine citizenship.

Rousseau concedes the validity of the *philosophes'* argument that the division of labor—and commercial society more generally—tends to produce great wealth. Supposing that there are ten people with ten different needs, he admits, it would be more efficient to have each of them work to fulfill one of those needs for all rather than to have each of them work to fulfill all ten needs on his own: "Each will profit from the talents of the others as if he alone had them all. Each will perfect his own by continuous practice, and it will turn out that all ten, perfectly well provided for, will even have a surplus for others" (*Emile* III, 193; see also 185). And Rousseau was fully aware of how central the division of labor was to the societies of his time: immediately after the passage just quoted, he asserts that "that is the apparent principle of *all* our institutions" (*Emile* III, 193; italics added). Rousseau concedes that the division of labor allows people to perfect their crafts through specialization and encourages efficiency, thereby producing superfluity, but he expresses grave reservations regarding the consequences of this specialization and superfluity.

Rousseau argues that even though the division of labor helps produce great wealth, this wealth is spread so unevenly throughout the population that poverty still produces a great deal of misery. In wealthy societies a few people—because they are industrious and talented, or (more often) because they are greedy and unscrupulous—will become rich, and it is *because* they are rich that others are impoverished: "there are poor people only because there are rich ones, and that is true in more than one sense" (*Fragments,* 48; see also *CW* II, 48; *Emile* II, 105n; *SD,* 75). A select few can become rich only at the expense of the rest of society, and as a consequence, people's interests can be reconciled neither through state intervention nor through any kind of invisible hand. There is an inextricable connection between riches and poverty, so instead of commercial society creating the kind of general prosperity the *philosophes* claimed it would, "the wealth of an entire nation produces the opulence of a few private individuals to the detriment of the public, and the treasures of millionaires increase the misery of the citizens" (*Fragments,* 50).

Rousseau objects to these great inequalities, first of all, because they are unjust: "it is manifestly against the Law of Nature, in whatever manner it is defined, that . . . a handful of men be glutted with superfluities while the starving multitude lack necessities" (*SD,* 67). This is not to suggest that Rousseau advocates an equal distribution of wealth—he sees this notion as "chimerical" (*Fragments,* 49)—but rather that he sees the immense inequalities characteristic of most modern societies as patently unfair. Inequality of wealth is so problematic, for Rousseau, because with money it is possible to buy nearly anything. Thus, unequal wealth leads to unequal levels not only of material possessions but also of security, independence, political power, education, and so on. Hence, Rousseau maintains, the poor are destined to live a life of struggle and suffering: "the misery of the poor man comes to him from . . . the rigor of his lot, which weighs down on him. No habit can take from him the physical sentiments of fatigue, exhaustion, and hunger" (*Emile* IV, 225; see also *PE,* 165). The hardships and privations of the poor, in short, act as a standing reproof to commercial society and its "prosperity." So great was Rousseau's sense of injustice and personal injury concerning the prospects of the less fortunate that Judith Shklar has labeled him "the Homer of the losers."[23]

But the concentration of wealth and the misery of the poor were not Rousseau's only (or even chief) objections to the prosperity of the modern world.

---

23. Shklar, "Jean-Jacques Rousseau and Inequality," in *Political Thought and Political Thinkers,* 290.

In fact, he argues that commercial prosperity is every bit as psychologically damaging to the rich as to the poor; both the victors and the victims become corrupt and miserable. One of the key reasons for this corruption and misery, for Rousseau, is that modern societies—and especially commercial societies—are characterized not only by wealth but also by luxuries, the arts and sciences, and technology, all of which tend to make people weak and ignorant. The commodities and technology generated by these societies do give people greater power in some ways, Rousseau argues, but they are also dangerous because people invariably come to depend on these things (see *Final Reply*, 110–11). In the state of nature, people's needs were very few; in commercial society, people become so accustomed to comforts and luxuries that soon they become true needs as well, and thus "commerce and the arts, in providing for some imaginary needs, introduce a far greater number of real ones" (*Fragments*, 47). Reliance on commodities and technology thus weakens people's bodies and minds: "The more ingenious are our tools, the cruder and more maladroit our organs become. By dint of gathering machines around us, we no longer find any in ourselves" (*Emile* III, 176; see also *SD*, 21). And the weakness and ignorance of nearly all civilized people are particularly exacerbated in commercial society, according to Rousseau, by the specialization of tasks associated with the division of labor. In commercial society people are often forced to work in one-dimensional jobs, and these jobs make the people themselves one-dimensional; in these "stupid professions" the workers are "almost automatons," and so "it is a case of one machine guiding another" (*Emile* III, 200–201; see also *FD*, 19). Commercial society may make life easier, but it also (and thereby) makes people weaker and more ignorant.

Rousseau argues that the arts and sciences tend to reinforce the weaknesses already present in spades in commercial society by promoting refinement and politeness (see *FD*, 12–17). Even worse, refinement and politeness tend to replace virtue as standards for judging people; civility covers weakness by giving it a pleasing appearance. People often take their pettiness and lack of vigor to be virtues like refinement and urbanity, Rousseau argues, but in reality they have only "the semblance of all the virtues without the possession of any" (*FD*, 5; see also 6, 18–19; *Emile* IV, 335). This is a long way from *doux commerce* indeed.[24] In explicit response to the argument that

24. On Rousseau's relationship to the theory of *doux commerce*, see Rosenblatt, *Rousseau and Geneva*, 52–84.

commerce makes people gentle (*doux*), Rousseau writes: "For being gentler, are you less unjust, less vindictive, is virtue less oppressed, power less tyrannical, the people less crushed, does one see fewer crimes, are evildoers more rare, are prisons less full? What have you gained from softening yourselves? For vices which denote courage and vigor you have substituted those of small souls" (*OC* IV, 1089–90). People in commercial society even stop *caring* about their weakness and pettiness: "until the present time," he writes, "luxury—although often prevailing—had at least been regarded in all ages as the deadly source of an infinity of evils" (*Final Reply*, 128). In commercial society, however, wealth and luxury are often applauded as politically salutary (see *FD*, 14). In Rousseau's eyes, of course, encouraging luxury is dangerous rather than salutary; the idea that private vice leads to public benefits only serves to encourage private vice and public corruption.

Rousseau further argues that the weakness and luxury characteristic of the modern world—and, again, especially commercial societies—combine to undermine citizenship as it is properly understood, the kind that existed in Sparta and republican Rome. An overwhelming concern with commerce means rejecting civic virtue as the end of politics and of life; true citizens must devote time and energy to ensure and exercise their political freedom, and things like the pursuit of wealth and artistic and scientific endeavors lure people away from a patriotic sense of devotion. Furthermore, the large geographic size and large populations that are especially characteristic of commercial societies—and the cosmopolitanism they foster—serve to undermine the moral bonds of the community (see *Final Reply*, 122; *SC* II-9, 159 and III-1, 168). Thus, in the modern world there can be no true citizens: "these two words, *fatherland* and *citizen*, should be effaced from modern languages," Rousseau writes (*Emile* I, 40). In particular, there can no longer be any citizen-soldiers, for luxury and weakness destroy the military virtues. A citizen militia from a poor but robust nation is always stronger than a paid standing army from a rich and refined one, Rousseau maintains. Thus the people's weakness ultimately leads to the weakness of the state (see *FD*, 14–17; *Corsica*, 126–27; *Poland*, 210, 217–18).

The *philosophes* held the opposite view of the relationship between commerce and the greatness of the state because they took their bearings from things such as wealth, refinement, glory, and accomplishments in the arts and sciences. Rousseau, however, finds these things empty and frivolous when viewed from the perspective of virtue or happiness:

They can admire at their will the perfection of the arts, the number and the grandeur of their discoveries, the range and sublimity
of human genius; should we congratulate them for knowing all of
nature save themselves and for having discovered all the arts except
that of being happy? "We have," they cry out sadly, "the resources
for well-being, a host of commodities unknown to our fathers; they
were ignorant of a number of pleasures we enjoy." It is true that
you have softness, but they had happiness; you are reasoners, they
were reasonable; you are polite, they were humane; all of your pleasures are outside of you, theirs were within themselves. (*OC* IV,
1089; see also *Final Reply*, 120–21; *Poland*, 183)

Rousseau prefers the simplicity and vigor of the ancient republics to the
"greatness" of commercial society, for even if the latter societies are in some
ways more impressive at first glance, the *people* were more impressive in
the republics of old: "men formerly accomplished great things with small
means, and today we do just the opposite" (*Julie*, 49; see also *d'Alembert*,
274). Rousseau judges societies largely by the kind of people they produce
(see *Confessions*, 340), and on this basis he finds commercial society wanting indeed.

In short, Rousseau argues that in commercial society people tend to become internally divided—they are rendered weak and ignorant—by reliance
on commodities and technology and by one-dimensional jobs. Likewise,
he maintains that people are divided against one another by the presence
of great inequalities. Yet perhaps the biggest reason why Rousseau thinks
people are divided against one another in commercial society—their overwhelming concern for the opinions of others—remains to be examined.

4. THE EMPIRE OF OPINION

In some ways even worse than people's dependence on commodities and
technology in commercial society, in Rousseau's view, is the rise and spread
of *personal* dependence. Because an extensive division of labor renders people
weak and ignorant while at the same time greatly expanding their needs and
desires, he argues, they become utterly dependent on others for nearly *everything*. And once people become dependent in this way, their self-concern
necessarily leads to concern for the opinions of others; people cannot fulfill

their needs and desires on their own, so they must convince others to help them. Eventually, he contends, this concern for others takes on a life of its own and people come to view the world, including themselves, only through others' eyes. Rousseau goes so far as to say that this overwhelming concern for the opinions of others is the "genuine cause" of all of the differences between savages and civilized people: "the Savage lives within himself; the sociable man, always outside himself, knows how to live only in the opinion of others" (SD, 66; see also d'Alembert, 300). In other words, people are naturally asocial, but once *amour-propre* develops they become social to the core. Concern for others' opinions is found to some degree in every civilized society, according to Rousseau, and it becomes especially deep and problematic when it is connected to wealth and luxury and to commercial exchange. Thus, we will see in this section, it is especially in commercial society that what Rousseau calls "the empire of opinion" holds sway (d'Alembert, 266).

When people are dependent on others, Rousseau claims, they come to care more about being esteemed by them than anything else, and in order to get others to esteem them they have to be what others want them to be: they must spend their entire lives being pleasant, polite, and accommodating. In other words, they turn into phony role players; they rarely speak as they really think or feel, even with those closest to them. Hence, civilized people are never truly themselves, according to Rousseau: "The man of the world is whole in his mask. . . . What he is, is nothing; what he appears to be is everything for him" (*Emile* IV, 230). The poor and the weak are most obviously enslaved to others in this way since they must flatter and serve their superiors, but the rich and powerful cannot escape it either: "Even domination is servile when it is connected with opinion, for you depend on the prejudices of those you govern by prejudices. To lead them as you please, you must conduct yourself as they please. . . . You will always say, 'We want,' and you will always do what others want. The only one who does his own will is he who, in order to do it, has no need to put another's arms at the end of his own" (*Emile* II, 83–84). Commanding others in fact entails a good deal of dependence, Rousseau maintains, and thus "one who believes himself the master of others is nonetheless a greater slave than they" (*SC* I-1, 131; see also SD, 51–52).[25] The rich and poor alike, then, constantly play

25. This critique of mastery echoes Socrates' famous critique of tyranny in Plato's *Republic*. See especially Plato, *The Republic*, 579c–580a.

a role instead of truly being themselves because of their dependence on other people's opinions.

While a degree of concern for others' opinions is present in every civilized society, according to Rousseau, this concern becomes especially deep and problematic in commercial society because of the great emphasis on wealth and luxury in this kind of society. He argues that people's true goal is not to attain wealth and luxuries themselves but to receive the approbation and esteem that come with them: "One does everything to become rich, but it is in order to be esteemed that one wants to be rich" (*Fragments*, 35; see also *Poland*, 178). That people desire esteem more than riches is obvious, Rousseau argues, when one considers the fact that "instead of stopping at that moderate wealth that constitutes well-being, each wants to arrive at that degree of wealth that attracts all eyes" (*Fragments*, 35; see also *Emile* IV, 344–54). If people could detach themselves wholly from the opinions of others—if they could be like Robinson Crusoe on his island—their desires would be extraordinarily few; it is the desire to have others look up to them that makes people want more than this (see *Emile* III, 184–85). The rich are more interested in displaying their wealth than actually enjoying it; their luxuries are purely a matter of "conspicuous consumption."[26] Indeed, Rousseau contends that the rich only enjoy things insofar as the poor are deprived of them and that "they would cease to be happy if the People ceased to be miserable" (*SD*, 63; see also *Emile* III, 186).

In commercial society everyone must appeal to other people's self-interest because this is the only effective way to influence them, Rousseau argues, but these appeals will always be insincere since people do not truly *care* about others' welfare. When providing a good or a service for the market, one is forced to try to please others in the hope they will buy that good or service, and thus everyone must "incessantly seek to interest [others] in his fate, and to make them find their own profit, in fact or in appearance, in working for his" (*SD*, 52; see also *Emile* IV, 321). This falseness, Rousseau writes, creates a society of "double men, always appearing to relate everything to others and never relating anything except to themselves alone" (*Emile* I, 41).[27] Because they need others but do not truly care about their

26. On the idea that luxuries are valued only insofar as they are scarce and so bring attention to oneself, see Fridén, *Rousseau's Economic Philosophy*, 49.

27. As Allan Bloom writes: "The bourgeois . . . is the man who, when dealing with others, thinks only of himself, and on the other hand, in his understanding of himself, thinks only of others." Bloom, "Introduction," in Rousseau, *Emile, or On Education*, 5.

well-being, people are always silently but thoroughly in competition with one other. Thus, "suspicions, offenses, fears, coldness, reserve, hate, betrayal will hide constantly under that uniform and false veil of politeness, under that much vaunted urbanity which we owe to the enlightenment of our century" (*FD*, 6; see also *CW* II, 49; *Fragments*, 20; *SD*, 51–52). Underneath the pretense of concern for others invariably lies an aspiration to succeed at their expense, so this pretense serves as a cover for exploitation and injustice. As Melzer writes, according to Rousseau "the modern commercial republic . . . necessarily creates a society of smiling enemies, where each individual pretends to care about others precisely because he cares only about himself."[28] Indeed, Rousseau claims that "one can make a very just estimation of men's morals by the multitude of business they have among each other: the more commerce they have together, the more they admire their talents and industry, the more they trick each other decently and adroitly, and the more they are worthy of contempt" (*Narcissus*, 194n; see also *Corsica*, 143).

Rousseau argues that the prevalence of deception and hostility in commercial society is a direct result of the effort to build society on people's selfish nature. Of this effort, he writes: "Our Writers all regard as the masterpiece of the politics of our century the sciences, arts, luxury, commerce, laws, and the other ties which, by tightening among men the ties of society from personal interest, put them all in mutual dependence, give them reciprocal needs, and common interests, and oblige each of them to cooperate for the happiness of the others in order to be able to attain his own" (*Narcissus*, 193). This passage constitutes a fair description of the *philosophes'* aspiration to base society on reliable motives such as self-interest and to create bonds among people through mutual dependence; by attributing this aspiration to *all* of "our writers," Rousseau indicates how common this viewpoint was in the eighteenth century. Yet he claims that the concentration on self-interest and interdependence, when examined "attentively and impartially," is not quite as advantageous as it might seem. Immediately after this passage, he continues:

> It is a very marvelous thing to have made it impossible for men to live among themselves without being prejudiced against, supplanting, deceiving, betraying, mutually destroying each other! Henceforth

28. Melzer, "Rousseau and the Modern Cult of Sincerity," in *The Legacy of Rousseau*, 282. See also Starobinski, *Jean-Jacques Rousseau*, 23.

we must beware of letting ourselves be seen as we are: for two men whose interests agree, a hundred thousand can be opposed to them, and there is in this case no other means to succeed than to deceive or ruin all these people. This is the deadly source of violence, treachery, perfidy, and all the horrors necessarily demanded by a state of things in which each—pretending to work for the fortune and reputation of others—seeks only to raise his own above them and at their expense. (*Narcissus,* 193)

While Rousseau agrees with the *philosophes* that human beings are naturally selfish, he denies that a healthy society can be built on this selfish nature; a kind of Spartan denaturing is necessary to make society function well, to make true citizens. Any society built on selfishness will result in nothing but exploitation and deception.

The *philosophes* believed that people's selfishness could be channeled toward the common good, that (to borrow Mandeville's terms) "private vices" could be turned into "public benefits" if institutions were set up to direct them in the right way. Rousseau, on the other hand, argues that selfishness cannot be so easily controlled and made useful, for he believes that people's selfish interests are always opposed to one another. People will always gain more from harming others than peacefully coexisting with them: "If I am answered that Society is so constituted that each man gains by serving the others, I shall reply that this would be very well, if he did not gain still more by harming them" (*SD,* 75). For all of the *philosophes'* talk about "enlightened self-interest," Rousseau claims, any minimally shrewd person can see that it is often easier to fill one's purse through cheating and manipulation than through honest work.[29] Hence, Rousseau has no faith in any kind of invisible hand that could reconcile people's selfish interests: "Far from there being an alliance between private interest and the general good, they are mutually exclusive" (*GM* I-2, 79; see also *Emile* II, 105n). Self-interest simply cannot create gentle (*doux*) or even mutually beneficial bonds among people in the way the *philosophes* claimed it could.

In short, Rousseau argues that people in commercial society tend to be overly concerned with the opinions of others and that this concern produces a great deal of role-playing, ostentation, deception, and immorality. As bad

---

29. On Rousseau's argument against the idea that economic exchange encourages integrity since "honesty is the best policy," see Grant, *Hypocrisy and Integrity,* 37–39, 43–44.

as all these things are, however, perhaps the *worst* effect of people's dependence on the opinions of others, we will see in the next section, is that it greatly expands their desires and thereby makes them miserable. This misery is one of the principal reasons why others' opinions are, as Shklar writes, "the knot in our swaddling-clothes and the nail in our coffin."[30]

5. THE PURSUIT OF UNHAPPINESS

As we have seen, the first two Rousseauian critiques of commercial society are rather broad and complex; the detrimental effects of the division of labor and of dependence on others' opinions are many and varied. The third critique, by contrast, is beguilingly simple: people's desires are greatly expanded in commercial society. Yet this simple idea is in some ways Rousseau's deepest and most damning argument against commercial society, both because emancipated desires are so central to commercial life and because he sees the effects of such desires as so grave and inescapable. Rousseau maintains that people's desires tend to be literally *endless* in commercial society because of the emphasis placed on wealth and luxury and because of the great concern people have for others' opinions; thus they almost inevitably spend their lives toiling in a vain attempt to attain a happiness that will always elude them. Indeed, their very pursuit of happiness is what ultimately renders them constantly unhappy.

As is evident from his depictions of the "pure" state of nature and of savage society, in which people were content because they were able to satisfy all or almost all of their limited desires, Rousseau believes that the material requirements for happiness are extraordinarily few: "The happiness of the natural man is as simple as his life. It consists in not suffering; health, freedom and the necessities of life constitute it" (*Emile* III, 177; see also II, 80; *SD*, 28, 86). The inhabitant of the state of nature, Rousseau says, "breathes only repose and freedom; he wants only to live and remain idle; and even the perfect quietude [*ataraxia*] of the Stoic does not approach his profound indifference for all other objects" (*SD*, 66). *Ataraxia*, a Greek term often translated as "tranquility," was a central aim of both the Stoics and the Epicureans and is remarkably similar to Rousseau's understanding of happiness: for Rousseau, happiness is produced by—or rather accompanies—

---

30. Shklar, *Men and Citizens*, 73–74. See also *Emile* I, 42–43.

a tranquil mind.[31] Just as the inhabitants of the state of nature are happy simply because of their self-sufficiency and lack of suffering, so too *ataraxia* is defined largely negatively: it denotes the state of being free from *tarachai* (troubles or worries), of not being frustrated or hindered in one's movements and desires.[32] Both Rousseau's happiness and the Greeks' *ataraxia* require a sort of permanence; they are lasting states of being and not momentary feelings or passions (see *Emile* IV, 229; *Fragments*, 40; *Reveries*, 45, 78). And they both require a degree of rest but not a complete lack of activity: "without movement, life is only lethargy," Rousseau writes, so "what is needed is neither absolute rest nor too much agitation, but a uniform and moderated movement having neither jolts nor lapses" (*Reveries*, 47). A state of tranquility or *ataraxia* produces happiness, according to Rousseau, and this state was easily achieved in the state of nature.

As we saw in Section 2, Rousseau claims that misery began to spread when people's desires were emancipated early in human history because of the rise of *amour-propre*, imagination, and foresight. In commercial society, people's desires are not only emancipated but also *encouraged*, since acquisitiveness is seen as the driving force behind the economy and the ultimate cause of prosperity. People in commercial society are told that by advancing their material lot they are in fact indirectly serving the common good—hence Rousseau's famous assertion that "Ancient Political thinkers incessantly talked about morals and virtue, those of our time talk only of business and money" (*FD*, 14; see also *Poland*, 210). Unlike in earlier societies, then, people in commercial society feel uninhibited in their constant pursuit of more and more material goods. Yet material goods ultimately do little to make people any happier, Rousseau argues, for people tend to become enslaved to their wealth and commodities in such a way that being deprived of them is more cruel than possessing them is sweet; they are "unhappy to lose them without being happy to possess them" (*SD*, 46; see also *Dialogues*, 11). The pleasure of having something wears off when its novelty does: no one wakes up in the morning thrilled to have indoor plumbing. Furthermore, material possessions are a great deal of trouble, for people must worry about buying, protecting, fixing, and replacing these goods.

31. Among the most helpful accounts of Rousseau's views on happiness are Cooper, *Rousseau, Nature, and the Problem of the Good Life*, 19–35; Grimsley, "Rousseau and the Problem of Happiness," in *Hobbes and Rousseau;* Melzer, *The Natural Goodness of Man*, 40–46, 63–68; Reisert, *Jean-Jacques Rousseau*, 114–23; and Salkever, "Rousseau and the Concept of Happiness."
32. See Annas, *The Morality of Happiness*, 238, 336, 408–10.

They are chains tying people down: "It is not without reason that Socrates, looking at a shop display, congratulated himself for having nothing at all to do with all that" (*Final Reply*, 128).

Rousseau claims that people's desires for empty goods are not just greatly expanded in commercial society; in fact, they are *limitless*. People tend to put a great deal of emphasis not only on material goods but also on money itself, he observes, but money is only a means to an end: "it is good for nothing by itself; one must transform it to enjoy it" (*Confessions*, 31; see also *Julie*, 449). Thus, people spend their entire lives pursuing the *means* to satisfy their desires rather than the satisfaction of the desires themselves; the inhabitant of commercial society "thinks less of enjoying than of multiplying for himself the instrument of enjoyments" (*Dialogues*, 122). And there is, of course, no limit to the amount of money or means one can acquire. Furthermore, as we saw in the previous section, people are pushed to obtain more and more money not only because it serves as a means to satisfying their desires but also (and especially) because of the esteem and admiration that come with it; they care more about keeping up with the Joneses than actually enjoying their possessions. In short, because the things that people desire above all in commercial society—wealth and recognition from others—can always be increased, the quest for these things is literally unending.

The most obvious consequence of limitless desires, of course, is that people are likely to spend their entire lives toiling in a vain attempt to fulfill them. Rousseau posits that the typical civilized person—in sharp contrast to people in the state of nature—"sweats, agitates himself, torments himself incessantly in order to seek still more laborious occupations" (*SD*, 66; see also *Dialogues*, 144). The result of this constant toil is not satisfaction or fulfillment but fatigue and empty achievements:

> When, on the one hand, one considers the vast labors of men, so many Sciences fathomed, so many arts invented, and so many forces employed, chasms filled, mountains razed, rocks broken, rivers made navigable, land cleared, lakes dug out, swamps drained, enormous buildings raised upon the earth, the sea covered with Ships and Sailors; and when, on the other hand, one searches with a little meditation for the true advantages that have resulted from all this for the happiness of the human species, one cannot fail to be struck by the astounding disproportion prevailing between these things, and to deplore man's blindness. (*SD*, 74)

All of this labor is undertaken in an attempt to make the world safer and more comfortable—to give people power over their environment—but in the end this attempt is futile since people's desires can never be completely fulfilled. The *philosophes'* attempt to use science and technology to conquer nature, in short, turns life into a kind of Hobbesian struggle for power after power that ceases only in death. No matter how wealthy an individual or a society becomes, people will spend the greater part of their lives working. The "leisure" made possible by the productivity of commercial society is in truth an illusion, Rousseau contends, for people's time is invariably filled in the endless pursuit of riches and esteem. People labor with the idea that their work will provide satisfaction for them at some point in the future, and so their entire lives are spent postponing gratification; they are always "on the way," looking to the future rather than enjoying and embracing the present moment.[33] "What madness," Rousseau laments, "for a fleeting being like man always to look far into a future which comes so rarely and to neglect the present of which he is sure" (*Emile* II, 82; see also IV, 211; V, 410–11; *Julie*, 42; *Reveries*, 46).

Because people in commercial society always desire more, Rousseau argues, they are never satisfied and hence never really happy. Rousseau associates happiness with tranquility and self-sufficiency, and these in turn require the ability to satisfy one's desires: "Our unhappiness consists . . . in the disproportion between our desires and our faculties. A being endowed with senses whose faculties equaled his desires would be an absolutely happy being" (*Emile* II, 80; see also *GM* I-3, 82). And since no amount of struggle or conquest will satisfy people's desires if they are limitless, "human wisdom or the road of true happiness" consists in "diminishing the excess of the desires over the faculties" (*Emile* II, 80). In other words, happiness is to be found in a posture of moderation and acceptance rather than of conquest or acquisitiveness: "It is less the strength of arms than the moderation of hearts which makes men independent and free" (*Emile* IV, 236; see also II, 84; IV, 354). It is only by pursuing a relatively small number of manageable desires—something that is nearly impossible in commercial society—that people can attain self-sufficiency, tranquility, and ultimately happiness. Commercial society may give people the means and the discretion to pursue happiness as they see fit, according to Rousseau, but the

33. Volume II, Part 2, Chapter 13 of Alexis de Tocqueville's *Democracy in America* contains a description of "why the Americans show themselves so restive in the midst of their well-being" that is remarkably Rousseauian. See Tocqueville, *Democracy in America*, 511–14.

acquisitiveness unleashed by this kind of society ensures that it will always be a pursuit and never an attainment.

This, then, is Rousseau's most fundamental critique of commercial society: it makes people miserable. While many Enlightenment thinkers advocated commercial society because they thought it would provide the conditions under which people could pursue their own happiness as they saw fit, Rousseau claims that this kind of society in fact makes attaining happiness nearly impossible. Even if the *philosophes* were to succeed in their efforts to provide the *conditions* under which people could pursue happiness—even if they could assure peace and prosperity—this would not guarantee happiness itself. As Melzer writes, "as loudly as violence and oppression may proclaim their evil, in the end one cannot escape the quiet fact that safety is not happiness and that a nation free of oppression can still be miserable or debased."[34] And, we have seen, Rousseau in fact had many reasons to think that commercial society *would* be miserable and debased, above all because the encouragement of acquisitiveness turns life into a joyless quest for joy.

The fact that commercial society renders people miserable is particularly disheartening, for Rousseau, because happiness was so simple to achieve in the state of nature. Human beings are *made* to be happy, but they almost never actually are. Perhaps the most famous argument for why life in commercial society is preferable to life in simpler, precommercial times is Locke's claim that the prosperity produced by commercial society improves the quality of life of even the poorest individuals. Speaking of the American Indians, Locke contends that "a King of a large and fruitful Territory there feeds, lodges, and is clad worse than a day Labourer in England."[35] Rousseau counters that even if Locke is right in his economic argument, he is wrong in a more fundamental sense because he ignores the psychological differences between these two individuals. As Allan Bloom writes: "Unimpressed by the moral qualities Locke finds in the English day laborer, Rousseau turned back toward the proud dignity and independence of the king."[36] Rousseau argues that wealth and comfort do not produce the real happiness that the savage enjoys, and he thinks the latter is of much greater consequence. The savage is happy and free, and the day laborer—despite (or rather because of) his commodities—is miserable and dependent. Thus,

---

34. Melzer, *The Natural Goodness of Man,* 84.
35. Locke, *Two Treatises of Government,* 297.
36. Bloom, "Rousseau's Critique of Liberal Constitutionalism," in *The Legacy of Rousseau,* 155.

the savage would loathe civilized life: "What a Sight the difficult and envied labors of a European Minister are for a Carib! How many cruel deaths would that indolent Savage not prefer to the horror of such a life?" (SD, 66; see also 34, 92).[37] People simply will not be satisfied in a society in which everyone is made richer if they still find themselves chasing a happiness that always remains one step ahead, if their artificially induced desires multiply faster than their means to satisfy them. "On the contrary," Rousseau writes, "the closer to his natural condition man has stayed, the smaller is the difference between his faculties and his desires, and consequently the less removed he is from being happy" (Emile II, 81).

In sum, Rousseau sees the commercial society that the philosophes so lauded as an unmitigated disaster: The division of labor produces great inequalities and makes people weak and ignorant, thereby undermining citizenship. Dependence on the opinions of others encourages a great deal of role-playing, ostentation, deception, and immorality. And the expansion of people's desires results in endless toil, constant postponement of gratification, and misery. Commercial society, in short, produces people who are good neither for themselves nor for others. According to Rousseau, we have procured prosperity at the cost of our goodness and our happiness.

6. THE POSSIBILITY OF ESCAPE

Rousseau sees the degeneration of humanity from the goodness and happiness of the state of nature to the corruption and misery of civilized society as the result of a series of accidents rather than an inevitable development; however, he also concedes that once people have reached this state, they cannot simply retrace their steps back to an earlier, happier time (see Dialogues, 213; SD, 79) and that doing so would not necessarily be desirable even if it were possible, since such a return would entail certain problems of its own (see GM I-2, 77–78; SC I-8, 141; SD, 63). Yet the fact that people cannot simply return to the state of nature does not render humanity's natural goodness meaningless, for Rousseau, because it may be possible to

37. The frontispiece of the Discourse on Inequality vividly illustrates this point: it depicts a native from the Cape of Good Hope who, after living in Europe for some time, chooses to renounce the trappings of civilized life to return to his savage roots (see SD, xxx; for Rousseau's comments on this episode, see 93). The significance of this story, for Rousseau, lies in the fact that one of the few individuals who was in a position to truly appreciate the advantages of both ways of life found that he was happier as a savage.

reconstruct some of the conditions or experiences of the state of nature in the civilized world. Indeed, many of Rousseau's works can be read as attempts to delineate various "escape routes" from the problems of civilized society: *The Social Contract* and Rousseau's other political works show how to surmount these problems through citizenship in a virtuous republic; his autobiographical works show how to escape them through a life of solitary reverie and contemplation; and *Emile* shows how to retain a measure of natural goodness through the proper kind of education. We will see, however, that even Rousseau himself ultimately seems to hold out little hope that any of these solutions are truly possible in the modern world.

The Social Contract attempts to show how to unite people in society while leaving them as free as before. Rousseau's paradoxical solution to this problem is "the total alienation of each associate, with all his rights, to the whole community" (*SC* I-6, 138). Complete commitment to the community is necessary to produce true citizens; people must abandon their natural freedom entirely in order to secure their civil freedom (see *SC* I-8, 141–42). In the ideal republic, as Rousseau outlines it, the citizens submit themselves not to an individual but to the community at large—or, more precisely, to the general will, the will of the whole community concerning its well-being. Obedience to the general will does not have the same drawbacks as dependence on other individuals, according to Rousseau, for the citizens submit themselves only to laws that they help make and so obey only themselves and remain as free as before (see *Mountain*, 261; *PE*, 146; *SC* I-6, 139; II-4, 150).

While Rousseau does not call attention to the fact, we can observe that such citizens are likely not *completely* free and content in the way that people were in the state of nature: Rousseau seems to admit that it is impossible to *entirely* eliminate the private will in civilized people, and thus that citizens will always be conflicted to some (ideally infinitesimal) degree (see *SC* I-7, 140–41; III-10, 186). Furthermore, public-spirited citizens would be too active to fully enjoy the tranquility that Rousseau sees as a necessary prerequisite of true happiness. Yet neither would they have the boundless longings and unsatisfied desires that prevail in commercial society; it is precisely because they are dedicated to the community (i.e., good for others) that Rousseau believes true citizens would be by and large satisfied or content (i.e., good for themselves).[38]

38. See Reisert, *Jean-Jacques Rousseau*, 113, 124, 134–35.

A republic of the kind that Rousseau advocates is most feasible, he notes, in a relatively small, homogenous, isolated, and agrarian community with minimal differences in wealth among the citizens (see *SC* III-4, 173–74). Yet he concedes that even under these conditions people must be transformed or denatured in order to become true citizens; they must be made into wholly civic beings, and their natural selfishness must be eradicated. This can be done, according to *The Social Contract,* through a kind of miraculous legislator who persuades people to devote themselves to the community by presenting himself as a prophet; he places his pronouncements "in the mouth of the immortals in order to win over by divine authority those who cannot be moved by human prudence" (*SC* II-7, 156–57).[39] And once the legislator has created true citizens and a common culture worthy of patriotic devotion, this devotion must be constantly reinforced through civic education and a civil religion (see *SC* IV-8, 222–23).

Much ink has been spilled concerning the exact nature of this ideal community and what precisely Rousseau means by the general will, yet one of the most remarkable features of Rousseau's political thought is often overlooked: he advocates true citizenship not for the good of the community as a whole, but primarily for the sake of the individual citizens themselves. As Bernard Yack writes, "he demands the complete subordination of the individual *for the sake of the individual,* not to further the collectively shared goals that constitute the community."[40] It is less the strength or stability or even the justice of the community than the healthy state of citizens' souls that leads Rousseau to admire Sparta and republican Rome.[41] The true citizen is less divided and less unhappy than the typical inhabitant of commercial

39. This manipulation of the legislator, along with Rousseau's rejection of any individual rights against the community and his talk about forcing people to be free (see *SC* I-7, 141), has led many commentators to accuse Rousseau of being a precursor to totalitarianism. Isaiah Berlin goes so far as to argue that Rousseau "was one of the most sinister and most formidable enemies of liberty in the whole history of modern thought." Berlin, *Freedom and Its Betrayal,* 49. For other readings that stress Rousseau's totalitarian tendencies, see Crocker, *Rousseau's Social Contract;* and Talmon, *The Origins of Totalitarian Democracy.* For attempts to defend Rousseau against this charge, see Leigh, "Liberté et autorité dans le *Contrat social,*" in *Jean-Jacques Rousseau et son oeuvre;* Plamenatz, "Ce qui ne signifie autre chose," in *Hobbes and Rousseau;* and Wokler, "Rousseau and His Critics," in *Rousseau and Liberty.*

40. Yack, *The Longing for Total Revolution,* 63; see also 66–67.

41. While the repressive features of Spartan society render this city-state largely unattractive to contemporary sensibilities, viewing it in a positive light was common in the eighteenth century. See, for example, the entry "Lacedaemon" in Diderot, ed., *Encyclopedia: Selections,* 160–87. Rousseau's praise of Sparta is perhaps better known, but it is Rome that he calls the "model of all free peoples" (*SD,* 4; see also *Mountain,* 233).

society, and this is why citizenship in a virtuous republic could serve as an escape route from the ills of this kind of society.

Yet Rousseau is extraordinarily pessimistic about the possibility of (re)-creating such a republic in the modern world. First of all, the founding of such a society would require a nearly God-like legislator who is "capable of changing human nature, so to speak" (*SC* II-7, 155). Furthermore, even if an extraordinary person like this were to arise, he would need to find a people capable of accepting good laws, and such a people is equally rare since "once a people has been corrupted, it has never been seen to return to virtue" (*CW* II, 53; see also *Fragments,* 33; *Narcissus,* 196; *PE,* 169; *SC* II-8, 158). And even if a miraculous legislator *were* to miraculously find a people capable of accepting good laws, the republic he founded would inevitably decline, for "the vices that make social institutions necessary are the same ones that make their abuse inevitable" (*SD,* 62; see also *Corsica,* 123; *SC* III-10, 186–88; III-11, 188). In short, Rousseau admits, healthy politics is all but impossible: "To put law over man is a problem in politics which I compare to that of squaring the circle in geometry" (*Poland,* 170; see also *CJJR* XXXIII, 243). Betrand de Jouvenel is essentially correct, then, when he argues that *The Social Contract* "is not a hopeful prescription for a Republic to come, but a clinical analysis of political deterioration" and that "Rousseau the social scientist predicts the destruction of what Rousseau the moralist recommends."[42]

At times Rousseau seems to suggest that creating a healthy republic might be possible since it *did* occur in Sparta and republican Rome (see *Final Reply,* 119), but he more often admits that these ancient peoples cannot serve as models for the modern world since they were so different in every respect (see *Fragments,* 65; *Mountain,* 292; *Poland,* 171). This kind of republic was, he says, "a continual miracle that the world ought not to hope to see again" (*PE,* 156–57). He laments that even his beloved Geneva succumbed to the commercial tendencies of his time: "let us not flatter ourselves that we shall see Sparta reborn in the lap of commerce and the love of gain," he writes of his native city (*d'Alembert,* 300).[43] In *The Social Contract,* Rousseau

---

42. Jouvenel, "Rousseau's Theory of the Forms of Government," in *Hobbes and Rousseau,* 487, 496. See also Melzer, *The Natural Goodness of Man,* 112–13, 218–20, 265–70, 278; and Peled, "Rousseau's Inhibited Radicalism," 1034.

43. On the idea that Geneva had become essentially commercial by this point, see *Julie,* 545, and d'Alembert's article "Geneva" in *Encyclopedia,* 128. On Rousseau's recognition that Geneva was probably past the point of real reform, see *Confessions,* 333; *Mountain,* 237, 254, 293.

argued that in all of Europe only the island of Corsica—because it was small, isolated, and relatively undeveloped—was fit for the kind of legislator that a true republic requires (see *SC* II-10, 162). And his *Plan for a Constitution for Corsica,* written later in life, explained to the Corsicans how to secure such a republic: he advised them to maintain a primitive agrarian economy in which everyone cultivated the land and served in a citizen militia, to enact sumptuary laws, to use the barter system instead of money to the greatest extent possible, to keep the island completely self-sufficient and largely isolated, and to have a minimal division of labor and no great extremes of wealth. Yet Rousseau ultimately admits that such a reactionary solution is bound to fail in the long run; even his work on Corsica ends on a note of pessimism, acknowledging that increases in population and contact with neighboring states will inevitably bring about the spread of commerce and all of the ills associated with it.[44]

In short, Rousseau recognized that it is impossible to stem the tide of "progress" forever. He held out almost no hope that the only conceivable collective solution to the ills of commercial society—the virtuous republic— was possible *anywhere* in the modern world. And if Rousseau's diagnosis of his own time was grim, his diagnosis of the future was even more so: at the outset of the *Discourse on Inequality,* he tells his contemporaries that the problems of their world "foretell even greater discontents for your unhappy Posterity" and that this thought must be "the dread of those who will have the unhappiness to live after you" (*SD,* 20). Since he thought that healthy politics was impossible in his (and our) time, he also proposed some ways that an individual might overcome or avoid the corrupting influences of commercial society.

The first individual-level solution is embodied in Rousseau himself as depicted in his autobiographical writings, especially *The Reveries of a Solitary Walker.* In these works, Rousseau takes on the persona of *"pauvre* Jean-Jacques," the solitary wanderer and dreamer, rather than "J. J. Rousseau, *citoyen de Genève,"* the republican patriot. His life, as he describes it in these works—or at least the happiest periods of his life, such as the time he spent on Saint Peter's Island—is largely spent in solitude, where he is able to enjoy

---

44. On Rousseau's ultimate pessimism concerning Corsica, see Peled, "Rousseau's Inhibited Radicalism," 1035, 1039–40, 1042. Rousseau is even more pessimistic in his advice to the Poles in *Considerations on the Government of Poland:* since Poland is a large, landlocked country with powerful neighbors and a tradition of feudalism, he holds, a healthy republic almost certainly would not be possible there.

leisure and innocent, simple, and immediate pleasures. For instance, he rapturously describes lying on his back in a boat, floating on Lake Bienne, where he is able to harmonize with nature and enjoy tranquility (see *Confessions*, 539; *Reveries*, 44). He spends a good deal of his time letting his mind wander in blissful reverie, although he occasionally botanizes in order to keep himself from being completely idle. In a word, he attains happiness by withdrawing from commercial society's corrupting influences. The simplicity of his life ensures that his desires do not constantly outstrip his faculties, and thus he is content in the way that people in the state of nature were (see *Dialogues*, 144; *Reveries*, 42). In fact, he may even be *more* content than people in the state of nature because he remains self-sufficient even with his more highly developed faculties; he enjoys "a sufficient, perfect, and full happiness which leaves in the soul no emptiness it might need to fill" (*Reveries*, 46). It seems, then, that Rousseau presents his own life as the highest possibility, the most complete escape from the ills of commercial society.[45]

Yet Rousseau concedes that a life like his would not be an appropriate goal for the vast majority of people. This is true in the first place because of his utter uniqueness: "I am not made like any of the [people] I have seen; I dare to believe that I am not made like any that exist," he writes (*Confessions*, 5; see also *Reveries*, 41). Rousseau presumably thinks it is his extraordinary genius and strength of soul that has allowed him to so fully escape the corrupting influences of commercial society, and in this case it would be unlikely that anyone else would be capable of reaching similar heights. Moreover, Rousseau's greatest happiness—the happiness he found on Saint Peter's Island—only arose through extraordinary circumstances, when he was cut off from the rest of society not by choice but by persecution (see *Reveries*, 41, 46–47). And the other moments of happiness he describes generally also arose from peculiar circumstances, such as the health problems that led him to believe he would die young and his somewhat perverse romantic involvement with Mme de Warens (see *Confessions* 90, 191).

It is also worth noting that Rousseau describes periods of great misery interspersed with his moments of great joy, particularly in the *Confessions;* he claims to have experienced "unparalleled misfortunes" and "a terrible . . . fate which has no precedent among mortals" (*Confessions*, 233, 351; see also 295, 410). The rapturous moments of reverie were, by his own account, the

---

45. This is a theme of Kelly, *Rousseau's Exemplary Life*.

peak of his existence but not a consistent way of life. And, to repeat, even the brief moments of perfect happiness that he describes were attained only through extraordinary genius and extraordinary circumstances, neither of which anyone else could hope to replicate. Rousseau's own life cannot ultimately serve as a model for most people, then, so he also attempts to describe a way to avoid the ills of commercial society that is open to an ordinary person.

The second individual-level "escape route" that Rousseau presents is embodied in Emile, the eponymous student in his work on education. In this work, Rousseau shows how an ordinary boy can be raised in such a way as to preserve much of his natural goodness. Emile's is the ultimate child-centered education: his seemingly omniscient and omnicompetent governor, "Jean-Jacques," spends nearly every waking moment of every day raising him, from birth to marriage. Emile is trained, first of all, to be tough and to cope with suffering, and this helps him accept necessity and makes him moderate (see *Emile* I, 47). Likewise, he is taught to think of himself as Robinson Crusoe on his island, and this perspective frees him from many of the prejudices and desires of society (see *Emile* III, 184–86). Above all, because of the artifice of his governor, Emile always feels free to do whatever he wants even though in fact he is largely controlled in all his actions (see *Emile* II, 85, 120). By never confronting Emile with another person's will or command, all the while manipulating his environment "behind the scenes," the governor ensures that Emile never feels his dependence on others and so has the illusion of self-sufficiency.[46] In the end Emile lives a simple life, largely independent of society, but he is not a solitary in the way that Rousseau is in his autobiographical writings: he is above all a "family man" whose domestic life serves as a refuge from society's corrupting influences. Just like the citizen and Rousseau the solitary dreamer, then, Emile avoids the key corrupting influences of commercial society: he is given

---

46. Just as in the *Social Contract*, where citizens are formed through the manipulation of the legislator, Emile feels free from dependence on others because of the manipulation of his governor. In both these cases, freedom is maintained not despite but *because of* deception; even if they are not truly free they at least *feel* free, and this is all that is necessary for a healthy soul. This technique of *la main cachée* or the "hidden hand" is one that Rousseau uses frequently to solve the problem of authority throughout his writings. See Burgelin, *La philosophie de l'existence de Jean-Jacques Rousseau*, 298–303; Crocker, *Rousseau's Social Contract*, 14, 18, 23, 167–68; Grant, *Hypocrisy and Integrity*, 125–39; Melzer, *The Natural Goodness of Man*, 244–49; and Starobinski, *Jean-Jacques Rousseau*, 100–101.

no duties that oppose his inclinations, he feels no dependence on others, and his moderation helps him limit his desires to those he can satisfy.

A life like Emile's would offer a way for ordinary people to escape the effects of commercial society if it were possible to imitate it, but this kind of life also ends up seeming to be impossible for all practical purposes. Like Rousseau's life, Emile's requires a person of extraordinary genius: not Emile himself, but the seemingly superhuman governor, Jean-Jacques. Such "a sublime soul" is hard to find indeed: "Is this rare mortal to be found? I do not know," Rousseau confesses (*Emile* I, 49–50; see also 59). And even if this extraordinary person were found, he would have to succeed in perfectly manipulating every element of the child's environment, including all of the other people with whom he comes into contact. This rigorous method must be followed to the letter, Rousseau says, for pursuing even a good method halfway would only plant contradictions in the child (see *Emile*, 34). In the end, Rousseau admits in *Emile* itself that the difficulties may be "insurmountable" (*Emile* II, 95). He makes this admission even more explicitly elsewhere: "You say, correctly, that it is impossible to make an Emile," he writes in a letter. "But I cannot believe that you take the book that carries this name for a true treatise on education. It is a philosophical work on the principle advanced by the author in other writings *that man is naturally good*" (*CJJR* XXI, 248; see also *Dialogues*, 213; *Mountain*, 211). Just like the lives of the true citizen and of Rousseau himself, then, Emile's life seems to be an impracticable alternative to commercial society rather than a truly viable option.

It is perhaps because he recognizes that the only conceivable alternatives to the misery of commercial society are not ultimately viable that Rousseau often suggests that human beings can simply no longer be happy. People's happiness can never be complete or permanent, he laments:

> Everything is in continual flux on earth. . . . There is nothing solid to which the heart might attach itself. Thus, here-below we have hardly anything but transitory pleasure. As for happiness which lasts, I doubt that it is known here. In our most intense enjoyments, there is hardly an instant when the heart can genuinely say to us: *I would like this instant to last forever.* And how can we call happiness a fleeting state which leaves our heart still worried and empty, which makes us long for something beforehand or desire something else afterward? (*Reveries*, 46 see also *Emile* II, 80)

Or again: "Happiness is a permanent condition which does not seem to be made for man here-below. . . . Thus, all our plans for felicity in this life are idle fancies. . . . I have seldom seen happy men, perhaps not at all" (*Reveries*, 78). In one of his last speeches to Emile before he marries, Jean-Jacques tells him that happiness "is the goal of every being which senses. . . . But where is happiness? Who knows it? All seek it, and none finds it. . . . Happiness leaves us, or we leave it" (*Emile* V, 442, 447; see also *Confessions*, 207). Civilized people would not be happy even if they could fulfill all of their desires, for they desire the wrong things: "Man once having renounced his original simplicity becomes so stupid that he does not even know how to desire. His wishes granted would all lead him to fortune, never to felicity" (*Julie*, 438n). Because of the circumstances of the civilized world and the transitory nature of life on earth, it seems that *no one*—not the citizen, Rousseau, or Emile, and certainly not the typical inhabitant of commercial society—can enjoy lasting happiness in the modern world.

In the end, then, Rousseau seems to concede that a healthy politics or even a healthy way of life is simply no longer attainable. Escape is impossible and the misery of commercial society is our fate.

CONCLUSION

All told, Rousseau's critique of commercial society is perhaps the deepest and most comprehensive critique ever made of this kind of society. Even if the various alternatives he offers are ultimately impracticable, his critique remains; while few people take Rousseau's "escape routes" fully seriously and at face value today (for good reason), the various elements of his critique are taken seriously indeed. In fact, the most serious critiques of commercial society made today seem to have already been anticipated to some degree by Rousseau. To take but a few of the most obvious examples: Rousseau's objections to the concentration of wealth and the injustice of poverty resemble similar objections from Marx to present-day antiglobalizationists. His disgust at people's weakness and pettiness resembles similar disgust from Nietzsche to present-day cultural declinists. His protests against conquering nature instead of treasuring it resemble similar protests from Thoreau to present-day environmentalists. His complaints about atomism and the undermining of citizenship resemble similar complaints from myriad communitarians and nationalists. His condemnation of people's vanity and moral corruption resembles similar condemnation from virtue ethicists and religious thinkers of all denominations. And his denunciation of people's acquisitiveness, postponement of gratification, and materialism resembles some of the most common themes of contemporary society: Western popular culture abounds in stories about the futility of the rat race, the lack of leisure even in the midst of prosperity, and how those who get to the top end up miserable. Even if they are not directly inspired by Rousseau, all of these complaints echo one part or another of Rousseau's critique of commercial society. And even if Rousseau's successors developed certain elements of his critique more fully, it is doubtful that any of them were as comprehensive in their approach. In many ways, then, Rousseau's critique presents the greatest challenge for someone who hopes to defend commercial society; any persuasive defense of commercial society would have to take all of the many and varied elements of Rousseau's critique into account. The remainder of this book will examine precisely such a defense from one of the first and greatest theorists of commercial society, Adam Smith.

T W O | SMITH'S SYMPATHY WITH ROUSSEAU'S CRITIQUE

Rousseau claims in his *Confessions* that "the *Discourse on Inequality* . . . found only a few readers who understood it in all of Europe, and none of these wanted to talk about it" (*Confessions* VIII, 326). We will see in this chapter, however, that Adam Smith not only understood this work and wanted to talk about it, but also was far more sympathetic to its arguments than is commonly acknowledged. Early in his career Smith wrote a review of Rousseau's famous work that urged his fellow Scots to take notice of it, and in that review he translated three long extracts from the *Discourse* that point to the three main Rousseauian critiques of commercial society that were discussed in Chapter 1. Later in life Smith continued to grapple with the issues raised by Rousseau; in his later writings he not only concedes a measure of validity to each of Rousseau's critiques of commercial society, but also on occasion comes close to appropriating Rousseau's own words in doing so. Of course, Smith was far from *wholly* sympathetic to Rousseau's arguments; we will see in Chapters 3 and 4 that he offers counterarguments and countermeasures for each of the three critiques and that in the end he is a firm supporter of commercial society. We will see in this chapter, however, that his support did not come at the expense of an appreciation of the possible problems associated with this kind of society. While Smith is often portrayed as an unabashed champion of commercial society, he in fact shared a number of the same misgivings as the great crusader against that kind of society.

We will begin, in Section 1, by looking at the historical connection between Smith and Rousseau. While Smith probably never met or corresponded with Rousseau and never explicitly discusses him in either of his principal works, we will see that he was well aware of Rousseau's great influence and that he discusses Rousseau's critique of commercial society explicitly in several of his shorter writings and implicitly a number of times in his principal works. Section 2 analyzes Smith's earliest and lengthiest writing on Rousseau—his review of the *Discourse on Inequality*—and shows that this review anticipates Smith's later engagements with Rousseau's arguments. The rest of the chapter, Sections 3 through 5, mirrors Sections 3 through 5 of the previous chapter, showing that Smith in fact expressed some sympathy with each of the three main Rousseauian critiques of commercial society: he, too, acknowledges that the division of labor produces great inequalities and can exact an immense cost in human dignity by rendering people feeble and ignorant; that people's great concern with the opinions of others can lead to problems such as ostentation and moral corruption; and that people tend to submit themselves to endless toil and anxiety in the pursuit of "trinkets and baubles" that in the end provide (at best) only fleeting satisfaction.

I. SMITH AND ROUSSEAU: THE HISTORICAL CONNECTION

It might at first glance seem surprising to argue that Rousseau had an impact on Smith's thought. After all, these two thinkers never corresponded and probably never met, much less shared ideas with each other; nor does Smith explicitly mention Rousseau in either *The Theory of Moral Sentiments* or *The Wealth of Nations*. But Smith (1723–90) and Rousseau (1712–78) were near contemporaries, thought and wrote largely during the same period, and in fact had many mutual acquaintances. As we will see, these two thinkers moved in similar circles within Europe's republic of letters, and Smith was well aware of Rousseau's great influence on the leading thinkers of their time. Furthermore, we will see that while Smith does not explicitly mention Rousseau in either of his principal writings, he does discuss Rousseau in a number of his shorter letters and writings—including a substantial review of the *Discourse on Inequality*—and there is strong evidence to support the idea that he had Rousseau in mind while writing several crucial passages of his two most famous works.

Smith toured the Continent between February 1764 and October 1766 as tutor of the young Duke of Buccleuch, and during this trip he met a number of the most prominent *philosophes,* including Voltaire, Diderot, d'Alembert, Helvétius, and the Baron d'Holbach (who had earlier supervised a French translation of *The Theory of Moral Sentiments*).[1] These men of letters, most of whom had once been friends and colleagues of Rousseau

1. For an account of Smith's Grand Tour, see Ross, *The Life of Adam Smith*, 195–219.

(with the exception of Voltaire) but who were by this point his adversaries, welcomed Smith with enthusiasm and affection. While the animosity between Voltaire and Rousseau ran deep, there was nothing but mutual admiration between Voltaire and Smith, who met on five or six different occasions at Ferney in 1765. Smith had earlier proclaimed Voltaire to be "the most universal genius perhaps which France has ever produced" (*Letter*, 254); and on their meeting, Voltaire exclaimed, "This Smith is an excellent man! We have nothing to compare with him, and I am embarrassed for my dear compatriots."[2] Smith met the other *philosophes*, as well as *économistes* such as Turgot, Quesnay, and Mirabeau, regularly in the salons of Paris in 1766, where his reputation, breadth of knowledge, and amiable absent-mindedness—as well as his friendship with Hume, affectionately known there as *le bon David*—made him almost universally respected by his hosts despite his poor spoken French. Smith returned their esteem and, according to Dugald Stewart, Smith's contemporary and first biographer, "some of them he continued ever afterwards to reckon among his friends" (*EPS*, 303).

Smith's acquaintance with many of the leading thinkers on the Continent is sufficient for us to surmise that he must have been well aware of Rousseau's peculiar place among them, but we need not rest on such inferences. The individual with the most significant link to these two thinkers, after all, was undoubtedly Hume, who was Smith's closest friend and whose quarrel with Rousseau created a considerable stir among Europe's republic of letters. At the prompting of the Comtesse de Boufflers, one of the most distinguished *salonnières* in Paris, Hume offered Rousseau a refuge in England from his persecutions (both real and imagined) on the Continent. They met in Paris in mid-December of 1765 and then traveled together to London in early January 1766. The two philosophers got along well enough at the outset, but by June their tenuous friendship had been ruptured after Rousseau accused Hume of participating in a conspiracy to damage his reputation and keep him buried in obscurity in England.[3]

Given that Smith probably arrived in Paris from Geneva sometime in

---

2. Quoted in Dawson, "Is Sympathy so Surprising?" 147.

3. For accounts of the famous Rousseau–Hume quarrel, see Cranston, *The Solitary Self*, 157–68; and Mossner, *The Life of David Hume*, 511–32. For a more popular account that is perhaps a bit too generous to Rousseau, see Edmonds and Eidinow, *Rousseau's Dog*. The best treatment will soon be found in Scott and Zaretsky, *So Great a Noise*. I am grateful to Scott for allowing me to read this forthcoming work.

December 1765[4] and that Hume and Rousseau did not leave for England until January 4, 1766, John Rae (whose influential *Life of Adam Smith* was published in 1895) assumes that "Smith must no doubt have met Rousseau occasionally with Hume during that last fortnight of 1765, though there is no actual evidence that he did."[5] The evidence, however, seems to point against such a meeting. In a letter from London at the end of January 1766, Hume wrote Smith to say, "I am sorry I did not see you before I left Paris" (*CAS*, 110).[6] This could conceivably mean that Hume was sorry he did not see Smith *again* in Paris (i.e., they had already met, and at that meeting they had promised each other they would meet again before Hume left); other evidence, though, suggests that a meeting between Smith and Rousseau never took place. Dugald Stewart omits Rousseau from the long list of French literary figures with whom Smith associated while in Paris (see *EPS*, 302–3)—an improbable omission if Smith *had* met Rousseau, given Rousseau's celebrity status—and Barthélemy Faujas de Saint-Fond, a French geologist who visited Edinburgh in late 1782, reports that Smith knew Voltaire personally but makes no similar claim when speaking of Smith's thoughts on Rousseau.[7] It is impossible to know for certain, then, but it seems unlikely that Smith and Rousseau met in Paris that December, and it is clear that they never met at any other time.

While Hume was contemplating whether to publish an account of his

---

4. Dugald Stewart reports that Smith returned to Paris "around Christmas 1765" (*EPS*, 302), and John Rae speculates, on the basis of a letter from Horace Walpole written on December 5 saying that the Duke of Buccleuch was expected to arrive in Paris the following week, that Smith "arrived in Paris about the middle of December, just in time to have a week or two with Hume before he finally left Paris for London with Rousseau." Rae, *Life of Adam Smith*, 194. Yet as Ian Simpson Ross notes, the first conclusive news of Smith being in Paris did not come until March 2, 1766, when Walpole recorded that he went to see an Italian play with Smith. Furthermore, a letter dated February 5 from George-Louis Le Sage, a Genevese physician, implies that he had seen Smith recently in Geneva. See Ross, *The Life of Adam Smith*, 209. Thus it is difficult to say exactly when Smith arrived in Paris (and consequently whether he would have been in that city at the same time as Rousseau). Given, however, that the authority of Stewart probably outweighs that of the rather imprecise evidence revealed by the letter from Le Sage, it seems fair to suppose that Smith arrived in Paris sometime in December 1765. Smith is said to have uncharacteristically kept a diary during his trip, but unfortunately no trace of it has been found since it was sold in the 1920s from a bookshop in Edinburgh. See Scott, "Studies Relating to Adam Smith During the Last Fifty Years," in *Proceedings of the British Academcy*, 273.

5. Rae, *Life of Adam Smith*, 196.

6. This letter from Hume was addressed to Smith through an M. Foley, a banker in Paris, further supporting the idea that Smith arrived in that city well before the first positive report of his being there on March 2 (see footnote 4 above).

7. See Saint Fond, *A Journey Through England and Scotland*, vol. 2, 245–46.

quarrel with Rousseau, Smith wrote to him urging him not to do so. "I am thoroughly convinced that Rousseau is as great a Rascal as you, and as every man here believes him to be," Smith wrote from Paris on July 6, 1766. "Yet," he continued,

> let me beg of you not to think of publishing anything to the world upon the very great impertinence which he has been guilty of to you. . . . By endeavouring to unmask before the Public this hypo-critical Pedant, you run the risk, of disturbing the tranquillity of your whole life. By letting him alone he cannot give you a fort-nights uneasiness. To write against him, is, you may depend upon it, the very thing he wishes you to do. He is in danger of falling into obscurity in England and he hopes to make himself consid-erable by provoking an illustrious adversary. (CAS, 112–13)

In the end, Hume refused to listen to his friend's plea for restraint. Con-vinced that Rousseau would publish his own version of the quarrel, he was determined to get into print first. Hume's pamphlet, "A Concise and Gen-uine Account of the Dispute between Mr. Hume and Mr. Rousseau," was published in French in October and in English in November.[8] Smith, like the rest of Europe's literary world, remained interested in the outcome of the quarrel, and he wrote to Hume in June of the following year to ask sar-castically, "What has become of Rousseau? Has he gone abroad, because he cannot continue to get himself sufficiently persecuted in Great Britain?" (CAS, 125). Hume's next reply to Smith contained no mention of Rousseau, so Smith persisted in another letter in September: "I should be glad to know the true history of Rousseau before and since he left England" (CAS, 132). Hume replied with a lengthy account of the "late heteroclite Exploits of Rousseau" on October 8 and added some corrections in a letter dated Octo-ber 17 (see CAS, 133–37).

While Smith understandably supported his close friend in this famous quarrel (as did most people who knew about it), and while there was a mutual feeling of admiration between Smith and many of Rousseau's ene-mies in France and Geneva, we should be wary of concluding that Smith's view of Rousseau was entirely negative. A little over a decade earlier he had written a letter to the editors of the *Edinburgh Review* in which he discussed

---

8. See Cranston, *The Solitary Self*, 168; and Mossner, *The Life of David Hume*, 530.

at some length "the late Discourse upon the origin and foundation of the inequality amongst mankind by Mr. Rousseau of Geneva" (*Letter*, 250). His review of the *Discourse on Inequality*, which will be examined in detail in the next section, is on the whole respectful and at times admiring. In the same letter he also bestows high praise on the *Encyclopédie* and mentions Rousseau as one of the several "very eminent" contributors who are "already known to foreign nations by the valuable works which they have published" (*Letter*, 246). Smith's next recorded mention of Rousseau came in 1761, five years before the quarrel with Hume, in his "Considerations Concerning the First Formation of Languages." Here he speaks of "the ingenious and eloquent M. Rousseau of Geneva" and attempts to resolve a problem that Rousseau had raised in the *Discourse on Inequality*, the question of how general names were first formed (*LRBL*, 205).[9] The last reference to Rousseau in Smith's own hand is found in an essay titled "Of the Nature of that Imitation which takes place in what are called The Imitative Arts," unpublished until after his death but written at some point after the quarrel.[10] In this work he discusses Rousseau's argument in the *Dictionary of Music* (1768) that music has the power to imitate sights and events as well as sounds; he carefully describes him as "an Author, more capable of feeling strongly than of analising accurately" (*EPS*, 198–99).

Smith's final recorded comment on Rousseau was made in 1782 to Saint-Fond, the French visitor to Edinburgh mentioned earlier. Saint-Fond reports that Smith "spoke to me of Rousseau with a kind of religious respect": "'Voltaire,' said he, 'sought to correct the vices and the follies of mankind by laughing at them, and sometimes even getting angry with them; Rousseau, by the attraction of sentiment, and the force of conviction, drew the reader into the heart of reason. His *Contrat Social* will in time avenge him for all the persecutions he suffered.'"[11] While this effusive praise may be a bit of an exaggeration from a Frenchman who wished to boast of the admiration that this "venerable philosopher" had for "all our best French authors,"[12] there is no reason to believe that Smith did not speak highly of Rousseau to his visitor. In any event, it is difficult to assess Smith's personal views of Rousseau: as we have seen, his comments range from describing Rousseau

9. Smith also mentioned Rousseau in a similar context in his lectures on rhetoric and belles lettres at the University of Glasgow in 1762 to 1763. See *LRBL*, 9.

10. The essay is difficult to date precisely; see Wightman's "Introduction" in *EPS*, 170–75.

11. Saint Fond, *A Journey through England and Scotland*, vol. 2, 246.

12. Ibid., 245.

as "ingenious and eloquent" to calling him a great "Rascal" and a "hypo-critical Pedant" and then perhaps back to speaking of him "with a kind of religious respect." One possibility is that Smith's comments on Rousseau varied according to their audience: the most favorable of these comments were addressed to a French visitor and the most negative were addressed to Hume during his quarrel with Rousseau, with the others adopting a more moderate stance. It is also possible that Smith's views of Rousseau changed over time—that he respected Rousseau early in his career, came to dislike him during the quarrel with Hume, and was later able to think of him in perspective, after distancing himself a certain amount from the quarrel.[13]

Regardless of Smith's views of Rousseau the *person*, what is important for our actual purposes is that he clearly had respect for Rousseau the *author*—that is, for Rousseau's writings and arguments. This claim will be sub-stantiated throughout this chapter, but a few observations are possible at the outset. First, we should note that Smith owned a number of Rousseau's works—all in French, which Smith knew relatively well even if he could not speak it well—including the *Letter to M. d'Alembert on the Theater* (1758), the *Discourse on the Sciences and Arts* and Rousseau's replies to his critics, the *Letter on French Music*, his comic play *Narcisse*, his opera *Le Devin du village* (*The Village Soothsayer*), the *Encyclopédie* entry on *Political Economy*, the *Discourse on Inequality* (all found in a collection of Rousseau's *Oeuvres diverses* from 1760),[14] *Julie, or the New Heloïse* (1761), *Emile* (1762), the *Letters Written from the Mountain* (1764), and a few miscellaneous volumes from later collections.[15] That Smith owned so many of Rousseau's writings—many of them the earliest editions of his works—is especially noteworthy given that obtaining French books in Britain during much of this period was made somewhat more difficult than usual by the Seven Years' War (1756–63).[16]

More important than the fact that Smith owned many of Rousseau's works, however, is the fact that he was influenced by them.[17] That he took

13. See Ross, *The Life of Adam Smith*, 212.

14. I am grateful to Christopher Kelly for identifying the works included in this two-volume collection.

15. See Mizuta, *Adam Smith's Library*, 217–18.

16. See Ross, *The Life of Adam Smith*, 147.

17. Smith was far from the only figure of the Scottish Enlightenment to be influenced by Rousseau: James Beattie, Hugh Blair, James Burnett (Lord Monboddo), James Dunbar, Adam Ferguson, John Gregory, Henry Home (Lord Kames), John Millar, and Thomas Reid are among the other important Scottish thinkers whose works display signs of Rousseau's influence dur-ing these years. For a brief look at the relationship between Rousseau and some of these figures, see Leigh, "Rousseau and the Scottish Enlightenment."

Rousseau's works—or at the very least the *Discourse on Inequality* and his entries in the *Encyclopédie*—seriously is demonstrated by the letter to the authors of the *Edinburgh Review* mentioned earlier. Rousseau's *Discourse* was published in late April 1755, and Smith's review of this work appeared less than a year later, in March 1756, in the second (and, as it turned out, final) issue of the short-lived *Review*.[18] It was written when Smith was only thirty-two years old, making it one of his earliest published writings. When Smith wrote the "Letter" in late 1755 or early 1756, he had already discussed moral philosophy, jurisprudence, and political economy (among other topics) in his public lectures in Edinburgh from 1748 to 1750 and in his lectures at the University of Glasgow as Chair of Logic in 1751 and as Chair of Moral Philosophy since 1752 (in which position he would continue until 1764, when he left for his tour of the Continent).[19] Smith's early writings on these topics would appear not long after the "Letter": the first edition of *The Theory of Moral Sentiments* was published in 1759, the lectures on jurisprudence for which we have student notes were delivered in 1762–64, and the "Early Draft" of *The Wealth of Nations* was probably written before April 1763.[20] Thus, Smith's encounter with Rousseau came at a time when he had already begun thinking about many of the issues that would occupy him throughout his career and during which he was still working out the arguments he would make in his writings.

As we will see later in this chapter, the arguments in the *Discourse on Inequality* had a demonstrable impact on Smith's works. In fact, in all of the works mentioned above—*The Theory of Moral Sentiments*, the *Lectures on Jurisprudence*, and the "Early Draft" of *The Wealth of Nations*—as well as in *The Wealth of Nations* itself, Smith demonstrates his awareness of Rousseau's critique of commercial society. In each case, he casts a sort of reply to Rousseau in which he shows a degree of sympathy with his arguments but also shows how commercial society might be defended on these scores. He does not mention Rousseau by name in these passages, but this is not particularly surprising: Smith rarely names contemporaneous authors in his major

18. The *Review* was short-lived, in its eighteenth-century manifestation, at least: Francis Jeffrey began publishing a magazine by the same name in 1802, which had a long and distinguished run.

19. See the "Introduction" to *TMS* by Raphael and Macfie, 1–5; the "Introduction" to *LJ* by Meek, Raphael, and Stein, 1–5; and Scott, *Adam Smith as Student and Professor*, 50–56, 111.

20. This latter work is difficult to date precisely; see Meek and Skinner, "The Development of Adam Smith's Ideas on the Division of Labor."

works, even the ones to whom he frequently and obviously refers, such as Hume. Instead, he much more often speaks of "an author of very great and original genius," "an agreeable philosopher," and the like, or omits mentioning the other philosopher at all.[21] The idea that several passages in Smith's works were at least partially inspired by Rousseau is suggested by the fact that he not only directly responds to the challenges posed by Rousseau, but also (as we will see) occasionally even uses phrases strikingly similar to ones in the *Discourse on Inequality* that he translated for the *Edinburgh Review*.[22] It is very likely, then, that Smith was to some extent responding to Rousseau in a number of important passages throughout his works, and there is no question that he was at the very least responding to the Rousseau*ian* critique of commercial society—that is, the critique that was becoming more prevalent in the mid to late eighteenth century largely as a result of Rousseau's enormous intellectual impact. Thus, Istvan Hont and Michael Ignatieff are correct to conclude that "Rousseau is an important if unavowed interlocutor in the passages in the *Theory of Moral Sentiments* which Smith devoted to the pursuit of wealth in modern society"[23]— and, we will see, in a number of other passages throughout Smith's works.

2. THE LETTER TO THE *EDINBURGH REVIEW*

In his letter to the *Edinburgh Review,* Smith urges the editors to extend the periodical's coverage beyond Scotland to include more works from England

21. The exception is Part VII of *The Theory of Moral Sentiments,* which examines a number of previous "Systems of Moral Philosophy." Even here, however, Bernard Mandeville and Smith's teacher Francis Hutcheson are the only two eighteenth-century thinkers who are treated at any length. For reasons why Smith might have declined to explicitly name the thinkers with whom he was engaging, even where it would normally be expected, see Griswold, *Adam Smith and the Virtues of Enlightenment,* 47.

22. The idea that some passages in Smith's works might have been inspired in part by Rousseau is far from novel: see, for example, the note by the editors of *TMS,* 183–84n5; Bonar, *A Catalogue of the Library of Adam Smith,* 161; Dawson, "Is Sympathy so Surprising?" 149; Leigh, "Rousseau and the Scottish Enlightenment," 11–12; Morrow, *Ethical and Economic Theories of Adam Smith,* 87; Raphael, *Adam Smith,* 71–72, 80; Ross, *The Life of Adam Smith,* 211; Roddier, *J.-J. Rousseau en Angleterre au XVIIIe siècle,* 40–42; Sewall, "Rousseau's Second Discourse in England from 1755 to 1762," 98–99; Teichgraeber, *"Free Trade" and Moral Philosophy,* 146; Todorov, "Living Alone Together," 4; Winch, "Adam Smith: Scottish Moral Philosopher as Political Economist," 103–4; Winch, *Riches and Poverty,* 60, 72–73; and Wokler, *Rousseau,* 33. See also footnote 8 in the introduction for several works that give more sustained attention to the Smith–Rousseau connection.

23. Hont and Ignatieff, "Needs and Justice in the *Wealth of Nations,*" in *Wealth and Virtue,* 10.

and the Continent.[24] Near the end of the letter he offers an account of Rousseau's *Discourse on Inequality* to give an example of the sorts of works that ought to be included. While this account of the *Discourse* is not terribly long—around two pages of commentary and two pages of translated passages—it is far and away the longest one he presents in the "Letter." Smith's overall stance toward Rousseau in the "Letter" is difficult to gauge: his review has been characterized both as "laudatory"[25] and as an "attack,"[26] and it has been claimed both that Smith "lavishes high praise on the work as a whole"[27] and that "Rousseau's argument . . . receives short and sharp treatment."[28] Smith's tone seems to me to be neither laudatory nor critical but rather by and large *respectful;* although he does not overtly address the validity of any of Rousseau's arguments here, it is clear that he thinks these arguments *matter* and that the issues Rousseau addresses are important to him.

Smith begins his review by claiming that "whoever reads this . . . work with attention, will observe" that the second volume of Bernard Mandeville's *The Fable of the Bees* "has given occasion to the system of Mr. Rousseau, in whom however the principles of the English author are softened, improved, and embellished, and stript of all that tendency to corruption and licentiousness which has disgraced them in their original author" (*Letter,* 250). After this opening statement, much of the remainder of the review consists of a comparison between Rousseau and Mandeville. It is striking that Smith chooses to compare Rousseau to Mandeville; it is even more striking that he contends that Mandeville's work *has given occasion to* Rousseau's. After all, the idea that "private vices" can lead to "public benefits"— the central argument of *The Fable of the Bees*—was almost the exact opposite of Rousseau's view of the matter, and Rousseau himself calls Mandeville "the most excessive Detractor of human virtues" (*SD,* 36; see also *Narcissus,* 191). Furthermore, as Smith immediately notes, their views of the state of nature seem at first glance to be utterly opposed: "Dr. Mandeville represents the primitive state of mankind as the most wretched and

24. For an analysis of the first part of the "Letter"—the part before the review of the *Discourse on Inequality*—see Lomonaco, "Adam Smith's 'Letter to the Authors of the *Edinburgh Review.*'"

25. Todorov, "Living Alone Together," 5. See also Fleischacker, *A Third Concept of Liberty,* 309n37.

26. Hundert, *The Enlightenment's Fable,* 220. See also Macfie, *The Individual in Society,* 44; and Wokler, "Todorov's Otherness," 51.

27. Leigh, "Rousseau and the Scottish Enlightenment," 12.

28. West, "Adam Smith and Rousseau's *Discourse on Inequality,*" 68.

miserable that can be imagined: Mr. Rousseau, on the contrary, paints it as the happiest and most suitable to his nature" (*Letter*, 250).[29]

Yet as Smith shows, Rousseau and Mandeville have a surprising amount in common.[30] First, they both maintain "that there is in man no powerful instinct which necessarily determines him to seek society for its own sake" (*Letter*, 250; see also *TMS* VII.iii.1.1, 315). In other words, even though Rousseau sees the state of nature as an attractive state and Mandeville sees it as an unattractive one, they both see it as an extremely asocial and primitive condition; in this state people's cognitive endowments are meager and they are driven wholly by their impulses, none of which encourage them to seek the company of others. Second, Smith notes that Rousseau and Mandeville "suppose the same slow progress and gradual development of all the talents, habits, and arts which fit men to live together in society, and they both describe this progress pretty much in the same manner" (*Letter*, 250–51). Unlike Hobbes and Locke, in other words, these two thinkers underscore the gradualness of humanity's development from its rude beginnings to civilized society; they both maintain that this development occurred very slowly as a result of events like the rise of language, the development of the division of labor, and the invention of tools and money.[31] The final similarity that Smith notes between Rousseau and Mandeville is that "according to both, those laws of justice, which maintain the present inequality amongst mankind, were originally the inventions of the cunning and the powerful, in order to maintain or to acquire an unnatural and unjust superiority over the rest of their fellow-creatures" (*Letter*, 251). This is undoubtedly a reference to Rousseau's claim in the *Discourse on Inequality* that the social contract was really a cunning trick played by the rich on the poor (see *SD*, 53–54), as well as to Mandeville's argument that lawgivers used "dextrous Management" to gain political control over people.[32] In sum, Rousseau and Mandeville are at one in their view of humanity's natural asociality and extreme primitiveness, of the gradualness of humanity's development from

---

29. When Smith speaks of "the primitive state of mankind" with respect to Rousseau here, it is not entirely clear whether he is referring to the "pure" state of nature described in Part 1 of the *Discourse* or the "savage" or hut societies of Part 2. He does note the distinction between the two on the following page, but he does not scrupulously maintain this distinction throughout his review.

30. One possible reason for these commonalities is that Rousseau and Mandeville shared several common sources of inspiration, above all Book V of Lucretius' *De Rerum Natura*.

31. For a more detailed analysis, see Jack, "One State of Nature."

32. See Mandeville, *The Fable of the Bees*, vol. 1, 42, 369.

this natural state to a more civilized one, and of the manipulative origins of law and political society.

Smith then immediately notes that "Mr. Rousseau however criticises upon Dr. Mandeville: he observes, that *pity*, the only amiable principle which the English author allows to be natural to man, is capable of producing all those virtues, whose reality Dr. Mandeville denies" (*Letter*, 251). The fact that Mandeville admits that pity is natural is in fact Rousseau's clinching argument for the naturalness of this sentiment in the *Discourse on Inequality*: he writes, "I do not believe I have any contradiction to fear in granting man the sole Natural virtue that the most excessive Detractor of human virtues was forced to recognize" (*SD*, 36). Rousseau then attempts to show that Mandeville "did not see that from this quality alone flow all the social virtues he wants to question in men. In fact, what are generosity, Clemency, Humanity, if not Pity applied to the weak, to the guilty, or to the human species in general? Benevolence and even friendship are, rightly understood, the products of a constant pity fixed on a particular object" (*SD*, 37). As Smith indicates, whereas Mandeville accorded pity a rather limited role, for Rousseau people's natural pity can, if channeled and encouraged in the right way, produce nearly all of the important social virtues (see *Emile* IV, 221–26, 253).

Next Smith notes that according to Rousseau pity "is possessed by savages and by the most profligate of the vulgar, in a greater degree of perfection than by those of the most polished and cultivated manners" (*Letter*, 251).[33] Given that Smith takes careful note of Rousseau's conception of pity here and that a related notion, sympathy, acts as the lynchpin for Smith's understanding of morality, it has occasionally been argued that Smith's conception of sympathy was inspired by Rousseau's conception of pity. Henri Roddier claims, for instance, that Rousseau "seems to have directly inspired [Smith] to make sympathy the basis of a system,"[34] and Richard Sewall goes so far as to say that the first paragraph of *The Theory of Moral Sentiments* "is little more than a restatement of Rousseau's conception of pity."[35] Yet this

33. As Rousseau writes in the *Discourse on Inequality*, pity "must have been infinitely closer in the state of Nature than in the state of reasoning," for civilized people's reason isolates them and shows them that they are not the ones who are suffering; the civilized person "says in secret, at the sight of a suffering man: perish if you will, I am safe" (*SD*, 37).

34. Roddier, *J.-J. Rousseau en Angleterre au XVIIIe siècle*, 40.

35. Sewall, "Rousseau's Second Discourse in England from 1756 to 1762," 98. For similar but slightly more qualified claims, see Force, *Self-Interest before Adam Smith*, chap. 1; Leigh, "Rousseau and the Scottish Enlightenment," 12; Pack, "The Rousseau-Smith Connection," 46–47; and Winch, *Riches and Poverty*, 72–73.

is one area, I believe, where Rousseau was likely *not* a main source of influence on Smith: a much more obvious and plausible candidate here is Hume
(and perhaps Hutcheson).[36] Rousseau's pity is something like empathy; it
comes out when one person identifies with another person and feels what
he or she feels. He writes that pity "is only a feeling that puts us in the position of him who suffers" (*SD*, 37; see also *Languages*, 306). Smith, on the
other hand, uses the term "sympathy" in a technical sense to denote not
only "fellow-feeling with the sorrow of others," but also "fellow-feeling with
any passion whatever" (*TMS* I.i.1.5, 10). Smith's "sympathy" is similar to
Rousseau's "pity" in that it describes a situation in which someone puts
him- or herself in the place of another, but it is different in four important
ways: first, it denotes a correspondence with any kind of feeling, not just
suffering or sorrow; second, it is a *mechanism* or a correspondence between
feelings rather than a feeling or sentiment itself; third, it is what the *spectator* feels in any given situation that is crucial for Smith's system of morality, not what the actor feels; and finally, since Smith's sympathy is a rather
complicated process that sometimes requires elaborate assessment, it is
stronger and more refined in civilized people than in savages.[37]

This is not the place to enter into a more detailed comparison of the
thought of Rousseau and Mandeville (especially since this work has already
been ably done by E. G. Hundert and Malcolm Jack),[38] but it is worth noting what is perhaps the most important similarity between Rousseau and
Mandeville in this context, one that Smith does not explicitly point out: they
concur in thinking that commercial society is based on vice. Both these
thinkers famously argue that a number of the key features of commercial
society—things like wealth, luxury, and the arts and sciences—encourage
and are encouraged by passions like vanity, greed, and hypocrisy. It could
even be argued that Rousseau "took Mandeville's *Fable* as commercial society's most truthful and self-incriminating expression."[39] Mandeville would
have answered the question of the *Discourse on the Sciences and Arts*—the
question of whether the arts and sciences tend to purify or corrupt morals—

36. Compare *TMS* VII.iii.3.17, 327, and Hume, *A Treatise of Human Nature*, 357–65, 575–91.
37. Smith does offer some instances in which "sympathy may seem to arise merely from
the view of a certain emotion in another person" (*TMS* I.i.1.6, 11), such as when a smiling face
cheers a spectator, but he also goes on to offer a much more complicated vision of the way
sympathy normally occurs. See Campbell, *Adam Smith's Science of Morals*, 94–97.
38. See Hundert, *The Enlightenment's Fable*, 105–15; "The Thread of Language and the Web
of Dominion"; Jack, *Corruption and Progress*, 155–83; and "One State of Nature."
39. Hundert, *The Enlightenment's Fable*, 178.

with the latter answer, just as Rousseau had. They simply take opposite views regarding whether this corruption is too high a price to pay; they *describe* commercial society in similar terms but *evaluate* it differently.[40] Thus, Smith's comparison of Rousseau and Mandeville is of interest for one of the same reasons I believe a comparison of Rousseau and Smith is of interest: in both cases the two thinkers share a good deal of common ground in their assumptions about commercial society but nevertheless view it in a very different manner. In both cases the question is *why* they view commercial society so differently, given their common assumptions. The answer, I believe, is connected to Smith's next comments on Rousseau.

The "Letter" continues with some observations on Rousseau's depiction of savage life. People usually picture the life of a savage, Smith writes, as "a life either of profound indolence, or of great and astonishing adventures," and he adds that "in the descriptions of the manners of savages, we expect to meet with both of these." Yet he notes that Rousseau emphasizes only the former aspect: "Mr. Rousseau, intending to paint the savage life as the happiest of any, presents only the indolent side of it to view." Smith next praises Rousseau's writing style and says, in perhaps the key sentence of his review, that "it is by the help of this style, together with a little philosophical chemistry, that the principles and ideas of the profligate Mandeville seem in him to have all the purity and sublimity of the morals of Plato" (*Letter,* 251). The obvious question, of course, is what kind of "philosophical chemistry" could perform this trick.

In one of few scholarly works to treat Smith's review of Rousseau at any length, Pierre Force posits that Smith's use of the term "philosophical chemistry" is meant to suggest that "Rousseau is an alchemist who transformed Mandeville's vile metal into pure gold."[41] This reading forms a part of Force's broader argument: that Smith essentially appropriates Rousseau's civic

40. Given the important similarities that Smith indicates exist between Rousseau and Mandeville, it stands to reason that when Smith takes issue with some of Mandeville's arguments in *The Theory of Moral Sentiments* (see especially *TMS* VII.ii.4, 306–14), he is also implicitly arguing with Rousseau on some of these matters. See Winch, *Riches and Poverty,* 60. This is especially important because, with the exception of Smith's teacher Francis Hutcheson, Mandeville is the only eighteenth-century thinker who is considered at length in *The Theory of Moral Sentiments.* Although Smith writes that "the notions of [Mandeville] are in almost every respect erroneous" (*TMS* VII.ii.4.6, 308), he also contends that his system "could never have imposed itself upon so great a number of persons, nor have occasioned so general an alarm among those who are friends of better principles, had it not in some respects bordered on the truth" (*TMS* VII.ii.4.14, 313).

41. Force, *Self-Interest before Adam Smith,* 34.

republican critique of commercial society. He writes, for instance, that the parallels between Smith and Rousseau center on "the principal themes of civic humanism: critique of the corrupting influence of luxury and wealth, praise of poverty and virtue. . . . Smith saw Rousseau as someone who shared his republican values, but expressed them in an extremist fashion."[42] While Force is correct to note that Smith shows some sympathy with Rousseau's critique of commercial society, I believe that his reading drastically overestimates the extent of this sympathy. Smith ultimately leaves no doubt that he is a proponent of commercial society, and Force does not adequately explore this side of Smith's thought. Force's claim that Smith is a "secret admirer of Rousseau,"[43] and even more, his claim in an earlier article that he is a "good disciple of Rousseau,"[44] overstate the case considerably. As we will see, Force's reading of this key passage—that Smith sees Rousseau as an alchemist who transformed Mandeville's vile metal into pure gold—both overestimates the extent of Smith's endorsement of Rousseau's "philosophical chemistry" and underestimates the extent of Smith's sympathy with Mandeville's position.[45] Smith likely *is* referring to Rousseau as an alchemist here, but he seems to think that Rousseau's "philosophical chemistry" is every bit as elusive as the philosopher's stone.

What, then, *does* Smith mean by the term "philosophical chemistry"? The answer, I think, can be found in the differences Smith notes between Rousseau and Mandeville. Smith observes several areas of agreement between these two thinkers but points to only two differences: first, Rousseau's vision of the state of nature is much more peaceful and happy than Mandeville's (in part because he "presents only the indolent side of it to view"), and second, Rousseau places a greater emphasis on the role of pity than Mandeville does. Both these differences are connected to what Rousseau often declares is the fundamental principle of his own thought (see *CW* V, 575; *CW* IX, 28; *Dialogues*, 212–13): the natural goodness of humanity, meaning both that people are naturally well ordered and self-sufficient and hence happy (they are good for themselves), and that they naturally have little inclination or reason to harm others and, owing to their pity, have an aversion to seeing them suffer (they are good for others).

---

42. Ibid., 159.
43. Ibid., 20.
44. Force, "Self-Love, Identification, and the Origin of Political Economy," 63.
45. Donald Winch, too, argues that Smith was in some ways closer to Mandeville than Rousseau, despite his rhetoric in this letter. See Winch, *Riches and Poverty*, 73.

I believe that it is Rousseau's belief in humanity's natural goodness that Smith is referring to as the "philosophical chemistry" by which he manages to make Mandeville's "profligate" ideas seem to have the "purity and sublimity" of Plato.[46] The idea that humanity is naturally good inspired Rousseau with a longing to transcend the ills of commercial society; Mandeville's denial of humanity's natural goodness led him to mock the idea of such transcendence. And it was Rousseau's longing to transcend commercial society—evinced in his moving descriptions of the innocence, simplicity, and contentment of savage life, as well as in his later portrayals of the citizen in *The Social Contract,* the solitary dreamer in *The Reveries of a Solitary Walker,* and the eponymous student in *Emile*—that made his writings seem idealistic (to have "purity and sublimity") despite his deep pessimism regarding the actual lot of humanity. Rousseau's belief in humanity's natural goodness, in short, is the main reason why he and Mandeville view commercial society so differently despite their common assumptions; a thinker's attitude toward commercial society will certainly be different if he takes a happy and peaceful state of nature as his benchmark rather than a harsh and unendurable one. And this crucial difference between Rousseau and Mandeville is, not surprisingly, connected with the differences between Smith and Rousseau: we will see in Chapters 3 and 4 that Smith's denial of humanity's natural goodness (in Rousseau's sense) is one of the key grounds for his defense of commercial society.

Following his statement about Rousseau's "philosophical chemistry," Smith translates three lengthy passages from the *Discourse.* Before looking at these passages, however, we should take note of Smith's concluding remark, a comment on Rousseau's dedication of the *Discourse* to Geneva. While most of Smith's statements on Rousseau are relatively neutral, this final comment adopts a much more admiring tone. He writes that the dedicatory preface addressed to Geneva "is an agreeable, animated, and I believe too, a just panegyric; and expresses the ardent and passionate esteem which it becomes a good citizen to entertain for the government of his country and the character of his countrymen" (*Letter,* 254). Rousseau's tribute to Geneva is, then, an example of the kind of patriotic sentiment that Smith thinks any good citizen ought to feel. But this statement should not be used as evidence of Smith's conservatism or quietism, as Peter Minowitz has

46. For a slightly different but related suggestion, see Melzer, *The Natural Goodness of Man,* 25–26.

attempted to use it.[47] First of all, far from being uncritical of Geneva, Rousseau's dedication was in fact intended to show the Genevans how far they had fallen short of their own ideals. That this was the dedication's purpose has been thoroughly demonstrated by a number of contemporary scholars.[48] It was also noted by others in Rousseau's own day[49] and acknowledged by Rousseau himself.[50] As Anne Cohler writes, in the dedication Rousseau "combined the rhetoric of a citizen who must make every effort to maintain his society with the awareness of the philosopher of its real problems and the limits of any political establishment."[51] It is not unreasonable to suggest that Smith realized that Rousseau was criticizing Geneva even through his exaggerated praise, especially since Rousseau's approach in the dedication is close to the one Smith himself claims a good citizen ought to take.

In *The Theory of Moral Sentiments*, Smith writes that "the love of our country seems, in ordinary cases, to involve in it two different principles; first, a certain respect and reverence for that constitution or form of government which is actually established; and secondly, an earnest desire to render the condition of our fellow-citizens as safe, respectable, and happy as we can" (*TMS* VI.ii.2.11, 231). Of course, these two principles would be incompatible in the case of a government that is oppressive or too weak to maintain order, and they would at least be in tension under *any* imperfect regime. Thus while "in peaceable and quiet times, [these] two principles generally coincide," at other times "even a wise man may be disposed to think some alteration necessary in that constitution or form of government, which . . . appears plainly unable to maintain the public tranquility" (*TMS* VI.ii.2.12, 231). Even if alteration is necessary, though, Smith is no advocate of wholesale change: he says that, unlike the "man of system" who will brook no deviation from some abstract ideal, "the man whose public spirit is prompted altogether by humanity and benevolence . . . will content himself with

47. Minowitz argues that "this concluding praise is rhetorically suggestive of Smith's conservatism" and that "it is Smith—not Rousseau—who treats the government of his country (and government in general) with kid gloves." Minowitz, *Profits, Priests, and Princes*, 30.
48. See the "Introduction" to *CW* III, xiv; Cohler, *Rousseau and Nationalism*, 159–64; Masters, *The Political Philosophy of Rousseau*, 192–95; Palmer, "The Citizen Philosopher"; and Rosenblatt, *Rousseau and Geneva*, 84–87, 159–63.
49. Jean-Louis Du Pan, the First Syndic of Geneva, for instance, wrote to Rousseau that "you depict us as we ought to be, not as we are" (*CJJR* III, 136–37). See also the contemporary reactions to the dedication cited by Starobinski in *OC* III, 1288.
50. See *CJJR* III, 55–60. As we have seen, Rousseau had no illusions about the actual state of Geneva's political and social condition; see footnote 43 in chap. 1.
51. Cohler, *Rousseau and Nationalism*, 163.

moderating, what he often cannot annihilate without great violence. . . . When he cannot establish the right, he will not disdain to ameliorate the wrong; but like Solon, when he cannot establish the best system of laws, he will endeavour to establish the best that the people can bear" (*TMS* VI.ii.2.16, 233; see also *WN* IV.v.b.53, 543). A good citizen, for Smith, should respect the government of his country even as he tries to improve it, much as Rousseau does in his dedication.

Yet, to return to Minowitz's claim, support of gradual change and a willingness to accommodate existing institutions and prejudices are not the same as conservatism; Smith stands squarely on the pragmatic middle ground between conservatism and radicalism.[52] Viewing Smith as a conservative would, in any case, flatly contradict both his own assertion that in *The Wealth of Nations* he had made a "very violent attack . . . upon the whole commercial system of Great Britain" (*CAS*, 251) and, even more decisively, the fact that he defended commerce mainly because it had played a key *progressive* role in European history (see *WN* III.iv.4, 412). Perhaps, then, Smith praises Rousseau's dedication so highly because while the *Discourse* as a whole might seem to endorse revolutionary change (given its radical critique of all existing societies), the dedication tempers this appearance by adopting a much more moderate stance, attempting to show the Genevans how to realize their own highest ideals rather than imposing an abstract model on them from above or undermining the foundations of their republic.

We can now turn to the three passages from the *Discourse* that Smith translates near the end of his review, which take up more than half the space he devotes to Rousseau. He includes these passages, he says, in order to present the *Review*'s readers "with a specimen of [Rousseau's] eloquence" (*Letter*, 251), yet they were surely not chosen *merely* for their eloquence, for they contain some of Rousseau's deepest arguments against commercial society. Indeed, they point to what we saw in Chapter 1 are *the* three fundamental critiques of commercial society in Rousseau's works. While these passages are too long to reproduce in full, I will transcribe enough of them to demonstrate that they point to the three critiques outlined in Chapter 1.[53] The first passage (given here in Smith's translation) points to what I have called the "division of laborers" critique:

52. See Griswold, *Adam Smith and the Virtues of Enlightenment*, 301–10.

53. Of course, no set of quotations, even as long as the ones that Smith translates, can encompass every element of Rousseau's critique; my account of Rousseau's critique of commercial society in Chapter 1 expands on the critiques outlined in these three passages.

> While men . . . applied themselves to such works as a single per-
> son could execute, and to such arts as required not the concurrence
> of several hands; they lived free, healthful, humane and happy,
> as far as their nature would permit them, and continued to enjoy
> amongst themselves the sweets of an independent society. But
> from the instant in which one man had occasion for the assistance
> of another, from the moment that he perceived that it could be
> advantageous to a single person to have provisions for two, equality
> disappeared, property was introduced, labour became necessary,
> and the vast forrests of nature were changed into agreeable plains,
> which must be watered with the sweat of mankind, and in which
> the world beheld slavery and wretchedness begin to grow up and
> blosom with the harvest. (*Letter*, 251–52; see also *SD*, 49)

The second passage points to the "empire of opinion" critique:

> To be and to appear to be, became two things entirely different, and
> from this distinction arose imposing ostentation, deceitful guile,
> and all the vices which attend them. Thus man, from being free
> and independent, became by a multitude of new necessities sub-
> jected in a manner, to all nature, and above all to his fellow crea-
> tures, whose slave he is in one sense even while he becomes their
> master; rich, he has occasion for their services; poor, he stands in
> need of their assistance; and even mediocrity does not enable him
> to live without them. He is obliged therefore to endeavour to inter-
> est them in his situation, and to make them find, either in reality
> or in appearance, their advantage in labouring for his. It is this
> which renders him false and artificial with some, imperious and
> unfeeling with others, and lays him under a necessity of deceiving
> all those for whom he has occasion, when he cannot terrify them,
> and does not find it for his interest to serve them in reality. (*Letter*,
> 252; see also *SD*, 51–52)

And finally, the third passage points to the "pursuit of unhappiness" critique:

> Man . . . in his savage, and man in his civilized state, differ so essen-
> tially in their passions and inclinations, that what makes the supreme
> happiness of the one, would reduce the other to despair. The savage

breathes nothing but liberty and repose; he desires only to live and
to be at leisure; and the *ataraxia* of the Stoic does not approach his
profound indifference for every other object. The citizen, on the
contrary, toils, bestirs and torments himself without end, to obtain
employments which are still more laborious; he labours on till his
death, he even hastens it, in order to put himself in a condition to
live, or renounces life to acquire immortality. He makes his court
to the great whom he hates, and to the rich whom he despises. . . .
It belongs not to my subject to show, how . . . in the midst of so
much philosophy, so much humanity, so much politeness, and so
many sublime maxims we have nothing but a deceitful and frivolous exterior; honour without virtue, reason without wisdom, and
pleasure without happiness. (*Letter*, 253–54; see also *SD*, 66–67)

Because Smith claims that he is translating these passages to demonstrate
Rousseau's eloquence and because of the obvious differences in the thought
of Smith and Rousseau, E. G. West concludes that Smith's commendation
of the *Discourse on Inequality* "seems to be in spite of Rousseau's argument
rather than because of it" and that "he was intrigued not by the philosophy
but by the literary style."[54] It is true that Smith says that Rousseau's work
"consists almost entirely of rhetoric and description" (*Letter*, 251) and that
several of his references to Rousseau in other works also mention his eloquence (see *EPS*, 198–99; *LRBL*, 205), but it is difficult to imagine why
Smith would have chosen Rousseau's work to review at such length, among
all those he mentions in the "Letter," if he was uninterested in the arguments put forth in it. Given that the three passages Smith translates point
to Rousseau's deepest criticisms of commercial society—a subject on which
Smith had already been lecturing and on which he was beginning to write—
it is hard to believe that he was intrigued only by the style of these passages,
that the arguments they contained did not interest the future author of *The
Wealth of Nations*. We will see that Smith in fact took these arguments
quite seriously, for in his view they pointed to the deepest and seemingly
most intractable problems of the emerging commercial societies of his time.

54. West, "Adam Smith and Rousseau's *Discourse on Inequality*," 68–69. See also Wokler's claim that "Smith was impressed by Rousseau's eloquent style, not the substance of any
of his arguments," and Ryan Hanley's claim that Smith "respects Rousseau's style if not his
substance." Wokler, "Todorov's Otherness," 52; Hanley, "Rousseau's Diagnosis and Adam
Smith's Cure," ms. 13.

The remainder of this chapter will explore the extent to which Smith sympathized with the critiques of commercial society outlined in these three passages. While most Smith scholars writing in recent years acknowledge that Smith was not the crude advocate of laissez-faire capitalism that he is often thought to be, the full range and extent of his sympathy for the arguments *against* commercial society is not often appreciated, and a comparison with Rousseau can help us gain such an appreciation and thus take more seriously the depth and complexity of his thought. Unlike many latter-day "Smithians," Smith is no simple champion of commercial society; although he is convinced that it is the best alternative available, he recognizes the deep problems that arise from it. I want to stress, however, that in the rest of this chapter I am focusing quite deliberately on Smith's awareness of the problems of commercial society rather than on his counterarguments and countermeasures relating to them. An examination of Smith's defense of commercial society will follow in Chapters 3 and 4. With this disclaimer in mind, I next consider the extent to which Smith sympathized with each of Rousseau's three critiques.

3. THE DIVISION OF LABORERS

In Book I of *The Wealth of Nations,* Smith affirms that the division of labor is in many ways *the* defining element of commercial society: "When the division of labor has been once thoroughly established," he writes, "it is but a small part of a man's wants which the produce of his own labour can supply. . . . Every man thus lives by exchanging, or becomes in some measure a merchant, and the society itself grows to be what is properly a commercial society" (*WN* I.iv.1, 37). He also makes it plain that an extensive division of labor not only brings about the social changes that give rise to commercial society, but also serves as the main engine driving the economy of this kind of society. Joseph Schumpeter has gone so far as to claim that "nobody, either before or after A. Smith, ever thought of putting such a burden upon the division of labor. With A. Smith it is practically the only factor in economic progress."[55] Thus it is all the more surprising, when one reaches Book V of *The Wealth of Nations,* to read some of the most disparaging words ever uttered regarding the deleterious effects of the division

55. Schumpeter, *History of Economic Analysis,* 187.

of labor on the laborers; Smith's description of the weakness and stupidity of people who spend their lives working on a single task is, we will see, more severe than anything Rousseau ever wrote on this topic. In fact, each of Rousseau's main strictures against the division of labor and the laborers' dividedness in commercial society can be found in Smith's writings as well. He, too, acknowledges the damage wrought by weakness, ignorance, and great inequalities and the decline of citizenship that results.

Like Rousseau, first of all, Smith believes that government was instituted by the rich as a way for them to maintain their wealth. Early in human history, Smith maintains, before much property had been accumulated, government was unnecessary; laws and political power came into being only to safeguard the inequalities that the introduction of property created. He writes that "civil government, so far as it is instituted for the security of property, is in reality instituted for the defence of the rich against the poor, or of those who have some property against those who have none at all" (WN V.i.b.12, 715). As is often the case, he is even more blunt in his Lectures on Jurisprudence; in a passage that Richard Teichgraeber notes "sounds exactly like a précis of Rousseau's position in the Discours sur l'inégalité,"[56] Smith claims that "laws and government may be considered . . . as a combination of the rich to oppress the poor, and preserve to themselves the inequality of the goods which would otherwise be soon destroyed by the attacks of the poor, who if not hindered by the government would soon reduce the others to an equality with themselves by open violence" (LJ, 208; see also 338). For Smith, however, unlike for Rousseau, the emergence of government was not a trick that the rich played on the poor; the poor were rather forced to consent because they depended on the rich to protect them. And, as we will see in Chapter 3, Smith believes that the poor ultimately benefit from this agreement. But Smith never denies the Rousseauian claim that law and government themselves are inextricably connected to property and inequality.

Furthermore, Smith acknowledges that this inequality is by no means ameliorated by the increase in productivity that commercial society brings about. In fact, he admits that "wherever there is great property, there is great inequality. For one very rich man, there must be at least five hundred poor, and the affluence of the few supposes the indigence of the many" (WN V.i.b.2, 709–10). While this is a strong statement, Smith's Lectures on

56. Teichgraeber, "Free Trade" and Moral Philosophy, 146.

Jurisprudence—as well as the "Early Draft" of *The Wealth of Nations*—are again even harsher. In both these works, Smith admits that the division of wealth will always be unfair: "with regard to the produce of the labour of a great society," he writes, "there is never any such thing as a fair and equal division" (*ED*, 563). This is true because, despite their disproportionate effort, the laborers are always compensated less: "those who labour most get least" (*ED*, 564; see also *LJ*, 490), and thus "the labour and time of the poor is in civilized countries sacrificed to . . . maintaining the rich in ease and luxury" (*LJ*, 340). Smith further stresses, in these works, the oppressive (his word) nature of this inequality: "the poor labourer who . . . bears, as it were, upon his shoulders the whole fabric of society, seems himself to be pressed down below the ground by the weight, and to be buried out of sight in the lowest foundations of the building" (*ED*, 564; see also *LJ*, 341). Indeed, he says, "it may very justly be said that the people who cloath the whole world are in rags themselves" (*LJ*, 540). Although Smith tempers some of these statements in his published works, and although he argues even in his *Lectures* and the "Early Draft" that the productivity of commercial society is such that the laborers are ultimately better off than they would be in a less affluent society, the fact that he sets up this problem so starkly shows that he is well aware that the presence of great inequalities can still be problematic in commercial society.[57]

Smith's most critical statements about commercial society, however, come in his discussion of the debilitating effects of the division of labor on the laborers.[58] He observes that whereas in more primitive societies each individual takes on a variety of occupations, once the division of labor has advanced sufficiently "the employment of the great part of those who live by labour, that is, of the great body of the people, comes to be confined to a few very simple operations" (*WN* V.i.f.50, 781). Smith's most famous example of this phenomenon, of course, is that of pin making: he notes that this process can be broken up into eighteen distinct operations, and that in some cases a different laborer undertakes each of these operations (see *ED*, 564–65; *LJ*, 341–42, 490; *WN* I.i.3, 14–15). People whose labor consists in

---

57. For more detailed discussions of some of the similarities and contrasts between Smith and Rousseau on the issues of inequality and poverty, see Ignatieff, "Smith, Rousseau, and the Republic of Needs," 189–93, 197; and Winch, *Riches and Poverty*, 70–75.

58. In contrast to Rousseau, Smith attributes the potential for weakness and ignorance in commercial society much more to the effects of specialization than to people's dependence on commodities and technology, but the defects they describe in people's characters are similar.

performing such a specialized task will naturally have little opportunity to exert their minds while they are laboring. As a result, Smith writes—in as blunt a statement as can be found in his works—a laborer of this kind "generally becomes as stupid and ignorant as it is possible for a human creature to become" (*WN* V.i.f.50, 782). He follows this statement with a litany of criticism that surpasses anything Rousseau ever wrote on this score; this still-shocking passage is worth quoting at length:

> The torpor of his mind renders him, not only incapable of relishing or bearing a part in any rational conversation, but of conceiving of any generous, noble, or tender sentiment, and consequently of forming any just judgment concerning many even of the ordinary duties of private life. Of the great and extensive interests of his country, he is altogether incapable of judging. . . . It corrupts even the activity of his body, and renders him incapable of exerting his strength with vigour and perseverance, in any other employment than that to which he has been bred. His dexterity at his own particular trade seems, in this manner, to be acquired at the expense of his intellectual, social, and martial virtues. (*WN* V.i.f.50, 782; see also V.i.f.61, 788; *LJ*, 539–41)

While individuals whose occupations cannot be easily divided into many different operations, such as farmers, will be largely exempt from these ills, this harsh denunciation seems to apply to the majority of people in commercial society: "in every improved and civilized society this is the state into which the labouring poor, that is, the great body of the people, must necessarily fall, unless government takes some pains to prevent it" (*WN* V.i.f.50, 782; see also I.x.c.24, 143–44). It would be difficult to conceive of a more ringing condemnation of what is, after all, perhaps *the* central element of commercial society. As Charles Griswold writes, "perhaps no philosopher, with the possible exception of Marx, has described [the] human costs of the division of labor more bluntly and harshly than has Smith."[59] Indeed, it is not surprising that Marx himself took pleasure in quoting from these pages of Smith's work.[60]

59. Griswold, *Adam Smith and the Virtues of Enlightenment*, 17.
60. See Marx, *Capital, Volume One*, in *The Marx-Engels Reader*, 399. It is common among Marxist and Marxist-inspired scholars to subsume Smith's passages on the debilitating effects of the division of labor into Marx's notion of alienation; see, for example, West, "Adam Smith

Smith contends that even though most people in commercial society spend a preponderance of their time laboring, they tend to become weak and indolent. Like Rousseau, he maintains that "every savage undergoes a sort of Spartan discipline" and thus tends to acquire a "heroic and unconquerable firmness" (see *TMS* V.2.9–10, 205–7). In commercial society, by contrast, most people are constantly engaged in the pursuit of wealth and thus have little time to undertake any activities that require great courage or spirit. "By having their minds constantly employed on the arts of luxury," Smith claims in his *Lectures on Jurisprudence*, "they grow effeminate and dastardly" (*LJ*, 540; see also 411). This is a problem for two reasons. First, it renders people unfit for military service: unless "very particular pains" are taken to prevent this weakness, people in commercial society will be "incapable of defending [their] country in war" and thus will expose their country to attacks from more rugged peoples who are enticed by their wealth (*WN* V.i.f.50, 782; see also V.i.a.15, 697). Second, even aside from military considerations, this weakness is detrimental to society because it is detrimental to the people themselves: "even though the martial spirit of the people were of no use towards the defence of the society, yet to prevent that sort of mental mutilation, deformity and wretchedness, which cowardice necessarily involves in it, from spreading themselves through the great body of the people [is a problem warranting] serious attention" (*WN* V.i.f.60, 787).

By rendering the majority of the people so feeble and ignorant, Smith further concedes, commercial society also serves to undermine citizenship. In contrast to Rousseau, Smith seems fairly unconcerned about promoting patriotism or about ensuring that people devote themselves wholeheartedly to the common good, and he certainly has no desire for a citizenry that has been denatured in the way that Rousseau advocates in *The Social Contract* (see, for example, *TMS* II.ii.1.8, 81; *WN* IV.ii.9, 456). Yet he does admit that people's weakness and stupidity can be dangerous for the community as a whole. As we have just seen, Smith worries that the lack of a heroic or martial spirit will open a society to attacks from outsiders. In his *Lectures* he uses the example of the Jacobite Rebellion in Scotland, also known as

---

and Alienation," in *Essays on Adam Smith*. Such an assimilation seems not only anachronistic but also erroneous, however, given that Smith's concern is with the stultifying effects of the division of labor on the laborers and not with the ownership of the means of production or with the separation of the laborers from the products of their labor. As Gertrude Himmelfarb writes, for Smith "the factory worker in a socialist regime, or in any other form of cooperative or public enterprise, would suffer just as grievously as the factory worker under capitalism." Himmelfarb, *The Idea of Poverty*, 56.

"the 'Forty-Five": "In the year 1745 four or 5 thousand naked unarmed Highlanders took possession of the improved parts of this country without any opposition from the unwarlike inhabitants. They penetrated into England and alarmed the whole nation, and had they not been opposed by a standing army they would have seized the throne with little difficulty" (*LJ*, 540–41). Even more, however, Smith worries that the "gross ignorance and stupidity" of the lower classes will render them, first, more liable to "the delusions of superstition and enthusiasm" (i.e., religious zealotry) and hence more disorderly; second, more prone to disrespect the law and their superiors; and third, less capable of seeing through "the interested complaints of faction and sedition" (*WN* V.i.g.61, 788). Smith's concerns regarding citizenship are encapsulated in his observation that whereas in "barbarous societies, as they are called, every man . . . is a warrior" and "every man too is in some measure a statesman" (*WN* V.i.f.51, 783), in commercial society "every man . . . becomes in some measure a merchant" (*WN* I.iv.2, 37) instead and so cannot perform either of these other functions well.

To summarize, Smith and Rousseau both believe that the division of labor necessarily leads to great inequalities and that it can make people weak and ignorant and thereby undermine citizenship. Smith's statements regarding the injustice of inequality are somewhat more moderate than Rousseau's (particularly in his published works), and his worries about the decline of citizenship do not take quite the same form as Rousseau's, but he *does* share these concerns to some degree, and his anxieties about the weakness and ignorance caused by the division of labor are if anything *greater* than Rousseau's.

4. THE EMPIRE OF OPINION

Smith and Rousseau both stress that people tend to see themselves through others' eyes. For Rousseau this tendency arises only with the development of *amour-propre*. For Smith, by contrast, it is a natural phenomenon: the concern for the opinions of others has its basis in human nature and not an artificial faculty. Ultimately, however, both thinkers believe that the vast majority of civilized people tend to be greatly concerned about others' opinions, and they further believe that this concern can lead to problems such as a corruption of people's moral sentiments, selfishly motivated appeals to others' self-interest, and ostentation. In a word, we will see in this section that Smith shows a good deal of sympathy with several elements of the second Rousseauian critique outlined in Chapter 1, the "empire of opinion" critique, although we will also see that his sympathy here is not quite as broad as it is with Rousseau's other two critiques.

That people naturally care about others and their opinions is made clear beginning with the very first line of *The Theory of Moral Sentiments*, where Smith writes that "how selfish soever man may be supposed, there are evidently some principles in his nature, which interest him in the fortune of others" (*TMS* I.i.1.1, 9). This is so, of course, because people tend to put themselves in the position of others or to look at things through their eyes—to sympathize with them. As a result they come to see even *themselves* through others' eyes and hence desire to be approved or admired by them. This is true for nearly everyone, according to Smith:

> Rank, distinction pre-eminence, no man despises, unless he is either raised very much above, or sunk very much below, the ordinary standard of human nature; unless he is either so confirmed in wisdom and real philosophy, as to be satisfied that, while the propriety of his conduct renders him the just object of approbation, it is of little consequence though he be neither attended to, nor approved of; or so habituated to the idea of his own meanness, so sunk in slothful and sottish indifference, as entirely to have forgot the desire, and almost the very wish, for superiority. (*TMS* I.iii.2.8, 57)

In order to be beyond caring about the opinions of others, in short, one would have to be either a philosopher or a tramp. This cannot help but remind us of Rousseau's similar dichotomy whereby only the solitary dreamer of *The Reveries of a Solitary Walker* and the savage of the *Discourse on Inequality* are beyond (or beneath) caring about the opinions of others.[61] Since the overwhelming majority of civilized people fall between these two extremes, for Smith as for Rousseau, most people care a great deal about the opinions of others.

Also like Rousseau, Smith claims that people are especially concerned with the opinions of the rich and that their esteem for the rich can corrupt their moral sentiments. Indeed, he writes that the "disposition to admire,

---

61. It is also reminiscent of Aristotle's famous statement that a person "who is in need of nothing through being self-sufficient"—that is, someone who is independent of others and their opinions—must be "either a beast or a god." Aristotle, *The Politics*, 1253a.

and almost to worship, the rich and the powerful, and to despise, or, at least, to neglect persons of poor and mean condition" is "the great and most universal cause of the corruption of our moral sentiments" (*TMS* I.iii.3.1, 61). He maintains as well that most people put wealth ahead of virtue: "they are the wise and virtuous chiefly, a select, though, I am afraid, but a small party, who are the real and steady admirers of wisdom and virtue" (*TMS* I.iii.3.2, 62). Unlike Rousseau, however, Smith does not ascribe this problem to commercial society in particular: that people esteem the rich and powerful more than the wise and virtuous has, he says, "been the complaint of moralists in all ages" (*TMS* I.iii.3.1, 62). And while Smith concedes that people's moral *sentiments* are corrupted by their desire for wealth, he does not believe that their *actions* will always be immoral as well (for reasons we will see in more detail in Chapter 3). While he concedes that "the candidates for fortune too frequently abandon the paths of virtue" (*TMS* I.iii.3.8, 64), unlike Rousseau he ascribes this tendency principally to people in "the superior stations of life" rather than to everyone in commercial society. It is especially in aristocratic circles that people pursue wealth and greatness through unscrupulous means, Smith argues, for in those circles success often depends not on the respect of one's equals—as it does for those in "the middling and inferior stations of life"—but on "the fanciful and foolish favour of ignorant, presumptuous, and proud superiors" who are easily prevailed upon by "flattery and falsehood" (*TMS* I.iii.3.5–8, 63–64). In other words, while nearly everyone *cares* more about wealth than virtue, it is only in "the superior stations of life" that this sense of priority generally encourages immoral actions. Thus, while Smith, like Rousseau, shows some concern about people's admiration for the rich and powerful rather than the wise and virtuous—since their moral sentiments are corrupted by this admiration—he attributes immoral *actions* for the sake of riches and power especially to "the superior stations in life" and not to everyone in commercial society.

Smith grants, once again like Rousseau, that in commercial society people are, unlike in the earliest societies, dependent on others for nearly everything (see *LJ*, 334–35, 487–88; *WN* II.intro.1, 276). He illustrates this point nicely by pointing to the stunning number of people necessary to produce even the commodities enjoyed by an ordinary laborer, a number that "exceeds all computation" (*WN* I.i.11, 22–23). Yet no one can count on the benevolence of all of these people, the preponderance of whom are strangers: "in civilized society [a person] stands at all times in need of the cooperation and assistance of great multitudes, while his whole life is scarce sufficient to gain the friendship of a few persons" (*WN* I.ii.2, 26). Hence in commercial society people must, as Rousseau bemoans, appeal to the self-interest of others even when their primary concern is their own welfare. Instead of appealing to people's benevolence, Smith writes, a person in this situation "will be more likely to prevail if he can interest their self-love in his favour, and shew them that it is for their own advantage to do for him what he requires of them" (*WN* I.ii.2, 26; see also *ED*, 571).

This last sentence recalls the second passage from Rousseau's *Discourse* that Smith translates in the "Letter," in which Rousseau claims that, given people's great dependence on others in civilized society, each individual must "endeavour to interest them in his situation, and to make them find, either in reality or in appearance, their advantage in labouring for his" (*Letter*, 252).[62] The main substantive difference between the two sentences, of course, is Rousseau's addition of the phrase "either in reality or in appearance"; in other words, Rousseau stresses that the appeals to other people's self-interest will often be deceitful, that people will frequently try to harm others even as they pretend to care about them. Smith, on the contrary, seems to think that people's appeals to the self-interest of others will, in the majority of cases, be genuine; even if these appeals are selfishly motivated, they will not be fraudulent.[63] In one of the most famous lines in his writings, he notes that "it is not from the benevolence of the butcher, the brewer, or the baker, that we expect our dinner, but from their regard to their own interest. We address ourselves, not to their humanity but to their self-love, and never talk to them of our own necessities but of their advantages" (*WN* I.ii.2, 26–27; see also *ED*, 571–72; *LJ*, 348, 493). There is no hint that "we" are trying to deceive the butcher, brewer, or baker here, although it *is* clear that our primary motive is our own welfare.

While Smith does not accuse the majority of people in commercial society of being deceitful in their appeals to others' self-interest, he *does* make

---

62. The similarity of these passages has been noted by several scholars; see Colletti, *From Rousseau to Lenin*, 196; Force, *Self-Interest Before Adam Smith*, 130–31; and Hanley, "Rousseau's Diagnosis and Adam Smith's Cure," ms. 15–16.

63. It should be noted, however, that in an earlier formulation of this passage in the *Lectures on Jurisprudence* Smith, too, had hinted that these appeals might be deceitful: "Man continually standing in need of the assistance of others, must fall upon some means to procure their help. This he does not merely by coaxing and courting; he does not expect it unless he can turn it to your advantage *or make it appear to be so*" (*LJ*, 347, italics added).

this accusation with respect to wealthy merchants and manufacturers.[64] Smith's statements about the malicious activities of rich and powerful merchants could hardly be more critical; Nathan Rosenberg goes so far as to say that his attitude toward them is "hypercritical and almost pathologically suspicious."[65] Smith envisions merchants and manufacturers as constantly forming a "conspiracy against the publick" (*WN* I.x.c.27, 145) and says that they "have generally an interest to deceive and even to oppress the publick, and . . . accordingly have, upon many occasions, both deceived and oppressed it" (*WN* I.xi.p.10, 267). He speaks of "the impertinent jealousy," "the mean rapacity, the monopolizing spirit," and the "interested sophistry" of these groups (*WN* IV.iii.c.9–10, 493–94). Of the laws that merchants and manufacturers have "extorted from the legislature, for the support of their own absurd and oppressive monopolies," he writes that "like the laws of Draco, these laws may be said to be all written in blood" (*WN* IV.viii.17, 648). And, as hard as it may be to believe for those who think of Smith as a mere apostle for free enterprise, these statements are fairly typical of his posture toward these groups. But Smith does not attribute this kind deceitfulness and rapacity to merchants and manufacturers because he thinks they are particularly deceitful or rapacious *people*. Rather, it is their circumstances that allow or encourage them to act in this way; almost anyone else would act similarly if they were in the merchants' and manufacturers' situation (see *WN* I.vi.8, 67; IV.vii.c.107, 641). This only seems to impugn commercial society all the more, however, for it shows that this kind of society sometimes puts people in a position where they can easily gain by illicitly taking advantage of others.

Furthermore, Smith claims—yet again like Rousseau—that the concern for others' opinions is the main reason why people pursue wealth and why the rich are ostentatious with their riches.[66] "It is chiefly from . . . regard to the sentiments of mankind, that we pursue riches and avoid poverty," he writes (*TMS* I.iii.2.1, 50). It is obvious that people do not pursue wealth simply "to supply the necessities of nature," he tells us, because people's

64. When he speaks of merchants in this context, Smith is clearly not referring to everyone who engages in trade, for this would encompass nearly everyone in commercial society. Rather, his argument is directed at traders or "middle men," especially those who possess great wealth.

65. Rosenberg, "Adam Smith and Laissez-Faire Revisited," in *Adam Smith and Modern Political Economy*, 21.

66. Pierre Force brings out this similarity nicely; see *Self-Interest before Adam Smith*, especially 44–45, 123–25.

true needs are relatively few: "the wages of the meanest labourer can afford them" (*TMS* I.iii.2.1, 50). Rather, people want wealth and luxuries because of the attention it brings them: "it is the vanity, not the ease or the pleasure, which interests us" (*TMS* I.iii.2.1, 50; see also VI.i.3, 212–13). The real benefit that the rich derive from their riches is that people are more prone to sympathize with them and approve of them; whereas "the poor man goes out and comes in unheeded. . . . The man of rank and distinction, on the contrary, is observed by all the world" (*TMS* I.iii.2.1, 51). What is even more amazing, for Smith, is that people tend to esteem the rich not because they expect any advantages from them, but rather simply because they sympathize more easily with joy than with sorrow and tend to assume—usually erroneously—that the rich must enjoy a greater happiness because of their riches (see *TMS* I.iii.2.2, 51–52).[67] This false assumption, in turn, is the main cause of ostentation: the rich "parade" their riches because it is their wealth that makes people sympathize with them and approve of them (see *TMS* I.iii.2.1, 50–51). For Smith and Rousseau alike, then, wealth is to some extent a "positional good," to use Fred Hirsch's terminology: its value depends in large part on its contribution to one's rank or status, and therefore its worth depends predominantly on its exclusiveness.[68]

Smith further admits that the desire to seem more successful than others can lead to a degrading servility and obsequiousness. This can be seen in a story he tells in *The Theory of Moral Sentiments* about a "poor man's son, whom heaven in its anger has visited with ambition" (*TMS* IV.1.8, 181). Because he admires the advantages of the rich and imagines how much happier he would be were he in their situation, this young man not only spends much of his life toiling to acquire the advantages of wealth, but also goes to great lengths to make others think he already enjoys them (so that they will admire him in turn). In his attempt to distinguish himself, however, he ends up having to debase himself: "he makes his court to all mankind; he serves those whom he hates, and is obsequious to those whom he despises" (*TMS* IV.1.8, 181). This sentence strongly resembles one in the third passage from Rousseau's *Discourse on Inequality* that Smith had translated for the *Edinburgh Review*, where Rousseau contends that the civilized person "makes his court to the great whom he hates, and to the rich whom

---

67. A similar point is made in Hume, *A Treatise of Human Nature*, 365.
68. See Hirsch, *The Social Limits to Growth*.

he despises" (*Letter,* 253).[69] Here is another example of Smith not only show-ing a good deal of sympathy with Rousseau's argument—that people's van-ity leads them to flatter others and to be what others want them to be—but also coming close to using Rousseau's own words in doing so. Smith does not place the same emphasis as Rousseau does on the fact that people are constantly forced to play a role instead of truly being themselves, but he does acknowledge that the desire to be esteemed by others can sometimes take a particularly degrading form.

Smith's sympathy with Rousseau's second critique of commercial soci-ety is not quite as broad as his sympathy with the first Rousseauian critique (or with the third, as we will see in the next section). He does not place the same emphasis on the problem of role playing that Rousseau does, and his complaints about immoral *actions* and deceitfulness are applied especially to specific groups—to those in "the superior stations in life" and to wealthy merchants and manufacturers, respectively—rather than to everyone in commercial society. Yet Smith shows a greater degree of sympathy with this critique than might be expected: he acknowledges that people tend to be greatly concerned with the opinions of others and that this concern can corrupt people's moral *sentiments,* that the interdependence of commercial society encourages selfishly motivated appeals to others' self-interest, and that great wealth almost invariably leads to greed and ostentation. Further-more, his condemnation of the deceitfulness of merchants and manufac-turers—important groups in commercial society—is especially severe. As we will see in the next section, however, Smith and Rousseau both main-tain that the *worst* effect of concern for others' opinions is that it leads peo-ple to constantly strive for ever more wealth and material goods.

5. THE PURSUIT OF UNHAPPINESS

As we saw in Chapter 1, Rousseau's most profound critique of commercial society is that it expands people's desires far beyond their capacities and in this way makes them miserable. For Rousseau, people's desires were first emancipated early in human history but are expanded exponentially in commercial society, in part because of the great emphasis on wealth in this

69. The similarity of these passages, too, has been noted by other scholars; see Force, *Self-Interest Before Adam Smith,* 158–59, 180; and Hanley, "Rousseau's Diagnosis and Adam Smith's Cure," ms. 20.

kind of society. Once again, Smith disputes Rousseau's claim about human nature—for him there was no happy and peaceful natural state in which everyone's desires were limited to those that could easily be fulfilled. But once again, he is of a similar mind regarding the present predicament, in this case the fact that in commercial society people's desires are expanded well beyond their capacities, which leads to a great deal of toil and postponement of gratification. He does not go quite so far as Rousseau does in maintaining that commercial society almost unfailingly makes people *miserable,* but he does accept that the things people tend to strive for in commercial society—wealth and luxury, in order to secure the approval of others—ultimately do little if anything to make people happier. Smith joins Rousseau in associating happiness with tranquility, and he recognizes that people have little chance to enjoy tranquility when they spend their entire lives striving for more and more wealth.

Of course, in defending commercial society Smith could simply have claimed that Rousseau took the wrong view of happiness; Rousseau's view of happiness as consisting of tranquility is certainly not the only one available or possible. The connection between happiness and tranquility is an ancient one, going back at least to the Stoics and Epicureans, yet there is another view of happiness that can claim an equally venerable lineage: Aristotle's view of happiness as *energeia* (activity), that is, an activity of the soul in accordance with virtue or excellence.[70] Hume, too, parts from the view of happiness as tranquility, maintaining that happiness consists of three ingredients—action, pleasure, and indolence—and placing greater emphasis on the former two.[71] He writes that "indolence or repose . . . seems not of itself to contribute much to our enjoyment; but, like sleep, is requisite as an indulgence to the weakness of human nature." He goes on to declare that "in times when industry and the arts flourish, men are kept in perpetual occupation, and enjoy, as their reward, the occupation itself, as well as those pleasures which are the fruit of their labour."[72] The idea that perpetual occupation can produce happiness is nearly the reverse of Rousseau's view of the matter, and Hume's view of happiness is much more obviously compatible with a positive view of commercial society. But Smith does *not* choose to dispute Rousseau's view here: he, too, links happiness with

---

70. See Aristotle, *Nichomachean Ethics,* 1098a. For a discussion of both views of happiness, see Annas, *The Morality of Happiness,* chaps. 16, 18, and 19.

71. See Hume, "Of Refinement in the Arts," in *Essays,* 269–70.

72. Ibid., 270.

tranquility and thus shares the central assumption of Rousseau's key critique of commercial society, the "pursuit of unhappiness" critique.

"Happiness consists in tranquillity and enjoyment," Smith writes. "Without tranquillity there can be no enjoyment; and where there is perfect tranquillity there is scarce any thing which is not capable of amusing" (*TMS* III.3.30, 149; see also I.ii.3.6, 37). Like Rousseau, Smith consistently understands happiness as a lasting state of contentment, a state that is content precisely because it is not constantly disturbed by restless desires. Happiness, on this view, is produced above all by a state of inner harmony or balance—a lack of significant internal discord—and Smith claims that this is the "natural" or "usual" state that a person's mind takes when it is not disturbed by incessant desires or by strong fears or worries (*TMS* III.3.30, 149). He explicitly links this view to that of the Stoics, but he does not *wholly* adopt the Stoic view, for he recognizes that the eradication of all passions and feelings—which he generally refers to as "apathy" or "indifference"— is undesirable (see *TMS* II.3.14, 143; VII.ii.1.43–46, 292). A degree of emotion is necessary because while tranquility of mind is the key component of happiness, is not the *whole* of happiness; rather, it must be combined with "enjoyment" or pleasure. External fortune does, then, play a role in the attainment of happiness, and hence Smith says only that the Stoic view of happiness was "very nearly in the right" (*TMS* III.3.30, 149).[73]

Although external fortune plays a role in attaining happiness; however, great fortune is by no means necessary. It is not great achievements or vast ambitions that make people truly happy, on Smith's view, but rather simpler and calmer pleasures such as rewarding relationships with family and friends and the knowledge that one has acted virtuously. According to Smith, people are so constituted that they take pleasure in knowing they have acted in a praiseworthy manner, and in this sense virtue really is its own reward: warranted praise from others and warranted self-approbation are two of the surest sources of "inward tranquillity and self-satisfaction" and hence of happiness (*TMS* III.1.6, 113; see also III.5.6–7, 166; IV.2.1, 187). Personal relationships based on mutual affection and genuine sympathy are also crucial ingredients of happiness, on Smith's account (see *TMS* I.ii.4.1–2, 39; VI.ii.1.18, 224–25). He argues, for example, that it is better to advance slowly and steadily toward a higher station than to experience a "sudden revolution

---

73. Smith's relationship to the Stoics has received a good deal of scholarly attention; see, for example, Montes, *Adam Smith in Context;* Vivenza, *Adam Smith and the Classics;* and Waszek, "Two Concepts of Morality."

of fortune" (such as winning the lottery), since such revolutions tend to pro-
voke envy and thereby to alienate one's friends, and friendship is far more
important than fortune (*TMS* I.ii.5.1, 40–41). Indeed, in the midst of this discussion Smith posits that "the chief part of human happiness arises from
the consciousness of being beloved" (*TMS* I.ii.5.1, 41).

This kind of happiness requires little in the way of external goods, of
course, so Smith claims that the rich and powerful are no more likely to
attain it than the poor and weak. He asks rhetorically, "What can be added
to the happiness of the man who is in health, who is out of debt, and has a
clear conscience? To one in this situation, all accessions of fortune may properly be said to be superfluous" (*TMS* I.iii.1.7, 45; see also III.3.30, 149). In
fact, Smith sometimes even seems to imply that the poor may be *more* likely
to attain happiness than the rich:

> Except the frivolous pleasures of vanity and superiority, we may
> find, in the most humble station, where there is only personal lib-
> erty, every other which the most exalted can afford; and the plea-
> sures of vanity and superiority are seldom consistent with perfect
> tranquillity, the principle and foundation of all real and satisfactory
> enjoyment. Neither is it always certain that, in the splendid situa-
> tion which we aim at, those real and satisfactory pleasures can be
> enjoyed with the same security as the humble one which we are
> so very eager to abandon. (*TMS* III.3.31, 150)

Smith does not issue blanket statements about the worthlessness of material
goods in the way that Rousseau sometimes does; he harbors no illusions
about the importance of possessing the necessities and some of the conveniences of life. But even if *some* material goods are necessary, he argues,
the "trinkets and baubles" of the rich are often more trouble than they are
worth (see *WN* II.iii.42, 349; III.iv.15, 421). These goods cost a great deal of
trouble to buy, protect, fix, and replace, and they cannot relieve any of the
real ills in life; they "may save [their possessor] from some smaller incon-
veniencies," but they "leave him always as much, and sometimes more
exposed than before, to anxiety, to fear, and to sorrow; to diseases, to danger, and to death" (*TMS* IV.1.8, 183). Even further, Smith writes that "power
and riches" are "enormous and operose machines contrived to produce a
few trifling conveniences to the body, consisting of springs the most nice
and delicate, which must be kept in order with the most anxious attention,

and which in spite of all our care are ready every moment to burst into pieces, and to crush in their ruins their unfortunate possessor" (*TMS* IV.1.8, 182–83). For Smith as for Rousseau, then, a large number of the commodities produced by commercial society are ultimately useless—and perhaps even worse than useless.

Just as important as the fact that money can't buy happiness, for Smith, is the fact that the relentless *pursuit* of money tends to *detract* from people's happiness, for when people desire ever more wealth and material goods they often submit themselves to nearly endless toil and anxiety in the pursuit of them. People typically think they would be happier if they had more money, but Smith argues that this false belief actually tends to lead to *un*happiness: "the great source of both the misery and disorders of human life, seems to arise from over-rating the difference between one permanent situation and another" (*TMS* III.3.31, 149). It is precisely because people wrongly think they would be happier in a higher station that they forgo the happiness that is always within their power. To illustrate this point Smith relates a charming story told by Plutarch:

> What the favourite of the king of Epirus said to his master, may be applied to men in all the ordinary situations of human life. When the King had recounted to him, in their proper order, all the conquests which he proposed to make, and had come to the last of them; And what does your Majesty propose to do then? said the Favourite.—I propose then, said the King, to enjoy myself with my friends, and endeavour to be good company over a bottle.—And what hinders your Majesty from doing so now? replied the Favourite. (*TMS* III.3.31, 150)[74]

For Smith, people tend to strive for more and more wealth and consequently abandon the simple pleasures that are available to them at any time; as Rousseau laments, their entire lives are spent postponing gratification. Like Rousseau (but in stark contrast to Hume), Smith maintains that labor is "toil and trouble" (*WN* I.v.2, 47), that it requires a person to "lay down [a] portion of

74. Rousseau relates the same story in *Emile* and says that in this story "we see only a fleeting *bon mot;* but Emile will see a very wise reflection which he would have been the first to make and which will never be effaced from his mind." *Emile* IV, 242; see also *Confessions* V, 158. For Plutarch's version of the story, see Plutarch, *Lives of the Noble Grecians and Romans*, 529–30.

his ease, his liberty, and his happiness" (*WN* I.v.7, 50). He speaks of "all that toil, all that anxiety, all those mortifications which must be undergone in the pursuit of [wealth and greatness]; and what is of yet more consequence, all that leisure, all that ease, all that careless security, which are forfeited for ever by the acquisition" (*TMS* I.iii.2.1, 51). Happiness consists largely of tranquility, for Smith, and there is little tranquility to be found in toil and striving.

In short, Smith shows vividly that neither the pursuit nor the attainment of wealth brings true happiness. He also shows vividly, however, that the vast majority of people struggle mightily for wealth in any case. In a famous passage he writes that "the desire of bettering our condition . . . comes with us from the womb, and never leaves us till we go into the grave. In the whole interval which separates these two moments, there is scarce perhaps a single instant in which any man is so perfectly and completely satisfied with his situation, as to be without any wish of alteration or improvement, of any kind" (*WN* II.iii.28, 341). As Smith says time and again, people pursue wealth because they mistakenly associate it with happiness; everyone strives to attain (in the economist's phrase) a "higher standard of living," as if living well and having more money were the same thing.

It is nature, Smith says, that "imposes upon us . . . this deception which rouses and keeps in continual motion the industry of mankind" (*TMS* IV.1.9, 183). As we saw in the previous section, people are deceived into thinking that wealth and the things it can buy are important and fulfilling mainly as a result of their concern for the opinions of others; in the end, people forfeit leisure, ease, and security and undergo endless toil and anxiety in order to fulfill their vanity and avoid the contempt that comes from being poor. In short, the natural human faculty of sympathy deludes almost everyone into thinking that money can buy happiness. And even if there are moments when people see that neither wealth nor the fulfillment of their vanity will bring them happiness, such as when they are old or sick or depressed—or perhaps when they are enlightened by a book like *The Theory of Moral Sentiments*—they almost inevitably turn back toward the delusory pursuit of wealth since it is so difficult to constantly view things "in this abstract and philosophical light" (*TMS* IV.1.9, 183).

But if human nature conspires against people's happiness, it seems that commercial society aids and abets this conspiracy. For Smith, even if the "desire of bettering our condition" is natural and so has always been present, there is simply more to desire in commercial society; the combination of an extensive division of labor and a large market helps produce a great many luxuries and so makes available to people numerous things they could not otherwise desire. Whereas the desire for the necessities of life must be relatively limited since these things are fairly easily attainable, Smith claims, the desire for luxuries and "conveniencies" is "altogether endless" (*WN* I.xi.c.7, 181). And this continual pursuit of material goods is, of course, not just a minor component of commercial society but the very engine that drives it: "the uniform, constant, and uninterrupted effort of every man to better his condition [is] the principle from which publick and national, as well as private opulence is originally derived" (*WN* II.iii.31, 343). In a word, Smith accepts that both the rise of commercial society and continued economic growth *within* this kind of society are based on a delusion among the members of that society about their own happiness; the wealth of nations is made possible only by a massive self-deception about the true ends of human life.

Smith's explicit response to this problem in *The Theory of Moral Sentiments,* moreover, seems to do little to answer the question of why he ultimately defends commercial society. After discussing the fact that people strive for ever more material goods even though these goods cannot provide true satisfaction, he continues:

> And it is well that nature imposes upon us in this manner. It is this deception which rouses and keeps in continual motion the industry of mankind. It is this which first prompted them to cultivate the ground, to build houses, to found cities and commonwealths, and to invent and improve all the sciences and arts, which ennoble and embellish human life; which have entirely changed the whole face of the globe, have turned the rude forests of nature into agreeable and fertile plains, and made the trackless and barren ocean a new fund of subsistence, and the great high road of communication to the different nations of the earth. (*TMS* IV.i.10, 183–84)

Here, incidentally, is yet another example of Smith coming close to using Rousseau's words: whereas in the first passage from the *Discourse* that Smith translated for the *Edinburgh Review* Rousseau explains how "the vast forrests of nature were changed into agreeable plains" (*Letter,* 252), Smith here describes how people "turned the rude forests of nature into agreeable and fertile plains" (*TMS* IV.i.10, 183). Ignatieff notes that this "choice of words is so close to those of Rousseau . . . that it cannot be mere coincidence."[75] This passage, however, would seem to do little to explain why Smith defends commercial society; it seems merely to suggest that the delusion that money can buy happiness is good because it advances civilization, but this of course begs the question of why civilization is desirable in the first place. What good are all of these "improvements" (the arts and sciences and the rest), one might reasonably ask, if most of the individuals in commercial society remain deluded about the nature and basis of their own happiness?

Smith's defense of commercial society could be easily reconciled with his acknowledgment that it is based on this delusion if he was concerned only with how wealthy or civilized a society is and not how happy it is, but this is patently not the case: he writes in the very next paragraph that "all constitutions of government . . . are valued only in proportion as they tend to promote the happiness of those who live under them. This is their sole use and end" (TMS IV.1.11, 185). Smith's touchstone, then, is the happiness of the individuals who make up a society, and he seems to admit that commercial society cannot reliably make people happy and may even undermine their happiness in certain ways. If the central puzzle of Smith's thought is, as I have suggested, the question of why he advocates commercial society despite the many problems that are associated with it, then the "pursuit of unhappiness" critique can be seen as the most deeply puzzling part of this puzzle, for it shows that commercial society at least *seems* to fall short of Smith's *own measure* of a good society.

CONCLUSION

We should make no mistake: Smith is not Rousseau. As we have seen, Smith's sympathy with the "division of laborers" and the "pursuit of unhappiness" critiques is not total, his sympathy with the "empire of opinion" critique even less so. His statements regarding the injustice of inequality are somewhat more moderate than Rousseau's (particularly in his published works), and his worries about the decline of citizenship do not take quite the same form as Rousseau's. He does not place the same emphasis on the problem of role playing that Rousseau does, and his complaints about

---

75. Ignatieff, "Smith, Rousseau, and the Republic of Needs," in *Scotland and Europe*, 191. The similarity of these passages is also noted by the editors of *The Theory of Moral Sentiments*; see *TMS*, 183n5.

immoral actions and deceitfulness are applied only to specific groups—to those in "the superior stations in life" and to wealthy merchants and manufacturers, respectively—rather than to people in commercial society more generally. And he does not go quite as far as Rousseau does in scorning material goods as insignificant or in maintaining that commercial society necessarily makes people *miserable;* instead, he argues only that riches do not reliably produce happiness and *might* jeopardize it in certain ways. Even more important than these qualifications is that Smith provides counterarguments and countermeasures for even those portions of Rousseau's critique for which he shows some sympathy, as we will see in the next two chapters.

Yet the extent to which Smith *does* sympathize with Rousseau's three critiques is surprising, even given the more subtle picture of Smith that has emerged in the recent outpouring of Smith scholarship. Few contemporary scholars continue to portray Smith as a crude laissez-faire capitalist, but perhaps just as few appreciate the full breadth of his sympathy with the arguments *against* commercial society. As we have seen, Smith accepts that the division of labor necessarily leads to great inequalities and that it can make people weak and ignorant and thereby undermine citizenship—and his anxieties about weakness and ignorance are if anything stronger than Rousseau's. He recognizes that people tend to be greatly concerned with the opinions of others and that this concern corrupts people's moral sentiments, encourages selfishly motivated appeals to others' self-interest, and promotes ostentation. And perhaps most important, he concedes that in commercial society people's desires are expanded far beyond their capacities, that this expansion results in nearly endless toil and postponement of gratification, and that the things people strive for in commercial society—wealth and luxury, in order to secure the approval of others—ultimately do little if anything to make people truly happy. In short, Smith fully accepts that many real and important problems are associated with the kind of society he advocates. Yet in the end he *does* unambiguously defend and promote commercial society. The obvious question, given his deep sympathy with Rousseau's critiques, is why. Chapters 3 and 4 will provide an answer—or, rather, several answers—to this question and thus a solution to the central puzzle of Smith's thought.

T H R E E | THE EUROPEAN PEASANT AND THE PRUDENT MAN

We have seen that Smith was well aware of—even more, *insisted on*—the many problems associated with commercial society. Indeed, if taken in isolation his statements on the debilitating effects of the division of labor and on the rapacity of merchants and manufacturers would seem to comprise a devastating condemnation of this kind of society. It is perhaps not surprising, then, that at least one prominent scholar has argued that Smith's true conclusion regarding commercial society was that it would end in "material decline" and "moral decay."[1] But such a view ignores the entire tenor of his writings; while the common portrayal of Smith as an unabashed apostle of laissez-faire capitalism is surely a caricature, viewing him as anything but an advocate of commercial society requires a willful disregard for the substance of his thought.

Smith's advocacy of commercial society, we will see, is a sober and thoughtful one, based on a careful assessment of its potential costs and its undeniable benefits. While he recognizes the deeply problematic character of commercial society and concedes a measure of validity to the three-pronged Rousseauian critique, he is equally aware of the perhaps less obvious and longer-term benefits of this kind of society and so provides counterarguments and countermeasures for each of those critiques. In this chapter we will examine Smith's attempt to show that Rousseau's "division of laborers" and "empire of opinion" critiques are not finally convincing. He counters these critiques in a number of ways, but above all by showing, first, that the extraordinary productivity made possible by the division of labor allowed even a peasant in Europe to be materially better off than many an African king, and second, that the concern for others' opinions can serve as the very basis for moral conduct, especially by encouraging the type of person whom Smith calls the "prudent man."

Nearly every element of Smith's defense of commercial society consists

---

1. See Heilbroner, "The Paradox of Progress," in *Essays on Adam Smith*, 524.

of a comparison with previous societies. Thus I begin this chapter, in Section 1, with a preliminary synopsis of his view of human history. Sections 2 and 3 will consider Smith's response to the "division of laborers" critique. The first of these sections examines Smith's arguments regarding the productivity made possible by the division of labor and shows that he extols the prosperity of commercial society principally because it makes possible a rise in the living standards of the poor. In Section 3 we will consider the measures Smith advocates taking against the debilitating effects of the division of labor, focusing in particular on his emphasis on the importance of education in commercial society. The final two sections of the chapter examine Smith's response to the "empire of opinion" critique. Section 4 outlines Smith's claim that people's concern for the opinions of others, far from being unavoidably corrupting, can in fact serve as a basis of moral conduct. Finally, Section 5 centers on his argument that commercial society will encourage virtues like reliability, decency, cooperativeness, and strict adherence to society's norms of justice—the virtues of the "prudent man"—by ensuring that it is in people's best interests to exhibit these traits.

I. SMITH AS A HISTORIAN

Scholars have in general paid insufficient attention to the great weight that Smith places on the character of *pre*commercial societies. It is difficult to avoid noticing that several of Smith's most famous pronouncements about commercial society are cast as comparisons with earlier societies, and most scholars at least mention his "four stages" theory of history—which traces humanity's progress through its hunting, shepherding, agricultural, and commercial stages[2]—but few have stressed that the economic, moral,

2. The roots of this theory can be found in Montesquieu, and a similar theory can be found in the works of many of Smith's contemporaries, including Ferguson, Kames, Millar, and Robertson. For an extensive analysis of the precursors and exponents of the "four stages" theory, one which concludes that the fully developed theory was probably originated by Smith and Turgot independently and around the same time, see Meek, *Social Science and the Ignoble Savage*. For further evidence of the prevalence of this theory in the mid to late eighteenth century, see Hont, "The Language of Sociability and Commerce," in *The Languages of Political Theory in Early Modern Europe*. While the "four stages" theory bears only the slightest of resemblances to the history outlined in Rousseau's *Discourse on Inequality*, it is much closer to Rousseau's view in the *Essay on the Origin of Languages*. In the latter work, Rousseau divides history into "three states of man considered in relation to society": "The savage is a hunter, the barbarian a herdsman, the civil man a plowman" (*Languages*, 309; see also 307). For a

and political differences among these stages are in many ways *the* central subject and organizing principle of Smith's thought.

Placing a great emphasis on the history of human societies was more or less standard among thinkers in the Scottish Enlightenment; David Hume claimed of eighteenth-century Scotland that "this is the historical Age and this the historical Nation,"[3] and the titles of most of the major works written during this period bear witness to his claim.[4] Many thinkers of this period engaged in what Dugald Stewart dubbed "*Theoretical* or *Conjectural History*" (*EPS*, 293), endeavoring to determine not only the actual, empirical history of a particular society but also the "natural" or "typical" progress of human societies. Based on classical literature, civil and ecclesiastical law records, travelers' reports from primitive societies in Asia, Africa, and the Americas, and the palpable differences between the emerging commercial culture of the Scottish Lowlands and the relatively uncultivated Highlands, they attempted to reconstruct the progress of humanity from its rude beginnings to the more civilized state in which they found themselves.

Stewart notes that this sort of history "seems, in a peculiar degree, to have interested Mr Smith's curiosity" and that "something very similar to it may be traced in all his different works, whether moral, political, or literary" (*EPS*, 292). This is most obviously true for Smith's *Lectures on Jurisprudence*, where the focus is the historical development of law through the different ages of society and where the "four stages" theory is central. That *The Wealth of Nations* also fits this description is reasonably clear; Smith himself says that this work is part of "an account of the general principles of law and government, and of the different revolutions which they [have] undergone in the different ages and periods of society" (*TMS*, 3). Most of Books III and V of *The Wealth of Nations* are organized around the history of Europe since the fall of Rome and around the "four stages" theory,

---

comparison of Rousseau's view of history in these two works with the "four stages" theory, see Meek, *Social Science and the Ignoble Savage*, 76–91.

3. Hume, *The Letters of David Hume*, vol. 2, 230.

4. Think, for example, of James Dunbar's *Essays on the History of Mankind in Rude and Cultivated Ages*, Adam Ferguson's *An Essay on the History of Civil Society*, David Hume's *The History of England* (by far the most celebrated of his writings during his lifetime), Lord Kames's *Historical Law Tracts* and *Sketches of the History of Man*, John Millar's *An Historical View of the English Government* and *The Origin of the Distinction of Ranks*, Lord Monboddo's *Of the Origin and Progress of Language*, and William Robertson's *A View of the Progress of Society in Europe*. For an overview of the historical themes running through these and other writings during the Scottish Enlightenment, see Berry, *Social Theory of the Scottish Enlightenment*, especially chaps. 3 and 5.

respectively, and even the more straightforwardly "economic" parts of this work are remarkably full of historical material. Smith proceeds much more often by examining historical facts than by putting forward atemporal general principles. Finally, history plays an important role even in *The Theory of Moral Sentiments,* for Smith shows time and again that not only culture and customs but also moral judgments themselves are social in origin and so change with different stages of society.[5]

Like many other Enlightenment thinkers but dramatically unlike Rousseau, Smith views human history by and large as progressive. He adopts this viewpoint cautiously, continually stressing the failures of the modern world and the persistent obstacles to growth and improvement. But adopt it he does: through the "four stages" theory, he attempts to show how humanity advanced from hunting and gathering societies to the commercial societies of his day—in Walter Bagehot's mocking terms, "how, from being a savage, man rose to be a Scotchman."[6] History is, for Smith, a story of humanity's ever-widening conquest of nature; whereas people originally had to remain content with accepting what nature provided, in later stages of society they are able to control and harness nature and thereby ensure themselves a more comfortable existence.

The "lowest and rudest state of society," Smith maintains, is the hunting stage, such as could be found among the tribes of North America (*WN* V.i.a.1, 689–90; see also *LJ*, 15–16, 107, 201). In this stage there is no domestication of animals or raising of crops; people subsist by hunting, fishing, and gathering. There is very little division of labor or exchange, and so "every man endeavours to supply by his own industry his own occasional wants as they occur" (*WN* II.intro.1, 276; see also *LJ*, 583).[7] These societies must be relatively small in size and nomadic, Smith reasons, since it would be impossible to provide for a large population in a single location simply with game and wild vegetation. Thus, he estimates that hunting societies generally consist of only a few dozen families—around 150 people—who live and travel together for purposes of defense (see *LJ*, 201, 213, 407). Because their means of subsistence are extremely limited, these societies generally

5. See Skinner, *A System of Social Science,* 103–4.
6. Bagehot, "Adam Smith as a Person," in *Biographical Studies,* 275–76.
7. There could possibly be a rudimentary division of labor in hunting societies—for instance, a person who finds that he is especially skilled at making bows and arrows might make enough of them to use for exchange—but this division would have to remain extremely rudimentary because the population (the "market") is so limited (see *WN* I.ii.3, 27).

have little in the way of accumulated property or government: "there is scarce any property, or at least none that exceeds the value of two or three days labour; so there is seldom any established magistrate or any regular administration of justice" (*WN* V.i.b.2, 709; see also V.i.a.1, 690; *LJ*, 207). What little government there is at this stage tends to be relatively democratic; while one person may have more influence than the others because of his personal qualities (such as strength or intelligence) or his age, this influence is not institutionalized, so people are generally on an equal footing (see *LJ*, 202, 404; *WN* Vi.b.7, 712–13).

It is important to note here that while Smith claims that hunting societies are largely prepolitical, he does *not* argue that they are in any way presocial; whereas Rousseau posits a "pure" state of nature in which people lived solitary lives, the most primitive way of life that Smith envisions includes society and language. Even the most uncivilized people need others and tend to sympathize with others, Smith argues, and thus "man, who can subsist only in society, was fitted by nature to that situation for which he was made" (*TMS* II.ii.3.1, 85; see also II.ii.3.6, 88; III.2.7, 117). According to Smith, people also have a natural tendency to divide their labor: he contends in *The Wealth of Nations* that the "division of labor . . . is the necessary, though very slow and gradual consequence of a certain propensity in human nature . . . to truck, barter, and exchange one thing for another," and he elsewhere affirms that this propensity is ultimately a result of people's natural desire to persuade one another (*WN* I.ii.1, 25; see also *ED*, 570–71; *LJ*, 347, 352, 492–94; *TMS* VII.iv.25, 336). And since the division of labor is the driving force behind economic progress, over time people tend to develop more and more efficient means of subsistence and thereby bring about advances toward more civilized forms of society. Unlike for Rousseau, then, for Smith the causes of civilization are sown into human nature; society progresses as a result of people's innate abilities and propensities rather than through a series of accidents.[8]

The next step in the progress of society, in Smith's account, is the shepherding or pasturage stage, in which people have domesticated animals. His chief examples of this stage are the societies "such as we find . . . among the Tartars and Arabs," but he also includes in this group the most barbarous nations of Africa and the East Indies, as well as the inhabitants of the Scottish Highlands (*WN* V.i.a.3, 690; see also IV.vii.c.100, 634; V.i.a.26,

---

8. See Winch, *Riches and Poverty*, 70.

701; *LJ*, 15, 408, 583). Because subsistence is not quite as precarious in this stage as in the hunting stage—meat and milk are usually readily available—shepherding societies can be much larger than hunting societies, often numbering in the thousands (see *LJ*, 408, 583; *WN* V.i.a.5, 691). These societies are generally still nomadic since animals are relatively transportable and need fresh vegetation and a temperate climate in which to graze, but Smith does allow for the existence of stationary shepherds, such as the Highlanders (see *WN* V.i.a.3, 690; V.i.a.26, 701). The most important advancement in this stage, however, is that animals come to be regarded as property; the fact that property is extended beyond immediate possession makes possible great inequalities in wealth for the first time and thereby brings about a need for government to protect those inequalities (see *LJ*, 202, 208–9, 404; *WN* V.i.b.12, 715).

While government tends to remain theoretically democratic among shepherds, the rich tend to have an inordinate amount of influence, and the man with the greatest herds is always the chief (see *LJ*, 203; *WN* V.i.b.7, 712; V.i.b.11, 714). In fact, Smith claims of the shepherding stage that "there is no period of society in which the superiority of fortune gives so great authority to those who possess it" (*WN* V.i.b.7, 713; see also *LJ*, 202, 215, 405). Because there are almost no luxuries or manufactured goods in this stage, the only way for a wealthy person to use his wealth is to "maintain"—that is, to provide for—thousands of others, and this renders those thousands dependent on him (see *LJ*, 202, 405; *WN* V.i.b.7, 712). Given that the ability to accumulate property brings with it great inequalities, government, and dependence for the first time, "the step betwixt these two [the hunting and shepherding stages] is of all others the greatest in the progression of society" (*LJ*, 107).[9]

For Smith, government arises gradually and "naturally" with the progression of society and the increase of property (see *WN* V.i.b.12, 715); he follows Hume in rejecting the idea that political power is the result of any kind of formal social contract (see *LJ*, 315–18, 321, 402–4).[10] Rather, he claims

9. J. G. A. Pocock argues that Smith's most novel contribution as a historian was his contention that the shepherding stage is a decisive improvement over the hunting stage—that is, that the domestication of animals rather than the raising of crops is what brings about property, inequality, and government. "In most previous systems of this kind," Pocock contends, "the shepherd was little distinguished from the hunter, and the origins of civilization were located in the change from a nomadic to a sedentary way of life." Pocock, *Barbarism and Religion*, vol. 2, 316; see also 323.

10. Cf. Hume, "Of the Original Contract," in *Essays*.

that there are four qualities by which people naturally gain superiority over others: personal qualifications (such as strength, beauty, wisdom, or virtue), age, wealth, and birth (see *LJ*, 321, 401; *WN* V.i.b.4–8, 710–13). Only the former two qualities are meaningful in a hunting society; since there is no great wealth, there are no families that can claim entitlement by birth. But with the rise of extensive property and government in shepherding society the latter two qualities, wealth and birth, begin to predominate (see *LJ*, 215; *WN* V.i.b.9–12, 713–15). Recall here that in his letter to the *Edinburgh Review*, Smith had noted that Rousseau (like Mandeville) sees government as an invention of the rich, the purpose of which is to maintain "an unnatural and unjust superiority over the rest of their fellow-creatures" (*Letter*, 251). Smith, too, believes that government and political power arise in order to preserve inequalities in property; he denies, though, that for this reason they are either unnatural or unjust. He argues instead that inequalities and subordination arise naturally and spontaneously, not as a result of violence or fraud; as we will find, he also sees them as ultimately beneficial for all involved.

The third stage that Smith describes is the age of agriculture or husbandry, which arises when people begin devoting themselves to cultivating the land. By far his most detailed examination of this kind of society comes in Book III of *The Wealth of Nations*, in which he describes the allodial and feudal periods of Europe that followed the fall of the Roman Empire. In societies that subsist by farming, Smith maintains, a settled residence comes to replace the nomadic lifestyle (see *WN* V.i.a.7, 693), the notion of property is extended to include land (see *LJ*, 28), and the population can be still larger than in shepherding societies (see *LJ*, 15). The patterns of inequality and dependence that were found in the shepherding stage, however, are largely repeated: property remains a source of great power, though land comes to be more important than herds (see *LJ*, 244; *WN* V.i.b.16, 717), and the great landowners still have virtually nothing on which to spend their wealth except the maintenance of a large number of dependents, since at this stage there is generally still little foreign commerce and no manufactures outside those made by families for their own use (see *LJ*, 49–51, 248, 416; *WN* III.ii.3, 383; III.iv.5–7, 413–15; V.i.a.6, 692; V.i.f.51, 782–83). As a result of the greater size and population of society at this stage, government becomes much more complicated than it had previously been, but real power remains largely in the hands of the great landowners.

The fourth and apparently final stage in Smith's schema is the commercial stage, in which labor is divided to the point where "every man . . . lives by exchanging, or becomes in some measure a merchant" (*WN* I.iv.1, 37).[11] Some degree of exchange has existed since hunting society, he acknowledges (see *WN* I.ii.3, 27), but he points out that in commercial society people *live* by exchanging. As he notes in the first chapter of *The Wealth of Nations*, "in every improved society, the farmer is generally nothing but a farmer; the manufacturer, nothing but a manufacturer" (*WN* I.i.4, 15–16). In other words, in commercial society people specialize in a single task, and they do so with the explicit intention of exchanging their surplus with others in order to satisfy their needs. In this kind of society every good and service commands a price, and this allows people to divide their labor to the greatest extent possible, thereby generating an enormous increase in productivity. And just as individuals live by exchanging with one another, in the commercial stage nations, too, live by exchanging with one another (see *LJ*, 15–16). It seems that by the late eighteenth century this type of society had fully emerged only in parts of western Europe and North America, according to Smith; the only nations that he explicitly dubs "commercial" are Britain (excluding the Scottish Highlands), France, Genoa, Holland, Portugal, Spain, and the American colonies (see *WN* I.xi.e.38, 209; I.xi.m.4, 246; IV.i.5–6, 431).

It is important to distinguish Smith's comments on commercial society in general from his comments on the "system of commerce" or "commercial system" in Book IV of *The Wealth of Nations*. Smith uses these latter terms to denote the system that has come to be known as mercantilism, which comprises one form of commercial society. Another form of commercial society—the one Smith himself advocates—he dubs "the obvious and simple system of natural liberty" (*WN* IV.ix.51, 687) or "the natural system of perfect liberty and justice" (*WN* IV.vii.c.44, 606); this latter form of commercial society is closer to what we now call capitalism. The commercial

---

11. Smith never explicitly claimed that commercial society will be the final stage of human development; he was too cautious, too pragmatic, and too astute a historian to make rigid predictions of this kind. Partly because of his lack of forecasts about the future, there has been an intense debate as to whether he adequately anticipated the Industrial Revolution. (Most historians date the Industrial Revolution in Scotland from sometime in the 1780s, just after the first edition of *The Wealth of Nations*; see, for example, Smout, *A History of the Scottish People, 1560–1830*, 212–13.) For arguments that Smith failed to foresee the coming Industrial Revolution, see Caton, "The Preindustrial Economics of Adam Smith"; and Kindleberger, "The Historical Background," in *The Market and the State*. For an attempt to defend him on this score, see Hartwell, "Comment," in *The Market and the State*. Finally, for a more balanced— and perhaps more dependable—account, see Hollander, *The Economics of Adam Smith*, chaps. 3 and 7.

or mercantile system was the one that reigned in eighteenth-century Britain; Smith calls it "the modern system," the system that "is best understood in our own country and in our own time" (*WN* IV.intro.2, 428). By contrast, the system of natural liberty seems to him to be virtually beyond reach. "To expect . . . that the freedom of trade should ever be entirely restored in Great Britain," he writes, "is as absurd as to expect that an Oceana or Utopia should ever be established in it" (*WN* IV.ii.43, 471). Smith's criticisms of his own society and of mercantilism, then, are not *necessarily* meant to be applied to commercial society in general; on the contrary, he argues that many of the ills often associated with commercial society would be mitigated if mercantilism were to be replaced by the "system of natural liberty."

It is important to further note, though few scholars do, that Smith approaches mercantilism from two different directions.[12] On the one hand, this system and the monopolies that drive it are in some ways Smith's main antagonist in *The Wealth of Nations,* the subject of his "very violent attack . . . upon the whole commercial system of Great Britain" (*CAS,* 251). On the other hand, however, he sees mercantilism as a form of commercial society, one that shares a number of crucial elements with the "system of natural liberty" that he advocates. While Smith claims that mercantilism is harmful in many respects when compared to the potential benefits of his "system of natural liberty," he also sees it as a great improvement over the feudal age that preceded it in Europe. Indeed, his sometimes extravagant praise of the liberty and security that Britain affords its citizens must be ascribed at least in part to the mercantile system, since that was the system that prevailed there in Smith's time (see *LJ,* 121, 421–22; *WN* III.iv.20, 425; IV.v.b.43, 540; IV.vii.c.54, 610). That Smith defends the virtues of even his great antagonist over and against precommercial societies confirms just how significant an improvement he understands commercial society to be.

Before turning to the question of why Smith sees commercial society as such a great improvement, it should be noted that his view of history is not as crude or as one-dimensional as the "four stages" theory might seem to imply. While this theory is rather simple and straightforward, Smith fully recognizes that the history of human societies has actually been much more complicated. He never claims that the "four stages" theory is exhaustive, nor does he argue that history must move in a linear fashion. Indeed, he

---

12. A notable exception is Coats, "Adam Smith and the Mercantile System," in *Essays on Adam Smith,* 220–21.

maintains that "the natural course of things" is often diverted, such as in modern Europe, where the development of commerce preceded the improvement of the countryside (see *WN* III.iv.18–19, 422), and he accepts that societies can move backward, as Europe did after the fall of Rome (see *LJ*, 49; *WN* III.ii.1, 381–82). He also allows that societies can combine elements of different stages; for example, the Highland shepherds are stationary rather than nomadic (see V.i.a.26, 701) and the American Indian tribes have "some notion of agriculture" though none of shepherding (*LJ*, 15; see also 459). Moreover, it is unclear how ancient Greece and Rome fit into the fourfold classification; these societies seem to have developed past the agricultural stage, according to Smith's description, but it is unclear whether they attained all of the characteristics of a commercial society. In these societies, "commerce . . . naturally introduce[d] itself, tho' not, as now, particularly studied and a theory laid down" (*LJ*, 235; see also 91, 222; *Astronomy*, 51; *LRBL*, 150; *WN* IV.ix.47, 683–84; V.i.a.11–13, 693–97). All of these exceptions and ambiguities are sufficient to show that Smith intended the "four stages" theory less as a rigid framework for how societies must develop than as a loose outline or heuristic device that provides a means of comparing different forms of society.[13]

The fact that Smith uses the "four stages" theory more as a comparative tool than as a fixed model of development indicates that, contrary to an influential view of him, for Smith a society's mode of subsistence does not in any way "determine" the other features of that society. This view—propounded especially by Marxist and Marxist-inspired scholars—holds that Smith was a precursor of Marx in advancing a materialist interpretation of history, that his association of a society's mode of subsistence with its other features shows that he was by and large an economic determinist.[14] (Ronald Meek declares, with a nod to Marx, that Smith's view is "*a*, if not *the*, materialist conception of history.")[15] This thesis, however, has been to all intents and purposes refuted by the work of H. M. Hopfl, Knud Haakonssen, and Donald Winch.[16] These scholars have shown conclusively that many factors

13. See Berry, *Social Theory of the Scottish Enlightenment*, 114; Pocock, *Barbarism and Religion*, vol. 2, 322–23; and Skinner, *A System of Social Science*, 82.

14. The best-known presentations of this position are Meek, "The Scottish Contribution to Marxist Sociology," in *Economics and Ideology and Other Essays;* Pascal, "Property and Society," 167–79; and Skinner, "Adam Smith: An Economic Interpretation of History," in *Essays on Adam Smith.*

15. See Meek, "Smith, Turgot, and the 'Four Stages' Theory," in *Smith, Marx, and After*, 19.

16. See Hopfl, "From Savage to Scotsman"; Haakonssen, *The Science of a Legislator,* chap.

besides the mode of subsistence—including political and legal institutions, religious, geographical, and military considerations, accidents, and even the personalities of individual monarchs—are central to Smith's historical accounts and that they regularly override economic factors. As Haakonssen writes, Smith classifies societies based on their mode of subsistence but "he never mistakes taxonomy for explanation."[17] Smith's defense of commercial society was, as I have indicated, based above all on a comparison of this kind of society with previous societies. We now turn to one element of this defense: Smith's claim that commercial societies are far and away more prosperous than any other form of society.

2. PROVIDING FOR THE POOR

Smith's most famous argument for commercial society is almost certainly his contention that the extraordinary productivity of this kind of society makes everyone wealthier. He claims, echoing Locke, that "the accommodation of an European prince does not always so much exceed that of an industrious and frugal peasant, as the accommodation of the latter exceeds that of many an African king, the absolute master of the lives and liberties of ten thousand naked savages" (WN I.i.11, 24; see also 10; ED, 562–63; LJ, 338–41, 489).[18] In other words, commercial society makes possible such drastic increases in economic productivity that even though some people gain more than others, everyone gains to some degree in comparison to earlier stages of society. As we will see in this section, Smith attributes this prosperity above all to the extensive division of labor that is characteristic of commercial society. This is one of the main reasons why he defends the division of labor despite the deleterious effects it can have on laborers. We will also see that it is no coincidence that Smith uses the lot of the peasant to illustrate the prosperity produced by commercial society: he applauds the wealth produced in this kind of society especially because it opens the prospect of providing for the poor to an extent not previously possible.

8; Winch, "Adam Smith's 'Enduring Particular Result,'" in Wealth and Virtue, 258–60; and Winch, Adam Smith's Politics, 56–65. Andrew Skinner seems to have modified the position he took in the article cited in footnote 14, toward a less deterministic reading; see Skinner, A System of Social Science, chapter 4.

17. Haakonssen, The Science of a Legislator, 188.

18. Cf. Locke, Two Treatises of Government, 297.

In the "Early Draft" of *The Wealth of Nations* and in his *Lectures on Juris-prudence*, Smith sets up the prosperity produced by commercial society as a puzzle. He begins by noting two facts that would seem to suggest that the poor in commercial society would actually be *worse* off than people in ear-lier stages of society. First, he concedes that "in a civilized society the poor provide both for themselves and for the enormous luxury of their superiors," whereas "among savages . . . every individual enjoys the whole produce of his own industry" (*ED*, 563; see also *LJ*, 339–40, 489). Second, he grants that "with regard to the produce of the labour of a great society there is never any such thing as a fair and equal division" since "those who labour most get least" (*ED*, 563–64; see also *LJ*, 341, 490). Given these facts, he asks, how is it possible that the poor in commercial society are frequently better off (materially speaking) than even the rich in a less developed society? In other words, how can a peasant in commercial society enjoy a higher stan-dard of living than an African king even "in the midst of so much oppressive inequality" (*ED*, 564)? Smith's answer, in these works as well as in *The Wealth of Nations* itself, is well known: "the division of labor . . . can alone account for that superior opulence which takes place in civilized societies, and which, notwithstanding the inequality of property, extends itself to the lowest mem-ber of the community" (*ED*, 564; see also *LJ*, 341, 489; *WN* I.i.10, 22).

Smith shows that the division of labor produces this "superior opulence" by increasing the quantity and quality of work that people are capable of performing. It does this, he maintains, in three ways: it increases the dex-terity of the workers with respect to the operations they have to perform, it saves the time of switching from one task to another, and it encourages the development of time- and labor-saving inventions (see *ED*, 567–70; *LJ*, 345–47, 491–92; *WN* I.i.5–8, 17–21). All of this may seem rather simple and obvious, but Smith shows that the consequences of these improve-ments are startling: in his famous example of pin making, he shows that whereas one person working alone could only make somewhere between one and twenty pins in a day, when ten people divide the operations among themselves they are able together to make "upwards of forty-eight thousand" (*WN* I.i.3, 14–15; see also *ED*, 564–65; *LJ*, 341–42, 490). The difference that an extensive division of labor makes with regard to productivity is, in other words, astronomic. And since the division of labor is limited by the extent of the market (see *WN* I.iii.1, 31), it is only in commercial society—where the market is expanded to include all commercial nations—that this advan-tage can be fully exploited. Thus, in commercial society "so great a quantity of everything is produced that there is enough both to gratify the slothful and oppressive profusion of the great, and at the same time to supply the wants of the artisan and the peasant" (*ED*, 566).[19]

The simple fact of prosperity, however, would seem to do little to answer even the economic element of Rousseau's critique of commercial society. After all, Rousseau himself accepts that commercial society tends to produce great wealth, even if he does not celebrate this fact the way Smith does; he complains not about the lack of wealth but about its distribution, that is, about the injustice of the great inequalities characteristic of commercial society. In responding to this problem Smith shifts the focus somewhat: whereas Rousseau condemns the intrinsic injustice of inequality, Smith concentrates more on providing for the poor. One of the chief arguments against inequality, after all, is that, in Rousseau's words, "it is manifestly against the Law of Nature, in whatever manner it is defined, that . . . a handful of men be glutted with superfluities while the starving multitude lack necessities" (*SD*, 67). If Smith can show that the multitude will in fact be neither starving nor lacking in necessities in commercial society, he will have undercut Rousseau's critique by denying its premise.[20]

When Smith says that commercial society produces prosperity or opulence, he does *not* mean that it provides a great deal of luxury for the few.

---

19. Smith does raise the specter of a wealthy but "stationary" state in which capital does not increase and as a result the poor are unable to obtain adequate wages. He offers the example of China, which he says "has long been one of the richest . . . countries in the world" but where wages of labor are so low that "the poverty of the lower ranks of people in China far surpasses that of the most beggarly nations in Europe. . . . The subsistence which they find there is so scanty that they are eager to fish up the nastiest garbage thrown overboard from any European ship. Any carrion, the carcase of a dead dog or cat, for example, though half putrid and stinking, is as welcome to them as the most wholesome food to the people of other countries" (*WN* I.viii.24, 89–90). But Smith quickly sets this specter aside with the observation that as long as productivity keeps increasing and markets keep expanding, a nation's economy can grow indefinitely. See *EPS*, 322; *WN* II.iii.31–36, 343–46; IV.ix.28, 674; and Ignatieff, "Smith, Rousseau, and the Republic of Needs," in *Scotland and Europe*, 203. In other words, for Smith a "stationary state" can be avoided through wise policy; if China adopted better "laws and institutions"—if its government provided the poor with a modicum of security and allowed them to trade with foreign nations, for instance—it would be able to once again attain an expanding economy (*WN* I.ix.15, 111–12; see also IV.ix.40, 679–80). For a more detailed examination of the requirements and mechanisms by which commercial societies could continue to raise wages indefinitely, on Smith's view, see Hont, "The 'Rich Country-Poor Country' Debate," in *Wealth and Virtue*, 298–306.

20. Of course, there are other arguments against inequality, such as that it promotes envy and dependence. Smith's preliminary response to these arguments will be addressed after his thoughts regarding poverty. Other elements of his response will emerge over the course of this and the following chapter.

On the contrary, he writes, "that state is properly opulent in which opulence is easily come at, or in which a little labour, properly and judiciously employed, is capable of procuring any man a great abundance of all the necessaries and conveniencies of life. . . . National opulence is the opulence of the whole people" (ED, 567; see also LJ, 83, 343; WN I.viii.27, 91). This definition of opulence, of course, captures the standard of living of the poor in particular, since they face the greatest challenges in acquiring "the necessaries and conveniencies of life." Smith concentrates especially on the poor in part because of their sheer numbers. "Servants, labourers and workmen of different kinds, make up the greater part of every great political society," he notes, and so their condition should carry a great deal of weight when looking at a society's condition (WN I.viii.36, 96). But he also concentrates on them for reasons of justice. "It is but equity, besides," he maintains, "that they who feed, cloath and lodge the whole body of the people, should have such a share of the produce of their own labour as to be themselves tolerably well fed, cloathed and lodged" (WN I.viii.36, 96). The "wealth of nations" that Smith refers to in the title of his most famous work, then, refers not to a nation's GDP or any such aggregate sum, but rather to the prospects of *every individual* in the society, including (and especially) the poor. Indeed, in his *Essay on the Principle of Population* Thomas Malthus chides Smith for failing to differentiate between "the wealth of nations" and "the happiness and comfort of the lower orders of society."[21]

Smith's concern for the poor is all the more striking when we recall the context in which he was writing: in the eighteenth century, many if not most people who wrote about the poor maintained that they should be *kept* poor so that they would be willing to work hard and to respect their superiors and so that they wouldn't squander their money on vice (particularly alcohol).[22] To claim in this context that the wages and living conditions of

21. Malthus, *An Essay on the Principle of Population*, in *The Works of Robert Thomas Malthus*, vol. 1, 107. Carl Menger noted as long ago as 1891 that "A. Smith placed himself in all cases of conflict of interest between the rich and the poor, between the strong and the weak, *without exception* on the side of the latter. I use the expression 'without exception' after careful reflection, since there is not a single instance in A. Smith's work in which he represents the interest of the rich and powerful as opposed to the poor and weak." Menger, "Die Social-Theorien der classischen National-Oekonomie und die moderne Wirthschaftspolitik," translated in Rothschild, *Economic Sentiments*, 65.

22. See Baugh, "Poverty, Protestantism, and Political Economy," in *England's Rise to Greatness*, 85–86; Fleischacker, *On Adam Smith's Wealth of Nations*, 205–8; Muller, *Adam Smith in His Time and Ours*, 34, 56; and Rosenberg, "Adam Smith on Profits," in *Essays on Adam Smith*, 378–79.

the poor ought to be the standard for measuring a society's prosperity was undoubtedly controversial. Smith found it necessary to defend his position against "the common complaint that luxury extends itself even to the lowest ranks of the people, and that the labouring poor will not now be contented with the same food, cloathing, and lodging which satisfied them in former times" (WN I.viii.35, 96; see also I.viii.42, 99). His concern for the lot of the poor in an atmosphere that discouraged such concern led Gertrude Himmelfarb to maintain that even if *The Wealth of Nations* was not novel in its economic policy recommendations, "it was genuinely revolutionary in its view of poverty and its attitude toward the poor."[23]

Scholars have filled volumes on Smith's explanation of exactly how and why the poor are able to obtain the basic necessities of life in commercial society, and I do not propose to enter into their debates here.[24] Suffice it to say that on Smith's view, because so much more is produced in commercial society than can be consumed by the rich alone (see TMS IV.i.10, 184; WN I.xi.c.7, 180), and because an extensive and free market encourages competition and thereby lowers the price of food and the other necessities of life (see especially WN IV.v.b, 524–43), even the poor will have sufficient means to procure these necessities. Yet Smith never suggests that poverty will not be a problem in commercial society or that the distribution of goods will always be optimal; indeed, his sometimes harsh criticisms of the inequalities of commercial society would be directly at odds with such claims. On the contrary, he points to several means of improving the material lot of the poor *within* commercial society.

To begin with, one of the key reasons why he favors the "system of natural liberty" over mercantilism is that "it is the industry which is carried on for the benefit of the rich and the powerful, that is principally encouraged by our mercantile system. That which is carried on for the benefit of the poor and the indigent, is too often, either neglected, or oppressed" (WN IV.viii.4, 644; see also IV.viii.49, 660). By putting the interests of the merchant and the producer ahead of those of the consumer, in other words, mercantilism aggravates the problem of poverty. Even under the "system of natural liberty" there would be substantial inequalities, Smith concedes,

---

23. Himmelfarb, *The Idea of Poverty,* 46. Samuel Fleischacker concurs that "the dignified picture of the poor is . . . Smith's most novel contribution" in this work. Fleischacker, *On Adam Smith's Wealth of Nations,* 208.

24. A good starting place would be Hont and Ignatieff, "Needs and Justice in the *Wealth of Nations,*" in *Wealth and Virtue.*

because people tend to be paid more for doing jobs that are disagreeable, that require a great deal of training, that are irregularly available, that involve a great deal of trust, and that have a lower probability of success (see WN I.x.b.1, 116–17). But "the policy of Europe," he says, "occasions other inequalities of much greater importance" by discouraging imports and by allowing employers to combine to encourage low wages and high prices (WN I.x.c.1–2, 135).

Time and again in The Wealth of Nations Smith condemns the restrictive practices and laws of his time that he saw as hurting the poor, such as the Statute of Apprentices, which hampered the ability of workers to work where and when they desired (see WN I.x.c.12, 138); the Settlement Act, which limited the mobility of the poor (see WN I.x.c.45, 152); and the practices of primogeniture and entail, which kept large quantities of wealth in the same families for many generations (see WN III.ii.4–6, 383–85). In other words, on his view some of the greatest sources of inequality in commercial society—restrictive policies that give privileges to the wealthy—are not necessary features of this kind of society but rather specific to the mercantilist form of it; the poor, he feels, would be the chief beneficiaries of the implementation of the "system of natural liberty." While many people today think of free trade as harming the interests of the poor, Smith in his own time thought of it as advantageous to the poor because it entailed the elimination of the policies of his era that aided the rich.

But Smith does not leave the problem of providing for the poor strictly to free trade or the "invisible hand." Samuel Fleischacker notes that while Smith certainly does not put forward any large-scale program for state redistribution, he does advocate some positive measures to help the poor.[25] First of all, he advocates taxing the rich at a higher rate than the poor in some instances, such as by levying a heavier road toll on luxury vehicles so that "the indolence and vanity of the rich is made to contribute . . . to the relief of the poor" (WN V.i.d.5, 725), and by instituting a tax on house rents that would fall more heavily on the rich (see WN V.ii.e.6, 842). "It is not very unreasonable," Smith argues in this context, "that the rich should be made to contribute to the publick expence, not only in proportion to their revenue, but something more than in that proportion" (WN V.ii.e.6, 842).[26] Smith also advocates using tax revenues to provide services that benefit the poor

---

25. See Fleischacker, On Adam Smith's Wealth of Nations, 205.
26. See also McLean, Adam Smith, Radical and Egalitarian, 90–98; and Pack, Capitalism as a Moral System, 66–69.

more than the rich. As we will see in more detail in the next section, easily the most important of these services is compulsory and state-supported education aimed expressly at the poor (see *WN* V.i.f.55, 785). In addition, as Himmelfarb notes, Smith "conspicuously did not . . . challenge the poor law itself, the obligation to provide relief for those who could not provide for themselves."[27] Finally, Smith's harsh statements about the problems caused by poverty and inequality in commercial society were surely meant to urge people to recognize and contend with these problems.

To many people today, needless to say, the remedies that Smith proposes to deal with the problem of poverty may not seem like much, but they are unquestionably a far cry from the argument that the poor should be *kept* poor. And as Fleischacker writes, we should not be surprised by the lack of any significant program for state redistribution in Smith's works:

> The notion that states should redirect economic resources so as to eradicate poverty had never so much as been suggested by any serious philosopher, politician, or political movement among Smith's contemporaries and predecessors. Poor *relief* had of course been around for many centuries, but that was designed simply to enable disabled and starving people to survive, not to help them rise out of poverty altogether. . . . The idea that governments should institute a redistribution of wealth out of fairness to the poor was simply not on the table.[28]

Fleischacker presents the most persuasive argument available to support the idea that Smith would support redistribution if he were alive today—in other words, that redistribution coheres with his general outlook—but this contention cannot be established conclusively, as Fleischacker himself recognizes.[29] While Smith does not deny the need for positive action to remedy the shortcomings of the market with respect to poverty, he focuses much more on maximizing the production of goods to ensure that the poor can be provided for than on distributing these goods to promote equality.

As we have seen, however, Smith accepts (with Rousseau) that inequality can have harmful effects other than the hardships of poverty, especially

27. Himmelfarb, *The Idea of Poverty*, 61.
28. Fleischacker, Review of Griswold, 919; see also *On Adam Smith's Wealth of Nations*, 205, 213–14.
29. See Fleischacker, *On Adam Smith's Wealth of Nations*, chap. 10.

by producing envy and thereby leading people to always desire more than they can attain. While Smith's full answer to these problems will not emerge until the next chapter, we can note here that he sees inequality as a necessary part of any economy productive enough to provide for the poor. Since inequalities arise naturally through market interactions, he maintains, removing them altogether would be impossible without a great deal of oppressive measures, and even if this *were* possible it would mean condemning not only some but *all* to a life of poverty (see *LJ*, 195; *WN* I.viii.1–5, 82–83; V.i.b.7, 712).[30] It would mean, in the words of Istvan Hont and Michael Ignatieff, "an eternity of egalitarian barbarism."[31] Since the suffering caused by poverty is one of Smith's biggest concerns, he is willing to brook some inequalities in order to ameliorate this problem; perhaps this is why he refrains from calling the inequalities of commercial society "oppressive" in his published works. In the commercial nations of Smith's day even peasants were able to work for a wage with which they could adequately meet their needs of food, clothing, and shelter, and Smith seems to reason that this baby should not be thrown out with the bathwater of inequality (see *WN* I.i.10, 22; I.viii.28–33, 91–93).[32]

In part because of Smith's deep concern for the welfare of the poor, Haakonssen has claimed that *The Wealth of Nations* is "the greatest workingperson's tract ever written."[33] But could this really be the case, one might ask, if Smith's work promotes a kind of society that has the debilitating effects on workers that he describes so severely in Book V? In other words, what good is a higher standard of living in material terms if the majority of the people are rendered feeble and ignorant by the division of labor? It is to this problem that we turn in the next section.

3. EDUCATION AND THE ROLE OF THE STATE

The harshest denunciation of commercial society in Smith's writings is undoubtedly his castigation of the deleterious effects of the division of labor

---

30. See also Berry, *Social Theory of the Scottish Enlightenment*, 99; and Ignatieff, "Smith, Rousseau, and the Republic of Needs," 197.

31. Hont and Ignatieff, "Needs and Justice in the *Wealth of Nations*," 10.

32. See Muller, *Adam Smith in His Time and Ours*, 32–33, and the works cited there for evidence that this was perhaps the first society in history in which nearly everyone was able to fulfill these basic needs.

33. Haakonssen, "Adam Smith," in *The Routledge Encyclopedia of Philosophy*, vol. 8, 820.

on the laborers, that is, the ignorance and weakness caused by the extreme specialization of tasks (see *WN* V.i.f.50, 781–82). Critics of commercial society from Marx to the present have delighted in quoting this passage in an attempt to demonstrate that even the great theorist of this kind of society could not endorse it wholeheartedly. Even if Smith is right in claiming that commercial society produces prosperity, these critics reason, his acknowledgment of the gross deformation of the majority of people by the division of labor undermines his attempt to defend the means of procuring this prosperity. We will see in this section, however, that Smith does not in fact regard the deleterious effects of the division of labor as an inescapable feature of commercial society. While he is certainly concerned with the problems that specialization can produce—and in fact this is one of his *biggest* concerns, as his harsh language demonstrates—he maintains that the state can ameliorate these problems by promoting education and perhaps some kind of martial training.[34]

As we have seen, Smith contends that the extensive division of labor in commercial society renders the laborer "as stupid and ignorant as it is possible for a human creature to become" and that "his dexterity at his own particular trade seems . . . to be acquired at the expense of his intellectual, social, and martial virtues" (*WN* V.i.f.50, 782). The long and severe passage from which these lines are taken is almost always removed from its context and presented on its own, as it was in Chapter 2. But the context is crucial here: Smith's denunciation of the effects of the division of labor is found not within a discussion of the benefits and drawbacks of the division of labor or of commercial society but rather within a discussion of education. After examining a number of different approaches to education that have been taken in various ages and nations (chiefly ancient Greece and Rome), he asks whether and how the state ought to attend to the education of the common people (see *WN* V.i.f.48, 781). The answer to this question, he suggests, will be different in different societies. In some societies— especially those in the hunting and shepherding stages—people are naturally placed in a position where they will acquire the abilities and virtues

---

34. That Smith entrusts the state to perform such a crucial, character-forming role should be evidence enough that he is not the proponent of a minimalist or "night-watchman" state that he is often thought to be. On Smith's departure from strict libertarian principles, see Fleischacker, *On Adam Smith's Wealth of Nations*, 233–36; Muller, *Adam Smith in His Time and Ours*, chap. 11; Pack, *Capitalism as a Moral System*, chap. 4; Viner, "Adam Smith and Laissez Faire," in *Adam Smith*, 138–55; and Winch, *Riches and Poverty*, 114–21.

that are required of them; in others, they are not placed in such a position, so the state must take action to remedy this shortcoming (see *WN* V.i.f.49, 781; V.i.f.51, 782–83).

It is against *this* backdrop that Smith launches into his diatribe against the effects of the division of labor on the laborers in commercial society; because the extensive division of labor keeps the workers from undertaking varied or demanding occupations, he maintains, there is a greater need to instruct them. Thus, he concludes the passage on the division of labor by pointing to the role of the state in ameliorating its negative effects: "in every improved and civilized society this is the state into which the labouring poor, that is, the great body of the people, must necessarily fall, *unless government takes some pains to prevent it*" (*WN* V.i.f.50, 782; italics added). After this passage he immediately returns to his discussion of education, now addressing its crucial role in commercial societies. In other words, when read in its proper context, the purpose of the passage on the deleterious effects of the division of labor seems to be less to demonstrate the downfalls of commercial society than to underscore the importance of education in this kind of society.[35]

Smith devotes very little space in his corpus to describing how education ought to take place; there is no Smithian equivalent to Rousseau's *Emile*. But he does strenuously argue that education ought to play a central role in commercial society, and in Book V of *The Wealth of Nations* he writes at greater length on education than on any other positive role of the state. He advocates universal public schooling in commercial societies, largely at government expense: "the publick can facilitate, can encourage, and can even impose upon almost the whole body of the people, the necessity of acquiring [the] most essential parts of education . . . by establishing in every parish or district a little school, where children may be taught for a reward so moderate, that even a common labourer may afford it" (*WN* V.i.f.54–55, 785). This proposal, which is modeled on the innovative parish schools of Scotland, is directed especially at the poor; while children in the middle and upper classes generally have the time and means to acquire education

---

35. That Smith has at least a modicum of confidence in the ability of government-supported education to alleviate the mental ills caused by the division of labor is perhaps suggested by his earlier discussion of the division of labor, in which he suggests that factory workers are often responsible for inventions and technological improvements (see *LJ*, 351; *WN* I.i.8, 20–21). See also Rosenberg, "Adam Smith on the Division of Labor: Two Views or One?" For a contrary view, see West, "Adam Smith on the Cultural Effects of Specialization."

without the public's help, Smith says, the children of the "common people" do not and so require more attention from the state (see *LJ*, 539–40; *WN* V.i.f.52–53, 784–85). Smith further suggests that an individual should have to pass examinations in the sciences "before he [is] permitted to exercise any liberal profession, or before he [can] be received as a candidate for any honourable office of trust or profit" (*WN* V.i.g.14, 796).[36] Once again Smith's proposals were rather progressive for his time, when it was common to deny that the poor had the intellectual capacity to benefit from education and to worry that too much education would render them disobedient.[37]

Smith argues that the state "derives no inconsiderable advantage" from the instruction of the people, especially because it helps tame religious fanaticism, makes people more likely to respect the law, and enables them to see through "the interested complaints of faction and sedition" (*WN* V.i.f.61, 788). This latter advantage is especially important, he notes, for "in free countries, where the safety of the government depends very much upon the favorable judgment which the people may form of its conduct, it must surely be of the highest importance that they should not be disposed to judge rashly or capriciously concerning it" (*WN* V.i.f.61, 788). In short, Smith believes that education can help produce more dutiful and more informed citizens. But this is not to say that he endorses education strictly for purposes of "social control" or that, as Marx contemptuously puts it, "Smith recommends education of the people by the State, but prudently, and in homeopathic doses."[38] He is in fact resolute in maintaining that education is good in itself and not only as a means to economic or political ends. Because "the proper use of the intellectual faculties of a man" is such an "essential part of the character of human nature," he writes, "though the state was to derive no advantage from the instruction of the inferior ranks of people, [their education] would still deserve its attention" (*WN* V.i.f.61, 788). Education, for Smith, helps produce not only better workers and better citizens but also (and especially) better human beings.

36. Science education is not only important in itself, for Smith, but also has the added benefit of taming fanaticism: he writes that "science is the great antidote to the poison of enthusiasm and superstition"—eighteenth-century bywords for religious zealotry (*WN* V.i.g.14, 796). Smith holds that the arts, too, can help ameliorate the deleterious effects of the division of labor, but he argues that, unlike the sciences, they should be left to private initiative rather than supported by the government; for a discussion of why this is so, see De Marchi and Greene, "Adam Smith and Private Provision of the Arts." For a comparison of Smith and Rousseau on similar issues, see Hanley, "From Geneva to Glasgow."
37. See Himmelfarb, *The Idea of Poverty*, 58–60; and Rothschild, *Economic Sentiments*, 99.
38. Marx, *Capital, Volume One*, in *The Marx–Engels Reader*, 399.

Education, then, can help alleviate the problem of ignorance caused by the division of labor. But what of the problem of feebleness or weakness—the lack of martial spirit—in the people? There are actually two separate problems here, for Smith: the worry that a refined, civilized populace might be unable to defend itself against more rugged, barbarous peoples, and the concern about the deformity this feebleness causes in people's characters. The solution to the first problem, he argues, is the institution of a professional standing army. An alternative solution would be to raise militias, but this would require "a very vigorous police" and would be against "the whole bent of the interest, genius and inclinations of the people" (WN V.i.a.17, 698; see also V.i.f.60, 787).[39] Besides, as Smith shows through numerous historical examples, "a militia . . . in whatever manner it may be either disciplined or exercised, must always be much inferior to a well disciplined and well exercised standing army" (WN V.i.a.23, 700; see also V.i.a.24–39, 700–706; LJ, 543).

Smith concedes, like Rousseau, that militias from barbarous nations are usually superior to militias from civilized nations since the former tend to be superior in ruggedness and martial spirit; contrary to Rousseau, however, he argues that the training and discipline of a standing army can more than bridge this gap (see WN V.i.a.39, 705–6).[40] Another key advantage enjoyed by civilized nations is the development of military technology: since only civilized societies are able to afford the expense of modern firearms and since this advantage is decisive in any conflict with barbarous peoples, Smith maintains, "the invention of fire-arms, an invention which at first

39. Smith's preference for standing armies over militias placed him in opposition to a number of his contemporaries, most prominently Adam Ferguson (see CAS, 193–94). Smith notes that "men of republican principles have been jealous of a standing army as dangerous to liberty" (WN V.i.a.41, 706), but he takes the opposite stand: as long as the civil and military authorities work together and as long as the standing army is not "overgrown," he argues, a standing army "can never be dangerous to liberty" (WN V.i.a.41, 707; see also IV.ii.43, 471). In fact, Smith argues that a standing army can be *favorable* to liberty because "the security which it gives the sovereign renders unnecessary that troublesome jealousy, which, in some modern republicks, seems to watch over the minutest actions, and to be at all times ready to disturb the peace of every citizen" (WN V.i.a.41, 707). The debate between Smith and Ferguson on the militia issue has received a great deal of scholarly attention; see especially Sher, "Adam Ferguson, Adam Smith and the Problem of National Defense."

40. Thus in Smith's example of the 1745 Jacobite uprising, he recognizes that Britain's standing army was key: "In the year 1745 four or 5 thousand naked unarmed Highlanders took possession of the improved parts of this country without any opposition from the unwarlike inhabitants. They penetrated into England and alarmed the whole nation, and *had they not been opposed by a standing army* they would have seized the throne with little difficulty" (LJ, 540–41, italics added).

sight appears to be so pernicious, is certainly favourable both to the per-
manency and to the extension of civilization" (WN V.i.a.44, 708). Smith
acknowledges that the progress of civilization experienced numerous set-
backs throughout history (such the fall of Rome) because of the greater
ruggedness and martial spirit of barbarous nations, yet he believes that modern commercial societies can avoid this fate because of the development of
professional armies and the invention of gunpowder.

While the institution of a professional standing army provides an answer
to the problem of how to protect a civilized nation against more rugged
peoples, this measure does not solve the second problem, the deformity in
the character of the people. Thus, in contrast to the section of Book V of *The
Wealth of Nations* dealing with defense, in the section on education Smith
seems to be suggesting that a standing army alone is insufficient. He argues,
first, that a degree of martial spirit in the people would help reduce the size
(and hence also the cost) of the requisite standing army and "would necessarily diminish very much the dangers to liberty, whether real or imaginary,
which are commonly apprehended from a standing army" (WN V.i.f.59,
787). More important in this context, he further argues that "even though
the martial spirit of the people were of no use towards the defence of the
society, yet to prevent that sort of mental mutilation, deformity and wretchedness, which cowardice necessarily involves in it, from spreading themselves through the great body of the people, would still deserve the most
serious attention of government" (WN V.i.f.60, 787; see also *LJ*, 541).

While Smith maintains that preventing weakness and cowardice should
be one of the state's educational responsibilities, he takes no unequivocal
stand on how this responsibility ought to be fulfilled. He refers to the compulsory military exercises of the ancient Greeks and Romans and the prizes
they awarded to those who excelled in them, but he declares once again
that the modern equivalent, raising a militia, requires "the continual and
painful attention of government" because it is so contrary to the spirit of
commercial ages (WN V.i.f.60, 787). Whether and precisely how Smith
thinks the government ought to promote martial spirit is not in the end
entirely clear, though he emphasizes that the problem of weakness should
be a central concern in commercial society and trusts that steps can be taken
toward remedying it. (We will also see in Section 5 of this chapter that Smith
sees an *excess* of martial spirit and toughness as just as problematic—if not
more problematic—than a lack of it.)

This, in short, is Smith's response to the "division of laborers" critique:

he defends the division of labor despite its negative effects because it is the greatest source of prosperity in commercial society. While there will inevitably be great inequalities in this kind of society, it also gives rise to the possibility of providing for the poor to an extent not previously possible. (As we will see in the next chapter, Smith also contends that even though inequalities remain in commercial society, their negative effects—particularly personal dependence—are alleviated to a considerable degree by the interdependence of the market.) Smith further argues that the deleterious effects of the division of labor can be mitigated by promoting education and perhaps some kind of martial training. So while Smith acknowledges that problems often arise in commercial society as a result of the division of labor, he maintains that its advantages ultimately far outweigh its disadvantages.

4. THE CONCERN FOR OTHERS' OPINIONS
AND THE FOUNDATION OF MORALITY

Smith's response to the "empire of opinion" critique is based as well on a careful evaluation of the benefits and drawbacks of commercial society, but it takes a slightly different tack, in part because his sympathy with this critique is not quite as broad as it is with the other two critiques. As we saw in Chapter 2, he concedes that people tend to be greatly concerned with the opinions of others and that this concern can lead to a corruption of people's moral sentiments, selfishly motivated appeals to others' self-interest, and a good deal of ostentation. He further allows that those in "the superior stations in life" often "abandon the paths of virtue" in their pursuit of wealth (*TMS* I.iii.3.8, 64) and that merchants and manufacturers tend to be deceitful in their appeals to others' self-interest. But the fact that Smith attributes immoral actions and deceitfulness only to particular groups rather than to almost *everyone* in commercial society, as Rousseau does, points to an important difference in their premises: for Smith, unlike for Rousseau, the fact that people are concerned with the opinions of others can in fact serve as the very basis of moral conduct, *especially* in commercial society. In this section we will briefly examine the foundations of Smith's system of morality; then in the next we will see how this understanding of morality affects his view of the type of person who he thinks is likely to predominate in commercial society.

In *The Theory of Moral Sentiments*, Smith quietly rejects the idea of an independent moral standard, such as natural law or divine commandments, as well as the idea that moral standards can be found through reason alone.[41] Instead he maintains that morality is based on feelings or sentiments (hence the title of the work) and that it is mediated through the faculty of sympathy—a term that, we have seen, he uses to denote people's "fellow-feeling with any passion whatever" (TMS I.i.1.5, 10). When people place themselves in the position of others—when they sympathize with them—they tend to approve or disapprove of their actions and judgments, and this approval or disapproval is the ultimate source of propriety and impropriety or right and wrong: "What is agreeable to our moral faculties, is fit, and right, and proper to be done; the contrary wrong, unfit, and improper" (TMS III.5.5, 165). For Smith, people generally sympathize with and approve of feelings and actions that are morally right—or, rather, these feelings and actions are morally right because people sympathize with them and approve of them. Furthermore, people naturally seek the sympathy and approval of others: "nothing pleases us more than to observe in other men a fellow-feeling with all the emotions of our own breast" (TMS I.i.2.1, 13; see also III.2.6, 116). Thus, people have something of an incentive to act morally: they want others to sympathize with them and approve of them, and for the most part this requires them to conduct themselves with decency and integrity.

This is not to say, of course, that people always do act morally—Smith acknowledges that there are commonly powerful incentives to do the opposite—but rather that when people act immorally it is usually not because they have been corrupted by their concern for others' opinions, as Rousseau maintains; on the contrary, it is the thought of how others would see them that most often restrains them. "If we saw ourselves in the light in which others see us, or in which they would see us if they knew all," Smith declares, "a reformation would generally be unavoidable. We could not otherwise endure the sight" (TMS III.4.6, 158–59; see also WN V.i.g.12, 795). Thus, in addition to making the empirical claim (with Rousseau) that people tend to care about what others think, Smith also (very much against Rousseau) encourages them to do so. Whereas Rousseau sees the fact that people are greatly concerned with the opinions of others as the source of innumerable problems, Smith sees it as the very basis of morality and moral

41. As Charles Griswold writes, Smith "is not so much 'antifoundationalist' (in the current jargon) as he is self-consciously nonfoundationalist." Griswold, Adam Smith and the Virtues of Enlightenment (Cambridge: Cambridge University Press, 1999), 165. See also Rothschild, Economic Sentiments, 231.

conduct. Indeed, he claims that it is only by seeing themselves through others' eyes that people become aware of themselves as moral beings at all; in a passage that Christopher Berry notes has "strong overtones of Rousseau,"[42] Smith writes that "were it possible that a human creature could grow up to manhood in some solitary place without any communication with his own species, he could no more think of his own character, of the propriety or demerit of his own sentiments and conduct, of the beauty or deformity of his own mind, than of the beauty or deformity of his own face" (TMS III.1.3, 110).

For Smith, then, the ultimate foundation of morality is approval and disapproval, but this does not mean that individual feelings are the only standard for moral judgment; rather, he shows how these feelings provide the basis for general rules of morality. He maintains that general rules naturally develop out of people's moral sentiments over time. When people consistently approve of a particular action in a given context it is eventually settled that this kind of action is praiseworthy; similarly, when people consistently disapprove of an action it is eventually deemed blameworthy by the community (see TMS III.4.7–8, 159; VII.iii.2.6, 319). In other words, moral norms arise as people coordinate their behavior in response to others; people learn through their upbringing and their interactions with others what is moral and what is not.[43] There may be a diversity of moral standards in different times and places, but the mechanism for determining them—the formation of general rules as people's moral judgments converge—remains the same. In short, moral systems arise spontaneously from a multitude of individual actions, much the same way markets do in economics.[44] Smith is under no delusion, however, that in either the economic or the moral realm everything will miraculously work out perfectly without any rules or guidance. As a bare minimum, just as economic transactions must be directed through the market (i.e., there must be competition rather than monopoly), individuals must correct for their own partiality in their moral judgments by obeying the general rules that are formed by their society.

42. Berry, "Adam Smith: Commerce, Liberty, and Modernity," in *Philosophers of the Enlightenment*, 124.

43. While no community will ever agree completely on everything, of course, Smith claims that there will usually be enough of a correspondence to afford "the harmony of society" (TMS I.i.4.7, 22).

44. See Haakonssen, *The Science of a Legislator*, 61; Hamowy, *The Scottish Enlightenment and the Theory of Spontaneous Order*, 13–14; and Otteson, *Adam Smith's Marketplace of Life*, 6 and passim.

While Smith seems to be more interested in examining the nature and source of people's moral beliefs than in providing a ground for them, at times he also appears to want to use the notion of spontaneous order to provide a basis for normative judgments that avoids both the Scylla of absolutism and the Charybdis of relativism. To at least some degree, he succeeds in this endeavor: by viewing moral rules as based on people's feelings and judgments he circumvents the need to appeal to any ultimate cause or ground beyond experience, and by viewing moral rules as generated by societal interaction he eludes the need to claim that individuals themselves "choose" or "make" them in any direct way. Commentators have frequently argued, however, that Smith's moral theory nevertheless entails a kind of "soft" or cultural relativism, since it does not ultimately seem to provide any way of appealing beyond the convergence of sentiments that occurs in one's own culture.[45] Smith is constantly struck by the ease with which entire societies have accepted practices that he views as appalling, such as slavery and infanticide (see *TMS* V.2.9, 206–7; V.2.14–15, 209–10), yet he seems to offer no means to judge one culture's moral standards as superior to another's, or to criticize a practice that an entire society has adopted.[46] He emphasizes that people can judge themselves and their actions according to how an "impartial spectator"—that is, someone who is fully sympathetic, informed, and unbiased or unprejudiced—would view them, regardless of how the people around them actually do view them (see *TMS* III.3.1–3, 134–35), but even an impartial spectator has no standard by which to judge an action other than the standards of his own society; he simply judges by these standards impartially.[47] Other scholars have noted, though, that Smith's notion of the impartial spectator does allow for some degree of independent conscience, especially because such a spectator would fully sympathize with each actor in a given situation—including, for example, a slave or an unwanted infant.[48] I am inclined to believe that Smith's moral theory offers a reasonable middle ground between absolutism and relativism,[49] but in

---

45. See, for example, Campbell, *Adam Smith's Science of Morals.*
46. See Otteson, *Adam Smith's Marketplace of Life,* 305–14.
47. See Fleischacker, *On Adam Smith's Wealth of Nations,* 52–53.
48. See Griswold, *Adam Smith and the Virtues of Enlightenment,* 198–202, 349–54, 363–64. Still other scholars have stressed that Smith's notion of the impartial spectator is inherently connected to a belief in the basic dignity of all other human beings and thus that it stands as a kind of precursor to Kant's categorical imperative. See Darwall, "Equal Dignity in Adam Smith"; "Sympathetic Liberalism"; and Fleischacker, "Philosophy in Moral Practice."
49. A nice discussion of both the relativist *and* universalist or absolutist sides of Smith's

any event this potential quandary does not affect the main point for our purposes, which is Smith's argument (contra Rousseau) that the concern for others' opinions often has positive moral effects.

We are now in a position to see why I claimed at the outset of this section that Smith's response to the "empire of opinion" critique takes a slightly different tack than his response to the "division of laborers" critique. With respect to the latter, Smith essentially agrees with Rousseau's premises— poverty is bad, weakness and ignorance are bad—but then he tries to show that the problems he points to can be largely ameliorated. With respect to the "empire of opinion" critique, however, Smith takes issue with one of Rousseau's key premises, namely, the idea that people generally desire only to be praised and not to be praise*worthy*.[50] Smith devotes an entire chapter of *The Theory of Moral Sentiments* to the argument that, on the contrary, "man naturally . . . desires, not only praise, but praiseworthiness; or to be the natural and proper object of praise" (*TMS* III.2.1, 113–14).[51] He contends that only the most superficial people could be satisfied by groundless praise or could fail to be satisfied by the knowledge that they had done something praiseworthy even if they are not actually praised (see *TMS* II.2.4– 5, 114–16). Even if people cannot judge themselves based on a transcendental standard that is external to their society, they can judge by a standard *internal* to their society—that of the impartial spectator—that corrects for bias and misinformation, and it is only when they meet this latter standard that people are truly satisfied with themselves. If nature had endowed people only with the desire for the praise of others, then it would "only have prompted [them] to the affectation of virtue, and to the concealment of vice"; whereas the desire to be praise*worthy* "was necessary in order to inspire [them] with the real love of virtue, and with the real abhorrence of vice" and hence to render them really fit for society rather than only apparently fit for it (*TMS* III.2.7, 117).

---

moral theory can be found in Fleischacker, "Smith und der Kulturrelativismus," in *Adam Smith als Moralphilosoph.*

50. Rousseau *does* distinguish between the desire to be praised whether one deserves it or not (*vanité* or vanity) and the desire to deserve praise (*orgueil* or pride); see footnote 17 in Chapter 1. But as we have seen, he argues that it is vanity, not pride, that is almost the sole motivating force for the vast majority of civilized people (see *Corsica*, 153); it is only in the extremely rare—if not impossible—cases like the citizen, Emile, and Rousseau himself that *amour-propre* takes the latter form.

51. For a helpful elaboration on Smith's argument here, see Griswold, *Adam Smith and the Virtues of Enlightenment*, 130–34.

Smith attributes the opposite position—the idea that people desire only to be praised and not to be praiseworthy—to Mandeville: "Dr. Mandeville considers whatever is done from a sense of propriety, from a regard to what is commendable and praise-worthy, as being done from a love of praise and commendation, or as he calls it from vanity" (*TMS* VII.ii.4.7, 308; see also III.2.27, 127). It was by treating "every thing as vanity which has any reference, either to what are, or to what ought to be the sentiments of others" that Mandeville "seemed to prove that there was no real virtue," Smith maintains, but this was in fact only one part of "the great fallacy of Dr. Mandeville's book," that of "represent[ing] every passion as wholly vicious, which is so in any degree and in any direction" (*TMS* VII.ii.4.12, 312–13). Given that Smith goes to such great lengths in his letter to the *Edinburgh Review* to point to the similarities between Mandeville and Rousseau, it seems reasonable to conclude that his response to Mandeville here can also be taken as a response to Rousseau's formulation of the problem of *amour-propre*—a problem that was neatly summarized in the second quotation from the *Discourse on Inequality* that he had translated in his letter.[52] Smith, then, more or less explicitly rejects one of the key premises of Rousseau's "empire of opinion" critique, the idea that people are only concerned with what others' opinions actually *are* rather than with what they *should* be. We will now turn to the very different conclusions that Smith reaches regarding commercial society based on his different premise about human nature and people's moral sentiments.

5. MORALS AND MARKETS

In Part VI of *The Theory of Moral Sentiments*, which was added in the sixth edition in 1790, Smith elaborates on his earlier discussion of prudence—"of all the virtues that which is most useful to the individual" (*TMS* IV.2.6, 189)—by painting an evocative picture of a "prudent man."[53] The prudent man, he says, desires abilities and understanding for their own sake and not to impress anyone else; he rests his reputation on his own talents and

---

52. See footnote 40 in Chapter 2.

53. A plausible claim can be made that the prudent man is the most direct link between *The Theory of Moral Sentiments* and *The Wealth of Nations*. See Griswold, *Adam Smith and the Virtues of Enlightenment*, 203; and Macfie, "Adam Smith's Moral Sentiments as Foundation for His Wealth of Nations," 223.

not on the favor of others; he is sincere and honest even if reserved in his speech and actions; although he is not particularly outgoing, his friendships are steady and faithful; he is always decent, polite, and inoffensive; he is industrious and frugal, and is willing to sacrifice some gratification while he is young for future security and tranquility; he doesn't meddle in other people's affairs or political disputes, but he always does his duty (see *TMS* VI.i.7–13, 213–16). It is clear from Smith's portrait that the prudent man aims primarily to obtain things like security, health, and prosperity; Joseph Cropsey aptly characterizes Smithian prudence as a "decent but thoroughgoing care of one's external interest."[54] But the prudent man is far from being a *Homo economicus* who is concerned only with his material well-being; he adheres strictly to his society's norms of justice, and he genuinely cares for others, especially his family and friends. Nor is he a vain bourgeois who is concerned only with what other people think of him; while he desires a good reputation, he is unwilling to compromise his integrity to gain the favor of others, and he strives more to be worthy of the approval of an impartial spectator than to actually gain the approval of those around him.[55] This kind of prudence is not particularly noble or endearing, Smith admits, but he insists that it is respectable and agreeable (see *TMS* VI.i.14, 216). While the prudent man is far from being a hero, in other words, he *is* dependable and decent, and this is Smith's vision of what we should realistically hope people to be.[56]

54. Joseph Cropsey, *Polity and Economy*, 47.
55. On these last two points, see Den Uyl, *The Virtue of Prudence*, 140–41; and Griswold, *Adam Smith and the Virtues of Enlightenment*, 205–6.
56. Smith also discusses a "superior prudence" that aims at nobler things than security, health, and prosperity; this kind of prudence requires, in addition to the virtues associated with ordinary prudence, "the utmost perfection of all the intellectual and of all of the moral virtues. It is the best head joined to the best heart" (*TMS* VI.i.15, 216). As his language here demonstrates, however, Smith seems to think such a combination of virtues out of reach for the vast majority. Furthermore, he contends that the individuals who might seem to come closest to approximating this superior prudence—the "spirited, magnanimous, and high-minded persons" who perform illustrious deeds and bring about revolutions in thought and action, ranging from Socrates to Caesar—often also suffer from "excessive self-estimation and presumption," and that their splendor tends to obscure "not only the great impudence, but frequently the great injustice of their enterprises" (*TMS* VI.iii.28–30, 250–52). In other words, even if individuals with these superior virtues are occasionally necessary, they are also often dangerous. In any case, Smith does not seem to be too concerned about ensuring that people will possess these virtues in commercial society, perhaps because he sees them as ultimately unnecessary in a well-functioning society, perhaps because he thinks they are more a product of nature than of societal arrangements and so will arise regardless of the circumstances, or perhaps because he does not believe that *any* kind of society can reliably generate (or contain) such individuals.

Smith argues that people in commercial society will tend to exhibit the virtues of the prudent man because for most people in this kind of society, most of the time, these virtues are the surest path to success. He claims that in "the middling and inferior stations of life"—that is, the nonwealthy and nonnoble classes—"the road to virtue and that to fortune, to such fortune, at least, as men in such stations can reasonably expect to acquire, are, happily in most cases, very nearly the same. In all the middling and inferior professions, real and solid professional abilities, joined to prudent, just, firm, and temperate conduct, can very seldom fail of success" (*TMS* I.iii.3.5, 63). Given that people in these stations depend heavily on their reputations in their interactions with others—since these interactions almost always take place among relative equals—and that they can seldom gain a good reputation without "tolerably regular conduct," Smith argues, "the good old proverb . . . that honesty is the best policy, holds, in such situations, almost always perfectly true" (*TMS* I.iii.3.5, 63; see also VII.ii.2.13, 298). Furthermore, people in these stations are almost never above the law and so are forced to act justly even in those rare cases where their advantage might lie elsewhere. And significantly, the preponderance of people in commercial society are found in these stations: "fortunately for the good morals of society, these are the situations of by far the greater part of mankind" (*TMS* I.iii.3.5, 63).

Moreover, it is not just by increasing the size of the middle class that commercial society encourages the virtues of the prudent man, for Smith: the activity of commerce itself helps perform this function.[57] Given that an extensive division of labor renders all people utterly dependent on others to satisfy their needs and desires, he argues, people in commercial society are forced to adapt their behavior to meet the expectations of others; people will only interact and exchange with those whom they trust and on whom they can depend. For this reason, Smith claims, commerce encourages traits like reliability, decency, honesty, cooperativeness, a commitment to keeping one's promises, and a strict adherence to society's norms of justice.

People might not care about truly meeting the expectations of others—they might only try to feign the virtues of the prudent man or even disregard them altogether—if they only interacted with other people occasionally,

---

57. Perhaps the most famous proponent of this argument at the time when Smith wrote was Montesquieu, who claimed that "the spirit of commerce brings with it the spirit of frugality, economy, moderation, work, wisdom, tranquillity, order, and rule." Montesquieu, *The Spirit of the Laws*, 48.

but since in commercial society people *live* by exchanging, this is far from a sensible course: "wherever dealings are frequent, a man does not expect to gain so much by any one contract as by probity and punctuality in the whole, and a prudent dealer, who is sensible of his real interest, would rather chuse to lose what he has a right to than give any ground for suspicion" (*LJ*, 538; see also *WN* I.x.c.31, 146). In other words, because of the frequency of interaction among people in commercial society, they will generally not be "smiling enemies" in the way that Rousseau suggests, for they must genuinely aim to satisfy the desires of others in order to secure their own long-term interests.[58] People's selfish interests are simply not always opposed in the way that Rousseau claims they are—it is possible to make mutual gains through trade—and so it is possible for people to truly help others even while helping themselves. Whereas Rousseau claims that commerce almost invariably undermines virtue, Smith contends that people must become (to some degree) virtuous in order to engage effectively in commerce. Thus, he claims that the virtues of the prudent man "are the principal virtues of a commercial nation" (*LJ*, 538; see also 528).[59]

Once again, Smith does not simply argue that commercial society is good in itself; he also shows that this kind of society is advantageous compared to other kinds of society. To begin with, he contrasts the virtues encouraged by commercial society with those found in the earliest stage of society: "Among civilized nations, the virtues which are founded upon humanity, are more cultivated than those which are founded upon self-denial and the command of the passions. Among rude and barbarous nations, it is quite otherwise, the virtues of self-denial are more cultivated than those of humanity" (*TMS* V.2.8, 204–5). This difference arises, as might be expected, because life is comparatively easier in commercial society than in primitive societies. Whereas "the soft, the amiable, and the gentle virtues" (those that involve sympathizing with others) tend to flourish with refinement and prosperity, "the great, the awful, and the respectable virtues" (those that involve tempering one's own emotions) rarely thrive without hardships, danger, and struggle (*TMS* III.3.35–37, 152–53; see also I.i.5.1, 23). "But," he dryly notes,

58. As Nathan Rosenberg notes, Smith's argument here "foreshadows issues that have become of central importance to modern game theory: the evolution of cooperative modes of behavior and the importance of reputation in repeated market relationships." Rosenberg, "Adam Smith and the Stock of Moral Capital," 12. Since people usually play positive-sum rather than zero-sum games in commercial society, according to Smith, they do not *need* to be enemies with one another to the extent that Rousseau says they do.

59. See also Berry, "Adam Smith: Commerce, Liberty and Modernity," 123–26.

"these are all masters to whom nobody willingly puts himself to school," and so the latter virtues tend to diminish with the easier conditions of commercial society (*TMS* III.3.37, 153).

Unlike people in commercial society, Smith writes, "every savage undergoes a sort of Spartan discipline, and by the necessity of his situation is inured to every sort of hardship" (*TMS* V.2.9, 205). But the extremes of self-command that savages often attain—Smith remarks on how they regularly endure torture without so much as displaying discomfort (see *TMS* V.2.9, 206)—typically come at the cost of their humanity or humaneness (see *TMS* III.3.37, 153). Because savages continually face danger and adversity and have to constantly worry about themselves, they tend to feel and care little for others (see *TMS* V.2.9, 205). And because they almost always try to subdue their passions and conceal their feelings, when they finally do give way to their passions they are "mounted to the highest pitch of fury," with the result that their actions are often "sanguinary and dreadful" (*TMS* V.2.11, 208). Savages are also less apt to accurately understand or adhere to norms of justice: "the rudeness and barbarism of the people hinder the natural sentiments of justice from arriving at that accuracy and precision which, in more civilized nations, they naturally attain to" (*TMS* VII.iv.36, 341). Smith notes, for instance, that it is not uncommon in the most primitive societies for people to torture prisoners of war to death or to abandon or outright kill infants and old and sick people (see *LJ*, 172, 239, 449, 548; *TMS* V.2.9, 206; V.2.15, 210; *WN* intro.4, 10). While the lack of toughness and courage in commercial peoples is one's of Smith's great worries, and while he accepts that commercial and savage nations have different moral balance sheets, each more suitable to its own situation than to the other (see *TMS* V.2.13, 209), at the end of the day he seems to prefer the humane virtues to the awful ones. For Smith, people living in "barbarous countries" are not the indolent and peaceful creatures of Rousseau's pure state of nature. Instead they are, well, *barbaric*—callous, inhumane, sometimes cruel and bloodthirsty—and this seems to Smith to be too high a price to pay for a greater degree of toughness and self-denial.

Whereas the hunting stage is marked above all by poverty and hardship, for Smith, one of the chief characteristics of the shepherding and agricultural stages is personal dependence, and hence he claims that these societies, too, produce adverse moral effects. Recall that, according to Smith, the wealthy in these stages of society, such as the feudal lords in medieval Europe, use their wealth to "maintain" or provide for thousands of others, and that this renders those thousands utterly dependent on them. Such dependence is a great evil in itself, for Smith, and furthermore it leads to depravity: "nothing tends so much to corrupt and enervate and debase the mind as dependency" (*LJ*, 333; see also 486). Dependence has this kind of negative effect because it forces people to rely on the goodwill of others— that is, it essentially places them in the position of slaves. And this position, for Smith, is the surest encouragement of vices like submissiveness, hypocrisy, and deceitfulness. Just as "a spaniel endeavours by a thousand attractions to engage the attention of his master who is at dinner, when it wants to be fed by him," a person who is dependent on the benevolence of others must attempt "by every servile and fawning attention to obtain their good will" (*WN* I.ii.2, 26). In other words, the vast majority of people in these stages of society—not just those with overweening ambition—are placed in the position of the "poor man's son" discussed in the previous chapter, who "serves those whom he hates, and is obsequious to those whom he despises" (*TMS* IV.1.8, 181). And the few who are not—the masters who exercise almost total control over their subjects—tend to acquire the opposite vices: they are apt to be arrogant, domineering, and uncaring (see *LJ*, 186). In short, the relations of dependence in the shepherding and agricultural stages render the moral balance sheet in these societies wanting indeed.

In commercial society, by contrast, people are generally free of direct, personal dependence on others; while people are greatly concerned with the *opinions* of others, Smith claims, they are generally *not* dependent on any particular individual for their survival or livelihood. We will examine the full rationale behind this key Smithian argument in much more detail in the next chapter; here I only note that even when people are dependent on others *in general* for nearly everything in commercial society because of the specialization that comes with an extensive division of labor, no one is absolutely dependent on any particular *individual* because there are generally a multitude of potential buyers, sellers, and employers. When people ask for meat, beer, or bread from a butcher, brewer, or baker, they address themselves "not to their humanity but to their self-love," and thus no one in commercial society has to "depend chiefly on the benevolence of his fellow-citizens" (*WN* I.ii.2, 27). Since people rely on others' self-interest rather than their benevolence in market transactions, they have an independence that the serf, the spaniel, and the ambitious poor man's son lack. And because people in commercial society are rarely dependent on any single person and rarely have others directly dependent on them, Smith maintains, they avoid the vices of both master and servant. Thus, after saying that "dependency" corrupts the mind, Smith immediately goes on to claim that "commerce is one great preventive of [this problem]" (*LJ*, 333; see also 486–87).

The connection between dependence and corruption helps shed light on why Smith claims that individuals in "the superior stations of life" often "abandon the paths of virtue" in their pursuit of wealth (*TMS* I.iii.3.8, 64). The noble classes lack the virtues possessed by the vast majority of people in commercial society, according to Smith, for the simple reason that they are exempt from the restraints imposed by the market. Oddly like the serfs of medieval Europe, aristocrats often depend on sycophancy and submissiveness to advance their interests: "in the courts of princes, in the drawing-rooms of the great, where success and preferment depend, not upon the esteem of intelligent and well-informed equals, but upon the fanciful and foolish favour of ignorant, presumptuous, and proud superiors; flattery and falsehood too often prevail over merit and abilities" (*TMS* I.iii.3.5, 63). Whereas in aristocratic circles everyone but the king has someone above him to whom he must defer, in the market the wealthy and the poor alike are on an equal playing field insofar as neither are directly dependent on another individual and both rely on the good opinion of others. Moreover, because aristocrats—also unlike the vast majority of people—are often above the law, they frequently try "not only by fraud and falsehood . . . but sometimes by the perpetration of the most enormous crimes . . . to supplant and destroy those who oppose or stand in the way of their greatness" (*TMS* I.iii.3.8, 64–65). One of the key advantages of commercial society, for Smith, is that it encourages the refinement and implementation of the rule of law and so forces *everyone* to abide by at least the principal norms of justice. Commercial society, then, helps alleviate the problems posed by the immorality of "the superior stations" both by enlarging the middle class and by promoting the rule of law.

The other groups that concern Smith, wealthy merchants and manufacturers, are clearly central in commercial society and so cannot be marginalized in the way that he hopes the aristocrats will be. Here the distinction between mercantilism and Smith's own "system of natural liberty" comes into play once again. Under the mercantile system that prevailed in Smith's time, wealthy traders and producers often eluded competition through political means; protected monopolies and strict and extensive regulations on imports and exports were unexceptional in eighteenth-century Britain.[60] Indeed, Smith repeatedly declares that "monopoly of one kind or another . . . seems to be the sole engine of the mercantile system" (WN IV.vii.c.89, 630; see also IV.i.35, 450; IV.viii.1, 642). And the presence of monopolies makes the virtues of the prudent man unnecessary; when people do not have to compete in the market, they do not have to be concerned with their reputations or with the opinions of others, so they need not be trustworthy and reliable in the same way that the majority of people must. As Jerry Muller succinctly puts it, "competition makes prudence and self-control necessary; monopoly makes them superfluous."[61] Like the aristocrats, then, wealthy merchants and manufacturers often fail to display the virtues of the prudent man because they are largely exempt from the pressures of the market under the mercantile system. And the ability of merchants and manufacturers to avoid the market, Smith argues, can be prevented through the proper institutional arrangements: "the monopolizing spirit of merchants and manufacturers . . . though it cannot perhaps be corrected, may very easily be prevented from disturbing the tranquillity of anyone but themselves" (WN IV.iii.c.9, 493). In other words, if these groups are denied political influence and if monopolies are limited through legislation, they can be rendered relatively harmless. (In contemporary economics terminology, rent seeking has to be prevented.)

Here we see that, contrary to a common reading of Smith, he does *not* argue that there is an automatic or spontaneous harmony of interests in society or that simply avoiding governmental interference is sufficient for an effective market economy. On the contrary, he claims that individual interests can be largely harmonized only if they are adequately channeled through the market, and that this requires the proper laws, institutions, and incentives.[62] Smith's famous "invisible hand,"[63] which serves to reconcile

---

60. See Rosenberg, "Adam Smith and Laissez-Faire Revisited," in *Adam Smith and Modern Political Economy*, 23.

61. Muller, *Adam Smith in His Time and Ours*, 138.

62. The classic work on this aspect of Smith's thought is Rosenberg, "Some Institutional Aspects of the Wealth of Nations."

63. Ryan Hanley speculates that Smith may have in fact been inspired by Rousseau to use this famous phrase. He provides three pieces of evidence to support this idea: first, Rousseau speaks in the dedicatory preface of the *Discourse on Inequality* of a "beneficent hand" (*main bienfaisante*) that "has created our happiness from the means that seemed likely to heighten our misery" (SD, 19; see also OC III, 127); second, Rousseau includes a quotation in one of the Notes to this work that uses the phrase "invisible hand" (*main invisible*)(SD, 72; see also OC III, 200); and third, Smith employs the phrase in a passage of *The Theory of Moral Sentiments*

private interests with the public good (see *TMS* IV.i.10, 184–85; *WN* IV.ii.9, 456), is not the hand of God or Nature but rather the hand of competition, and competition cannot be assumed but rather must be ensured through law. As Patricia Werhane writes, "the invisible hand, far from being the impartial spectator of the market, can operate only with the self-interested and cooperative actions of economic actors, and it is efficient only to the extent that it exists within the context of perfect liberty, coordination or economic harmony, equally advantageous competition, and fair play. . . . The invisible hand, then, is a dependent, not an independent, variable in economic activities."[64] If rules of fair play were adequately enforced—as Smith maintains they would be under his "system of natural liberty"—then wealthy merchants and manufacturers would be subject to the same competitive pressures as everyone else. In other words, Smith's harsh language regarding merchants and manufacturers is not meant to impugn commercial society so much as the mercantilist form of it.

What, finally, of the other problems that seem to be associated with the concern for others' opinions—the corruption of people's moral sentiments, selfishly motivated appeals to other people's self-interest, and the encouragement of ostentation? First of all, Smith does not see the corruption of people's moral sentiments as a problem associated only or even *especially* with commercial society. While it is true that he sees people's moral sentiments as corrupted by their tendency to admire the wealthy and to imagine that they must be supremely happy (see *TMS* I.iii.3.1, 61), we have seen that he also claims that people's esteem for the rich and powerful over the wise and virtuous has been "the complaint of moralists in all ages" (*TMS* I.iii.3.1, 62). There is simply no form of society in which the majority of people would reliably give wisdom and virtue the praise and esteem they deserve. Furthermore, the corruption of people's moral *sentiments*—the fact that they admire the wrong things—becomes less significant if these corrupt sentiments do not lead to immoral *actions*, and Smith argues that most people in commercial society will *not* in fact act immorally, because doing so would

---

that twice elsewhere comes very close to using Rousseau's words (see footnotes 69 and 75 in Chapter 2). See Hanley, "Rousseau's Diagnosis and Adam Smith's Cure," ms. 6–7. This is an intriguing suggestion, but, as Emma Rothschild has shown in her extraordinarily well-documented chapter on the invisible hand, this phrase was actually not an uncommon one; many other eminent authors had already used it, including Ovid, Shakespeare, and Voltaire, and it seems to me that any of them could have just as easily been Smith's "source" as Rousseau (if indeed there was a single source). See Rothschild, *Economic Sentiments*, chap. 5.

64. Werhane, *Adam Smith and His Legacy for Modern Capitalism*, 107, 110.

be contrary to their own long-term interests. In other words, he maintains that while people have always preferred wealth to virtue—and probably always will—in commercial society, unlike in many other societies, most people must possess at least a degree of the latter in order to consistently attain the former.

As for the second issue, the prevalence of selfishly motivated appeals to other people's self-interest, we have seen that this is not actually a *problem* at all, according to Smith. On the contrary, the fact that people in commercial society *can* appeal to others' self-interest instead of being forced to rely on their benevolence is precisely what keeps them from being directly dependent on any one individual. And again, even if these appeals are selfishly motivated, they will generally not be deceitful in the way that Rousseau says they will be, for the sheer multitude of exchanges and interactions in commercial society ensures that it is in people's long-term interests to treat others fairly. Both parties necessarily gain from market transactions under competitive conditions; since they are voluntary, such transactions will only take place if both sides feel that the exchange will make them better off (see *LJ*, 511; *WN* IV.iii.c.2, 489). (In economics terminology, it must be a Paretian exchange.) Hence, these selfishly motivated actions end up producing beneficial results without the harmful side effects that relying on the benevolence of others often has.

The final problem that Smith acknowledges can be associated with people's concern for the opinion of others—that it encourages ostentation and conspicuous consumption—is one of the chief problems that he admits really *is* exacerbated to some degree in commercial society. In earlier stages the problem of ostentation is not as great because there are few luxuries or manufactured goods; along with the increased productivity of commercial society come more things for people to show off, and Smith concedes that they will take every opportunity to do so. We will see in the next chapter that Smith argues that ostentation can lead to important political benefits, but he still accepts that it is something of a moral shortcoming (see *WN* II.iii.42, 349). This is just one more piece of evidence that Smith does not see commercial society as faultless or as a panacea; there is simply a different mixture of virtues and vices in commercial society than in other forms of society, and on the whole it seems to him to offer the preferable mixture. As we have seen, Smith (unlike Mandeville) does not argue that the economic benefits of commercial society are sufficient to answer the moral objections that thinkers like Rousseau level against it; there is no simple trade-off between productivity and corruption in his writings. Rather, Smith argues that even if commercial society gives rise to certain moral problems, it also has numerous moral benefits. For Smith, the good outweighs the bad in commercial society with respect to morality, just as it does with respect to economics, especially in comparison with previous forms of society.[65]

CONCLUSION

We have seen in this chapter that while Smith shows a degree of sympathy with both the "division of laborers" and "empire of opinion" critiques, in the end he does not think that either of these sets of arguments is sufficient to truly call the desirability of commercial society into question. As for the former critique, he acknowledges that the division of labor can produce harmful side effects, but he defends it in any case because it creates astronomic increases in productivity, thereby opening up the prospect of raising the living standards of the poor to levels not previously attainable. The inequalities produced by the division of labor are more than justified, for Smith, not only because *everyone* is better off in commercial society than they would have been in precommercial times—that is, because a European peasant is materially better off than an African king—but also because one of the worst effects of inequality, personal dependence, is significantly diminished by the interdependence of the market. Furthermore, he argues that the other problems associated with the division of labor—ignorance, weakness, and the consequent decline of citizenship—can be ameliorated through a comprehensive system of state-supported education and perhaps some kind of martial training.

As for the "empire of opinion" critique, Smith concedes that people tend to be greatly concerned with the opinions of others, but unlike Rousseau he claims that this is actually a *good* thing, for this concern can act as the very basis of moral conduct. It is the fact that people see themselves through others' eyes, he maintains, that gives rise to social standards of propriety and that leads people to (more or less) follow them. Smith further argues that commercial society encourages the virtues of the "prudent man"—virtues like reliability, decency, cooperativeness, and strict adherence to society's norms of justice—by ensuring that it is in people's best interests to

65. See also Muller, *Adam Smith in His Time and Ours,* especially chap. 10.

exhibit these traits. Whereas in the hunting stage toughness and self-denial are generally purchased at the price of inhumanity and in the shepherding and agricultural stages personal dependence generally gives rise to obsequiousness and deceitfulness, for the vast majority of people in commercial society the surest path to success is honest work. The groups that Smith concedes often do not exhibit these virtues—aristocrats and wealthy merchants—fail to do so only because they are in one way or another exempt from the competitive pressures of the market; under the "system of natural liberty," he maintains, these problems would be allayed.

One of the major problems that Smith accepts *is* exacerbated in commercial society is that of ostentation and conspicuous consumption. People simply *will* flaunt their wealth when there are a great deal of luxury goods available to be shown off, and this will tend to make others envious and cause them to strive for useless luxuries of their own. This problem, of course, points toward Rousseau's third critique, the argument that people's desires are expanded well beyond their ability to fulfill them in commercial society and that this keeps them from ever being happy. And this third critique seems in some ways decisive: even if the overall economic and moral balance sheets favor commercial society over other forms of society, as Smith argues they do, all of these advantages would seem much less important if everyone living in this kind of society remained miserable. But are people really less happy in commercial society than they were in previous societies, according to Smith? And if so, then why does he defend it? It is to these questions that we turn in the final chapter.

In *The Theory of Moral Sentiments,* Smith states that "all constitutions of government . . . are valued only in proportion as they tend to promote the happiness of those who live under them. This is their sole use and end" (*TMS* IV.1.11, 185). In other words, Smith's standard for judging a society seems to consist much more in how happy it is than in how wealthy it is. Thus, Smith's best-known argument for commercial society—that it makes possible enormous increases in productivity and hence higher living standards—cannot be his ultimate reason for defending this kind of society unless he thinks that happiness can be found in material goods. On the contrary, however, we have seen that he accepts that material goods do little to make people any happier and that the relentless *pursuit* of material goods is in fact a major *obstacle* to true happiness. Here we arrive at one of the most fundamental and puzzling questions of Smith's thought: Why does he advocate commercial society if it undermines people's happiness—that is, if it falls short of his own measure of a good society? Or, conversely, why does he think commercial society promotes people's happiness, since he concedes that the desire for ever more material goods—the desire upon which commercial society is based—seems to keep people from enjoying true happiness?

Smith unequivocally states that *the* most important benefit of commercial society is that it provides a greater degree of liberty and security than precommercial societies were able to provide (see *WN* III.iv.4, 412), and I will argue that this statement points toward the ultimate solution to the apparent conflict regarding progress and happiness in his writings. Since dependence and insecurity are the chief obstacles to happiness and have been the hallmarks of most of human history, on Smith's view, the alleviation of these ills in commercial society constitutes a great step forward. While the fact that people tend to continually strive for more and more material goods might keep them from enjoying complete or unalloyed happiness, this tendency also plays a crucial role in paving the way toward liberty and security and thereby removing the great obstacles to happiness that had so dominated precommercial societies.

The first section of this chapter begins by considering two of the most prominent recent attempts to reconcile Smith's assertions about the delusions connected to the pursuit of wealth with his defense of commercial society and then turns to Smith's most explicit statement on why he ultimately defends commercial society, in which he claims that the most important effect of commerce is that it promotes liberty and security. Section 2 explores the relationship between liberty, security, and happiness through an analysis of Smith's presuppositions concerning the nature of happiness and his descriptions of the ills of previous stages of society. In Section 3 we turn to an investigation of how and why commerce leads to liberty and security, on Smith's account, focusing in particular on the political advantages that arose in and through the transition from the feudal age to the commercial age in Western Europe. Finally, Section 4 considers the question of what kind of government Smith thinks would be most effective in promoting people's happiness and shows that he endorses a mixed government with a powerful representative branch, one that is strong enough to effectively enforce order and administer justice but that carries out a relatively limited range of functions.

I. "BY FAR THE MOST IMPORTANT OF ALL THEIR EFFECTS"

As we saw in Chapter 2, Smith forcefully argues both that money really can't buy happiness and that the endless pursuit of wealth in fact tends to *detract* from people's happiness. The moving and oft-cited section of *The Theory of Moral Sentiments* that describes how people mistakenly associate wealth with happiness, however, is immediately followed by an assertion that this deception is in fact a *good* thing: "And it is well that nature imposes upon us in this manner. It is this deception which rouses and keeps in continual motion the industry of mankind. It is this which first prompted them to cultivate the ground, to build houses, to found cities and commonwealths, and to invent and improve all the sciences and arts, which ennoble and embellish human life" (*TMS* IV.1.10, 183). Yet the question inevitably arises: What good are all of these "improvements" if people remain deluded about the nature and basis of their own happiness? Smith has clearly not overlooked the importance of happiness here, for in the very next paragraph he asserts that the true measure of a government is the degree to which it "tend[s] to promote the happiness of those who live under [it]" (*TMS* IV.i.ii, 185). At this juncture there seems to be a conflict in his writings regarding the relative worth of wealth and civilization on the one hand and of happiness on the other. While many of the apparent conflicts in Smith's corpus have been analyzed and resolved in the many refutations of the "Adam Smith Problem" that have appeared over the past several decades, this conflict regarding happiness has received far less attention. Two of the best recent works on Smith, however, *do* address this conflict: Charles Griswold's *Adam Smith and the Virtues of Enlightenment* and Samuel Fleischacker's *On Adam Smith's Wealth of Nations*. Both these works offer insightful discussions of the place of happiness in Smith's thought, but I do not believe that either of them succeeds fully in resolving this apparent conflict.

In a discussion of Smith's views of commerce, progress, and happiness, Griswold notes the "comic irony" inherent in Smith's view that the wealth of nations is made possible only by a pursuit of wealth that leaves people "constantly dissatisfied."[1] He attempts to spell out Smith's reasoning by positing a distinction between what is good for society and what is good for the individual: "In both of his books Smith is recommending a society devoted to the improvement of the human lot but governed by a systematic self-deception about its own ends. Such a society is therefore inclined to private, though not necessarily public, unhappiness."[2] In other words, even if the deception associated with the pursuit of wealth renders the deceived individuals unhappy, it leads to "public happiness," by which Griswold essentially seems to mean economic development: "In the kind of twist so typical of his thinking, Smith explicitly argues that the fact that most individuals are *not* perfectly happy contributes to the 'happiness of mankind, as well as of all rational beings.' The deception of the imagination underlying the drive to better our condition . . . creates 'progress' or 'civilization,' that is, productive labor, which may increase the wealth of nations."[3]

1. Griswold, *Adam Smith and the Virtues of Enlightenment*, 222; see also 221–25, 262–63.
2. Ibid., 263; see also 288, 302. Similarly, Ryan Hanley writes that "modern commerce gives rise to a certain tragic paradox: that what is good for the society—the very scheme for the creation of public opulence—is in fact bad for the individual." Hanley, "Rousseau's Diagnosis and Adam Smith's Cure," ms. 11.
3. Griswold, *Adam Smith and the Virtues of Enlightenment*, 225. As Samuel Fleischacker notes, however, the internal quotation in this passage is in fact *not* taken from a discussion of the deception associated with the pursuit of wealth. Rather, Smith contends in this passage that "the happiness of mankind, as well as of all rational beings, seems to have been the purpose

That the deception associated with the pursuit of wealth is beneficial because it encourages productivity and drives the process of civilization is, we
have just seen, what Smith himself seems to imply in his own statement
about why this deception is a good thing (see *TMS* IV.i.10, 183). Yet we
have also seen that this argument alone does not seem to be enough to
resolve the problem, for Smith immediately claims that it is happiness and
not wealth or the degree of civilization that matters most, that the "sole use
and end" of a government is promoting people's happiness (*TMS* IV.i.11,
185). Furthermore, Smith elsewhere explicitly argues against the notion of
a "public happiness" that is separate from—indeed, opposed to—the happiness of each individual: "no society can be flourishing and happy, of which
the far greater part of the members are poor and miserable" (*WN* I.viii.36,
96).⁴ It is the happiness of *individuals* that counts, for Smith, not some
vague notion of "public happiness."⁵ Griswold is right to contend that, in
Smith's view, people generally fail to understand what true happiness is or
how it might be attained, but he never makes it entirely clear why Smith
advocates commercial society even though it expands and builds on this
confusion.

In a response to Griswold's argument, Samuel Fleischacker notes that
it does not make sense for Smith to have maintained that the pursuit of
wealth is conducive to unhappiness but to have also "applaud[ed] a social
system that depends upon, and encourages, that very pursuit."⁶ He attempts
to solve this puzzle by suggesting that later in life Smith changed his mind
about the relationship between commercial society and the deception associated with the pursuit of wealth: "TMS IV.i.10 [the passage which explains
why this deception is a good thing] is Smith's earliest published writing on
political economy, and he later significantly altered many of the views it expresses."⁷ Smith does not claim in *The Wealth of Nations* that the pursuit
of wealth is founded on the false supposition, aroused by vanity, that money

---

intended by the Author of nature, when he brought them into existence," and that this purpose
is furthered when we act "according to the dictates of our moral faculties" (*TMS* III.5.7, 166).
See Fleischacker, *On Adam Smith's Wealth of Nations*, 104.

4. As Smith says in a different context in *The Theory of Moral Sentiments*, "our regard for
the multitude is compounded and made up of the particular regards which we feel for the different individuals of which it is composed" (*TMS* II.ii.3.10, 89–90).

5. Rousseau, too, contends that a society cannot be happy unless the people in it are happy:
"That moral being you call public happiness is in itself a chimera. If the feeling of well-being
exists in no one, it is nothing" (*Fragments*, 41).

6. Fleischacker, *On Adam Smith's Wealth of Nations*, 104.

7. Ibid.

will buy happiness, Fleischacker argues; rather, Smith claims in his later work that the economy is driven by "the humble goods of the poor, not luxury goods," meaning that "the desire crucial to economic growth is not based on illusion."[8] The later Smith did not see commercial society as any more conducive than other societies to a delusory pursuit of wealth, and if he *had* held this view then advocating such a society would have been morally execrable according to his own terms.[9] Hence, Smith's earlier claim that people's vanity leads them to pursue meaningless luxuries, and that this pursuit is good because it is what drives the process of civilization, must not represent his settled views, and we ought to stress the later writings over earlier ones.[10] Fleischacker cites the fact that the section of *The Theory of Moral Sentiments* in question was written for the first edition in 1759 and received only "one tiny revision" over the course of the next five editions and suggests that Smith "may well have wanted to leave it in undisturbed in later editions whatever he thought of some of its implications" because it was "a beautiful piece of writing."[11]

Fleischacker's explanation, however, does not seem to fully solve the problem either. After all, the fact that luxury goods are not the primary driving force of the economy in *The Wealth of Nations* is entirely compatible with people's pursuit of wealth being fundamentally misguided,[12] and Smith gives no indication that striving and toiling for non-luxury goods is any less disruptive of people's tranquility and happiness than striving and toiling for luxury goods; we have seen that even in *The Wealth of Nations* Smith maintains that labor itself is "toil and trouble" (*WN* I.v.2, 47), that it requires a person to "lay down [a] portion of his ease, his liberty, and his happiness" (*WN* I.v.7, 50). Fleischacker's contention that a "slow, gradual 'bettering of one's condition' is perfectly compatible with contentment, for the later Smith"[13] seems to overlook Smith's insistence that this desire must be "uniform, constant, and uninterrupted" and hence generate nearly continuous labor in order for a nation or an individual to prosper (*WN* II.iii.31, 343).

Furthermore, the notion that Smith changed his mind about the deception

8. Ibid., 118, 111.
9. I am grateful to Fleischacker for personal correspondence clarifying this element of his argument.
10. See Fleischacker, *On Adam Smith's Wealth of Nations*, 108–11, 294n6.
11. Ibid., 108.
12. Fleischacker seems to largely concede this point at the end of his discussion; see ibid., 115, 120.
13. Ibid., 113.

associated with the pursuit of wealth but did not bother to change the passage in *The Theory of Moral Sentiments* that describes this problem so powerfully is also problematic. Fleischacker may be right to claim that Smith did not return to this passage with particular care in his revisions,[14] but the idea that he changed his mind about the larger point of the passage seems to be belied by his addition, in the final edition of this work in 1790, of an entire chapter on the corruptions associated with people's tendency to admire the wealthy and to imagine that they must be supremely happy—a chapter that would seem to reinforce the point made in the earlier passage on the delusory pursuit of wealth (see *TMS* I.iii.3, 61–66). Thus, it seems improbable that Smith changed his mind about this problem and simply chose to keep the earlier passage because he thought it was "a beautiful piece of writing"; the apparent paradox in Smith's writings on the issue of progress and happiness cannot be avoided by discounting the importance of one or another of his statements on the issue.

I believe that Smith's statements on this issue *are* ultimately consistent with one another and that the solution to the apparent paradox can be found in his account of the positive *political* effects of commerce. In a crucial passage in Book III of *The Wealth of Nations*, at the culmination of his account of the transition from the feudal age to the commercial age in Europe, he offers the most explicit statement of his entire corpus regarding why he ultimately defends commercial society: "Commerce and manufactures gradually introduced order and good government, and with them, the liberty and security of individuals, among the inhabitants of the country, who had before lived almost in a continual state of war with their neighbours, and of servile dependency on their superiors. This, though it has been the least observed, is by far the most important of all their effects" (*WN* III.iv.4, 412). The argument in this passage is, I believe, in many ways the key to Smith's defense of commercial society. Its importance is demonstrated not only by Smith's superlative language—the promotion of liberty and security is *by far* the most important of *all* of commerce's effects—but also by its age: as W. R. Scott has shown, Book III is the oldest part of *The Wealth of Nations* and may have originated as early as Smith's public lectures in Edinburgh

---

14. The "most striking clue" that Fleischacker offers to support the idea that this section of *The Theory of Moral Sentiments* received little attention in Smith's revisions is the fact that it contains an apparent praise of bounties (see *TMS* IV.i.11, 185), which of course would seem to be at odds with Smith's later economic thought. See Fleischacker, *On Adam Smith's Wealth of Nations*, 108–9, 295n8.

in 1748 to 1750—that is, well before Smith wrote *The Theory of Moral Sentiments* (the first edition of which was published in 1759).[15]

Other scholars have rightly emphasized that Smith's central aim in promoting commerce is political more than economic—that is, that his chief aspiration is liberty and security rather than wealth. Joseph Cropsey argues, for instance, that "Smith may be understood as a writer who advocated capitalism for the sake of freedom, civil and ecclesiastical,"[16] and Christopher Berry maintains that Smith defends commercial society "because the conditions that make opulence possible also, in a mutually complementary fashion, make possible a superior form of freedom—that of liberty under law, the hallmark of civilisation."[17] But even these scholars say very little about the importance of happiness for Smith. If the true measure of a society is, as Smith claims, the happiness of the people who live in it, then why does he say that liberty and security are the most important advantages of commercial society? In other words, what is the connection, for Smith, between liberty and security on the one hand and happiness on the other? We turn to these questions in the next section.

2. PREVENTING MISERY

The idea that liberty and security are key factors in solving the happiness puzzle in Smith's writings finds some initial plausibility in the fact that after he tells the story of how liberty and security were introduced in Europe, he asserts that this change constituted "a revolution of the greatest importance to the publick happiness" (*WN* III.iv.17, 422).[18] This idea is further reinforced by Dugald Stewart's "Account of the Life and Writings of Adam Smith, LL.D." (1793). Stewart prefaces his account of *The Wealth of Nations* with the observation that in modern times "the most wealthy nations are those where the people . . . enjoy the greatest degree of liberty" and that "it was the general diffusion of wealth among the lower orders of men, which

15. See Scott, *Adam Smith as Student and Professor*, 56. See also the note by the editors of *The Wealth of Nations* regarding the passage quoted above: *WN*, 412n6.

16. Cropsey, *Polity and Economy*, 112; see also xii–xiii, 100, 113.

17. Berry, "Adam Smith: Commerce, Liberty and Modernity," in *Philosophers of the Enlightenment*, 116. See also Rothschild, *Economic Sentiments*, 14, 70–71.

18. The context makes it clear that by "publick happiness" Smith means not some abstract entity along the lines that Griswold posits, but rather the happiness of every individual in the society (as opposed to the happiness of certain groups).

first gave birth to the spirit of independence in modern Europe" (*EPS*, 313). He then declares, in a revealing passage, that these comments on the relationship between wealth and liberty

> appeared to me to form, not only a proper, but in some measure a necessary introduction to the few remarks I have to offer on Mr Smith's Inquiry; as they tend to illustrate a connection between his system of commercial politics, and those speculations of his earlier years, in which he aimed more professedly at the advancement of human improvement and happiness. It is this view of political economy that can alone render it interesting to the moralist, and can dignify calculations of profit and loss in the eye of the philosopher. Mr Smith has alluded to it in various passages of his work, but he has nowhere explained himself fully on the subject. (*EPS*, 314–15)

In other words, Stewart, too, recognizes that Smith retained his concern for happiness when writing *The Wealth of Nations;* he also recognizes that Smith's "system of commercial politics," the rise of modern liberty, and the advancement of human happiness are all connected. The question to which we now turn is this: What *are* these connections to which "Mr Smith has alluded . . . in various passages of his work" but which he has "nowhere explained . . . fully"? Even if commercial society is able to provide a greater degree of liberty and security than previous societies, what does this have to do with *happiness?*

The first noteworthy point is that like Rousseau—and a long tradition of philosophers from Socrates to the present—Smith holds that a life of perfect, unalloyed happiness is simply unattainable. We saw in Chapter 2 that on Smith's account, incessant desires and continual fears and anxieties are the major obstacles to attaining the tranquility that is the key component of happiness. We have also seen that the "desire of bettering our condition" is not exclusive to commercial society, for Smith: he claims that people will *always* desire more than they have, whether they desire luxuries and refinements or more food and a better hut, since their chief desire is ultimately to impress others and fulfill their vanity rather than to actually enjoy the goods themselves (see *TMS* I.iii.2.1, 50). While some circumstances are undoubtedly more conducive to tranquility and happiness than others—given that continual fears and anxieties are *not* inescapable features of human nature as Smith depicts it—it seems that unfulfilled (and unful-fillable) desires will invariably hinder people's ability to attain perfect tran-quility under any conceivable circumstances. Rousseau's writings, too, seem to indicate that complete happiness is for all practical purposes unattain-able in the modern world. However, Rousseau sees the main cause of striv-ing (*amour-propre*) as adventitious, and this seems to lead him to also hold out a degree of (ultimately unrealizable) hope that people's natural happi-ness could be restored or retained—hence his vivid depictions of the hap-piness enjoyed by Emile, as well as by himself in the *Reveries of a Solitary Walker*. Rousseau inconsistently condemns commercial society for failing to produce an outcome (making people happy) that he himself acknowl-edges is all but unattainable; Smith, by contrast, seems much more willing to accept the fact that *no* set of circumstances can reliably produce com-plete happiness.

The idea that Smith accepts the limits to happiness might seem to con-tradict the fact that happiness is the standard by which he thinks a society ought to be judged. In truth, though, there is no contradiction here: Smith states only that a government should be valued insofar as it *tends* to *promote* the happiness of those who live under it—not that people must attain hap-piness without fail (see *TMS* IV.i.11, 185). And one of the surest ways to *promote* people's happiness, of course, is to alleviate the greatest sources of misery. Furthermore, preventing misery seems to be a more pressing task than ensuring happiness, on Smith's view, since pain is a more "pungent" sensation than pleasure and since suffering lowers people's spirits more than happiness can raise them: "pain . . . almost always, depresses us much more below the ordinary, or what might be called the natural state of our happiness, than [pleasure] ever raises us above it" (*TMS* III.2.15, 121; see also I.iii.1.3, 44). "Though between [the ordinary or natural state of happi-ness] and the highest pitch of human prosperity, the interval is but a trifle; between it and the lowest depth of misery the distance is immense and prodigious," and so it would seem even more crucial to assuage the deep-est miseries than to try to encourage the greatest joys (*TMS* I.iii.1.8, 45). Thus it seems that in the end, Smith's standard for measuring a society is not so much whether it ensures people's happiness—since this is impos-sible—as whether it *promotes* their happiness, if only by keeping them from being miserable.

I will argue that on Smith's view the key prerequisites for an individual to avoid misery—to attain a reasonable degree of tranquility and enjoyment—

are a sense of relative safety and freedom from direct dependence on an-other individual. In other words, when people feel safe and secure and do not feel subject to the caprices of others, they are less likely to experience the kinds of fears and anxieties that ruin almost any chance of finding a measure of tranquility. This conjecture will be substantiated throughout the rest of this chapter, but we can observe immediately the connection between these two prerequisites and Smith's description of the benefits of commerce in the passage whose importance I emphasized above. Smith writes there that whereas before the rise of commercial society people commonly "lived almost in a continual state of war with their neighbours, and of servile de-pendency on their superiors," these ills were finally alleviated in commer-cial society—a change that constitutes "by far the most important of all [of commerce's] effects" (WN III.iv.4, 412). I contend that these very effects—providing a greater degree of security and a greater degree of liberty, under-stood here as freedom from direct, personal dependence on others—are precisely the preconditions for attaining a meaningful degree of tranquil-ity and enjoyment, in Smith's view. In other words, the surest way of pro-moting people's happiness, for Smith, is to provide them with liberty and security. This reading neatly solves the puzzle described above, that of why Smith identifies liberty and security as the most important aspects of com-mercial society when he also says that the true measure of a society is the degree to which it promotes people's happiness.

The idea that liberty and security are the key prerequisites for any degree of happiness is, in fact, the entire point of Smith's claims that the rich tend to be no happier than the poor. Smith declares that "except the frivolous pleasures of vanity and superiority, we may find, in the most humble sta-tion, *where only there is personal liberty,* every other which the most exalted can afford" (*TMS* III.3.31, 150; italics added). In other words, Smith main-tains that personal liberty is *the* necessary ingredient for taking pleasure in life and that it is equally available to the rich and the poor. In his most extreme example of this claim, he writes that "in what constitutes the real happiness of human life, [the poor] are in no respect inferior to those who would seem so much above them. In ease of body and peace of mind, all the different ranks of life are nearly upon a level, and the beggar, who suns himself by the side of the highway, possesses that security which kings are fighting for" (*TMS* IV.1.10, 185).[19] Smith here essentially equates "the real

19. D. D. Raphael writes of this passage: "This piece of romanticism may be influenced

happiness of human life" with "ease of body and peace of mind" and with security; the poor and the beggar would not be "nearly upon a level" with the rich and the king with respect to happiness if they did not feel free and secure. Since this passage is found at the end of the paragraph in which Smith describes how the deception associated with the pursuit of wealth spurs industry and thereby advances civilization, it is relatively clear that the poor and the beggar here should be assumed to be living in a commercial society. The rich do not tend to be much happier than the poor in commercial society, according to Smith, because they both enjoy liberty and security under the law. We will see, however—and this is a crucial point— that this might not always be the case in societies that fail to provide as much liberty and security, for in these societies wealth may be the only means of avoiding dependence and insecurity.

While merely providing liberty and security might not seem to be a terribly lofty goal—as opposed to, say, promoting virtue or salvation—Smith shows that the vast majority of human societies have been unable to meet even this relatively modest objective. Indeed, significant portions of *The Wealth of Nations* and even larger portions of Smith's *Lectures on Jurisprudence* read like little more than extended descriptions of the astonishing range of ills that dominated previous stages of society. Smith maintains that in the earliest ages—the hunting stage—poverty is the keynote to all aspects of life (see *WN* V.i.b.7, 712). And whereas Rousseau sometimes waxes eloquent on the ruggedness and simplicity that come with poverty (in his descriptions of peasant life and savage life, for instance), Smith sees nothing redeeming about the kind of poverty that primitive societies face. He notes on the first page of *The Wealth of Nations* that many "savage nations . . . are so miserably poor, that, from mere want, they are frequently reduced, or, at least, think themselves reduced, to the necessity sometimes of directly destroying, and sometimes of abandoning their infants, their old people, and those afflicted with lingering diseases, to perish with hunger, or to be devoured by wild beasts" (*WN* intro.4, 10; see also *TMS* V.2.15, 210). Because of the scarcity that prevails in these societies, Smith writes, "every savage . . . is often exposed to the greatest extremities of hunger, and frequently dies of pure want" (*TMS* V.2.9, 205; see also *Astronomy*, 48). Competition for resources at this stage is cutthroat, and not only in a metaphorical sense:

---

by the egalitarianism of Rousseau, whom Smith seems to have had in mind when he wrote the whole paragraph." Raphael, *Adam Smith*, 80. See also Winch, *Riches and Poverty*, 63.

he graphically describes a prisoner of war among the American Indians being "hung by the shoulders over a slow fire," and then being "scorched and burnt, and lacerated in all the most tender and sensible parts of [the] body for several hours together" (*TMS* V.2.9, 206; see also *LJ*, 239, 548).

The inhabitants of hunting societies might seem to have a great deal of liberty or independence, at least, given that there is little or no government in this stage, but Smith claims that this is far from always the case. Before the rise of governmental power there was no authority that could intervene in family life, he notes, and so "the father possessed a power over his whole family, wife, children, and slaves, which was not much less than supreme" (*LJ*, 143–44; see also 176). Husbands "had absolute power over [their wives], both of death and of divorce," and fathers were not even obliged to provide for their children (*LJ*, 66; see also 172, 449). Even the adult males in these societies could not enjoy their relative independence, according to Smith, simply because life was so utterly precarious. He claims that without a reasonable level of security people must live in constant anxiety: "unprotected by the laws of society, exposed, defenceless, [a person in the first ages of society] feels his weakness upon all occasions; his strength upon none" (*Astronomy*, 48). Smith contrasts this kind of anxiety with "the general security and happiness which prevail in ages of civility and refinement" (*TMS* V.2.8, 205; see also *WN* V.i.g.24, 803). Whereas Rousseau envisions people in the state of nature as happy and free, Smith's descriptions of the earliest ages of society bear a much greater resemblance to the Hobbesian state of nature. While the life of a savage is not solitary, for Smith it is rather poor, nasty, brutish, and short.[20]

If the keynote of life in the hunting stage is poverty, in Smith's view, the defining element of both the shepherding and agricultural stages is dependence. He repeatedly asserts that given the relative absence of luxuries in these societies, the wealthy have little on which to spend their wealth other than "maintaining" or providing for a great multitude of tenants and

20. Although Smith's view of primitive societies is a dim one, I do not mean to imply that Smith was a follower of Hobbes in other senses, as has been contended by Cropsey, *Polity and Economy;* and Minowitz, *Profits, Priests, and Princes.* Contrary to the argument of these scholars, Smith does not see self-preservation as the primary end of human life, nor does he see commerce as incompatible with, or a substitute for, virtue. See Fleischacker, *On Adam Smith's Wealth of Nations,* 100–103. Just as important in the context of this chapter, Smith's view of happiness is nearly the opposite of Hobbes's contention that "felicity is a continual progress of the desire, from one object to another, the attaining of the former being but the way to the latter." Hobbes, *Leviathan,* 57; see also 34–35.

retainers (see *LJ*, 49–51, 202, 248, 405, 416; *WN* III.iv.5–7, 413–15; V.i.b.7, 712–13). And since government and the rule of law are generally not powerful enough in these stages to reach effectively into their estates, the wealthy remain largely free from external authority and have almost complete control over their dependents. Thus, to use Smith's chief example, in the allodial and feudal periods of Europe the lords held their tenants—who often numbered in the thousands—utterly at their mercy: "Every great landlord was a sort of petty prince. His tenants were his subjects. He was their judge, and in some respects their legislator in peace, and their leader in war. He made war at his own discretion, frequently against his neighbours, and sometimes against his sovereign" (*WN* III.II.3, 383; see also III.iv.7, 415; *LJ*, 51, 55, 128).[21] As a result of the nearly absolute power of the lords, people in these societies, too, enjoyed little security: "the law at that time . . . did not provide, nor indeed could it, for the safety of the subjects" (*LJ*, 55). The lords regularly used their power to make war on one another, according to Smith, so "depredations were continually committed up and down the country" (*LJ*, 416) and at times nearly the whole countryside was a scene of "violence, rapine, and disorder" (*WN* III.iv.9, 418; see also III.ii.1, 381; *LJ*, 520).

Just as detrimental as the general lack of security caused by the chiefs and lords in these stages, for Smith, was the near ubiquity of personal dependence itself. He repeatedly draws attention to the unfortunate condition of the tenants and retainers of medieval Europe, who had few rights of any kind: they could have no private property that was free from encroachment by their lord, they were bought and sold with the land and so were unable to move freely, they typically could not choose their own occupations, and they often had to obtain their lord's consent to get married (see *LJ*, 48, 53–55, 255; *WN* III.ii.8, 386–87). It is critical to recall that it was not just a few individuals but rather the overwhelming *majority* of people who lived in this condition in shepherding and agricultural societies. Precisely because almost everyone was so heavily dependent on the caprice of another person in these stages, Smith claims of them that "a more miserable and oppressive government cannot be imagined" (*LJ*, 414). In short, Smith shows that while subsistence is not as precarious in the shepherding and agricultural

---

21. Wealth brings its possessor great authority in a similar manner in shepherding societies, according to Smith—a fact that would have been especially palpable to him from his familiarity with the Scottish Highlands, where the chieftains held the power of life and death over their clans (see *LJ*, 54; *WN* III.iv.8, 416).

stages as in the hunting stage, the vast majority of people still have little liberty or security.[22]

To summarize, Smith argues that no society prior to the emergence of commercial society had been able to provide liberty and security for more than a relatively small number of individuals. And since dependence and insecurity are the greatest obstacles to happiness, on Smith's view, no pre-commercial societies were able to promote people's happiness as effectively as the commercial societies of his day that *did* provide their inhabitants with liberty and security. This is the main reason why Smith holds commercial society to represent such a marked advancement over the rest of human history. The question is this: Why are commercial societies able to succeed where every other society in history has failed? How exactly *does* commerce introduce "order and good government, and with them, the liberty and security of individuals" (*WN* III.iv.4, 412)?

3. COMMERCE AND PROGRESS

Smith's emphasis on the prevalence of dependence and insecurity in pre-commercial societies helps shed an interesting light on his famous comparison between the European peasant and the African king. Locke's equally famous statement along these lines holds that "a King of a large and fruitful Territory [among the American Indians] feeds, lodges, and is clad worse than a day Labourer in England."[23] The emphasis here is solely on material well-being. Smith's passage, however, adds an important political twist: "the accommodation of an European prince does not always so much exceed that of an industrious and frugal peasant, as the accommodation of the latter

22. The city-states of ancient Greece (particularly Athens) and republican Rome might seem to be a partial exception to this trend, since Smith accepts that they were in many respects the most civilized societies before the onset of modern commercial society (see *Astronomy*, 51; *LJ*, 91, 222, 235; *LRBL*, 150), but he insists that even Athens and Rome fell short of providing an adequate level of liberty and security. This was true, first of all, because they retained a number of harmful customs and habits from previous stages, such as infanticide and the nearly absolute rule of adult men over their families (see *LJ*, 47, 172–73, 440; *TMS* V.2.15, 210). Even more important, for Smith, is the fact that these societies had slavery—and a much harsher form of it than that found among the serfs in feudal Europe (see *LJ*, 183, 255, 451; *WN* III.ii.8, 386; IV.ix.47, 683–84). And Smith says that if a society is to be measured by how well it promotes people's happiness, any society marked by slavery—including Athens and Rome—fails to meet the test (see *LJ*, 185).

23. Locke, *Two Treatises of Government*, 297.

exceeds that of many an African king, *the absolute master of the lives and liberties of ten thousand naked savages*" (*WN* I.i.11, 24; italics added). The fact that the material conditions of the poor in Europe are higher than those of even a king in Africa is itself remarkable, but Smith also points here to something that is ultimately more significant: in contrast to the "ten thousand naked savages," no one is the absolute master of the life or liberty of the European peasant. In addition to increasing wealth, Smith indicates here and throughout his works, commercial societies are able to provide liberty and security for their inhabitants to an extent that far surpasses all previous societies.

Smith explains how commerce helped pave the way toward liberty and security in Book III of *The Wealth of Nations,* where he relates a now well-known story about how the nobles in feudal Europe squandered their authority over their dependents for the sake of frivolous luxuries. After the fall of the Roman Empire, Smith recounts, the great landowners throughout Europe possessed large estates over which they exercised complete control, since the authority of the sovereign was rarely strong enough to be effective throughout the country. The lords each maintained thousands of tenants and retainers who were utterly dependent on their patron for sustenance, accommodation, and protection. The inhabitants of the cities eventually sought to combine to protect themselves from the lords, Smith's narrative continues, and the kings tended to support their efforts toward independence in an effort to weaken the power of the lords and thereby extend the reach of their own authority (see *LJ,* 188, 256; *WN* III.iii.8, 402). Eventually, Smith writes—in a passage that closely prefigures the one to which I have attached so much importance—"order and good government, and along with them the liberty and security of individuals, were . . . established in cities at a time when the occupiers of land in the country were exposed to every sort of violence" (*WN* III.iii.12, 405). At this point, then, the burghers began to enjoy a greater degree of liberty and security under the protection of the king and the rule of law, but they constituted only a small proportion of the population. These individuals unsuspectingly helped pave the way toward liberty and security for the rest of the population, however, simply by engaging in commerce—especially by producing and importing luxuries and manufactured goods, which Smith claims were the ultimate cause of the lords' demise (see *WN* III.iii.15, 406–7).

The kings struggled for centuries without success to limit the power of the lords, Smith writes, "but what all the violence of the feudal institutions could never have effected, the silent and insensible operation of foreign commerce and manufactures gradually brought about" (*WN* III.iv.10, 418). Once luxuries were introduced, the lords finally had something on which to spend their wealth other than the maintenance of their dependents; these goods gave them a way to spend their wealth on themselves alone, one which they immediately adopted out of greed and vanity. Thus, "for a pair of diamond buckles perhaps, or for something as frivolous and useless, they exchanged the maintenance, or what is the same thing, the price of the maintenance of a thousand men for a year, and with it the whole weight and authority which it could give them" (*WN* III.iv.10, 418–19). Once the lords began to spend the bulk of their wealth on luxuries, in other words, they could no longer afford to keep their dependents. And once their dependents were dismissed, Smith writes,

> the great proprietors were no longer capable of interrupting the regular execution of justice, or of disturbing the peace of the country. Having sold their birth-right, not like Esau for a mess of pottage in a time of hunger and necessity, but in the wantonness of plenty, for trinkets and baubles, fitter to be the play-things of children than the serious pursuits of men, they became as insignificant as any substantial burgher or tradesman in a city. A regular government was established in the country as well as in the city, nobody having sufficient power to disturb its operations in the one, any more than in the other. (*WN* III.iv.15, 421; see also *LJ*, 264)

The decline in the power of the lords resulted in an enormous increase in the power of the kings, who were then able to establish a "regular government," meaning one that was strong enough to enforce order and administer justice throughout the country.[24] This is how the rule of law came to be enforced with reasonable fairness in most modern commercial nations, according to Smith, to the point where "in the present state of Europe, the

---

24. A number of thinkers in the Scottish Enlightenment related similar stories about how the introduction of luxuries led the feudal lords to dismiss their dependents and thereby made possible a more effective administration of justice; among the most prominent of these accounts were those of Smith's best friend, David Hume, and best student, John Millar. See, for example, Hume, *The History of England*, vol. 3, 76–77; *The History of England*, vol. 4, 383–85; "Of Refinement in the Arts," in *Essays*, 277; Millar, *An Historical View of the English Government*, in Lehman, *John Millar of Glasgow*, 375–78; and *The Origin of the Distinction of Ranks*, in Lehman, *John Millar of Glasgow*, 290–91.

proprietor of a single acre of land is as perfectly secure of his possession as the proprietor of a hundred thousand" (*WN* III.ii.4, 384; see also *LJ*, 55). Even more important than the fact that people are secure in their possessions, however, is the fact that they themselves feel sufficiently protected: "in modern commercial nations . . . the authority of law is always perfectly sufficient to protect the meanest man in the state" (*TMS* VI.ii.1.13, 223).

Of course, the downfall of the lords did not result in anything near economic equality, but Smith argues that inequalities in many ways *matter* less in commercial society because they do not result in personal dependence. Great wealth may give the rich a great deal of purchasing power, but (unlike in earlier societies) it does not give them any direct authority over others since everyone stands in a market relationship with everyone else and there are generally a multitude of potential buyers, sellers, and employers (see *WN* I.v.3, 48).[25] "Each tradesman or artificer derives his subsistence from the employment, not of one, but of a hundred or a thousand different customers," Smith writes, and thus "though in some measure obliged to them all . . . he is not absolutely dependent upon any one of them" (*WN* III.iv.12, 420; see also V.i.b.7, 712). Wealthy individuals in commercial society frequently support many others *indirectly* by employing them or by buying goods that they produce, of course, but Smith argues that this indirect support is not enough to place these people at their command; even if employees are likely to try to please their employers in order to keep their jobs, it is highly unlikely that they would surrender their rights to them or accompany them into battle, for example (see *LJ*, 50, 202; *WN* III.iv.14, 421). In the words of Knud Haakonssen, "the modern economy enables [the working poor] to sell their labour without selling themselves."[26]

25. Or, at least, there would generally be a multitude of potential buyers, sellers, and employers under the "system of natural liberty," in Smith's view; the fact that merchants and manufacturers are able to use their great wealth to maintain monopolies is of course one of his chief complaints against the mercantile system.

26. Haakonssen, "Adam Smith," in *The Routledge Encyclopedia of Philosophy*, vol. 8, 820; see also Griswold, *Adam Smith and the Virtues of Enlightenment*, 299. Smith is also well aware, however, that there is often an asymmetry between employers and workers in negotiating terms of employment; hence, he denounces combinations of employers and implicitly supports combinations of workers (i.e., trade unions) to combat them (see *WN* I.viii.12–13, 83–85). For the opposite argument, that Smith is insufficiently sensitive to Rousseau's (and Marx's) argument that the great inequalities and resulting asymmetries in bargaining positions in commercial society can lead to an important kind of unfreedom or enslavement among the workers (coercion by material necessity), see Neuhouser, "*Wealth of Nations* and Social Science," 235–36. Finally, for a (to my mind persuasive) rebuttal of Neuhouser's claim that also focuses on Smith and Rousseau, see Fleischacker, "On Adam Smith's 'Wealth of Nations': Response," 252–54.

Once the people were no longer personally dependent on the lords, then, they not only enjoyed greater security (because the rule of law was enforced by the king) but also greater freedom or discretion, such as the choice of where to live and what occupation to practice. It was only after people gained this kind of freedom of choice, Smith says, that they "became really free in our present sense of the word Freedom" (WN III.iii.5, 400). Whereas Rousseau seems to decry any kind of dependence on others,[27] Smith argues that it is impossible for people to be *entirely* independent in *any* society—human beings are simply not self-sufficient creatures—and that the key is rather to prevent direct, personal dependence on another individual in the way that the serfs were dependent on their lords in feudal Europe. Once this objective was realized with the onset of commercial society, a good deal of liberty and security were, for essentially the first time in history, extended to an entire society.

Alexis de Tocqueville would later famously claim that despite their economic and political subservience, the serfs of medieval Europe were actually in some ways better off than people in commercial society are because they were not driven by the same incessant drive to better their condition. Just as the aristocrats in these societies "are not preoccupied with material well-being because they possess it without trouble," he writes, the lower classes "do not think about it because they despair of acquiring it and because they are not familiar enough with it to desire it."[28] In other words, Tocqueville argues that the serfs knew their situation could not substantially change and so eventually became reconciled to their poverty and insignificance. People in commercial societies, on the other hand, face no legal barriers confining them to their current station and so continually have their eyes set on more and more wealth and prestige, and according to Tocqueville their boundless desires undermine their happiness in precisely the way that Rousseau—and indeed Smith himself—so forcefully describes.

Smith's response to Tocqueville's argument would, I think, be twofold. First, Smith would argue that the desire of bettering one's condition is an integral component of human nature and so could not be as easily curbed

27. Rousseau does depict some instances in which dependence does not have negative effects, such as that of Emile on his tutor and that of a true citizen on the community or the general will, but the negative effects are absent in these instances only because Emile and the citizen are deceived into *feeling* independent by the manipulation of the tutor and the legislator (see footnote 46 in Chapter 1). In other words, any *felt* dependence is alienating, according to Rousseau.

28. Tocqueville, *Democracy in America*, 507.

or eliminated as Tocqueville seems to assume. Smith stresses that this desire is ultimately a result of people's natural concern for others' opinions—their desire for sympathy or approbation (see *TMS* I.iii.2.1, 50)—and this concern presumably cannot be eliminated by any political or economic situation. In other words, even if the serfs' desire to better their condition in the feudal age was not displayed as visibly as it is by most people in commercial society because it was not afforded the same kind of outlet, the desire itself was still present and still disrupted their tranquility. Second, while Smith agrees with Tocqueville that the ability to reconcile oneself to one's situation is a key ingredient of tranquility and happiness (see *TMS* III.3.30–33, 149–51), he maintains that insecurity and personal dependence are circumstances to which people cannot simply reconcile themselves. The serfs were utterly dependent on the caprice of another person, and in this kind of situation "life and fortune are altogether precarious," and thus attaining tranquility seems extraordinarily unlikely (*LJ*, 414).

The fact that people constantly strive for meaningless luxuries, then, turns out to in some ways be a crucial *advantage* of commercial society, in Smith's view, for if there were no luxuries, or if people were not inclined to strive for them in order to show them off, then the wealthy would instead be likely to spend their money on maintaining vast numbers of dependents. Smith never tires of asserting that owning slaves—which is essentially what the tenants and retainers were, in feudal Europe (see *LJ*, 48, 189)—is in reality unprofitable, since slaves have no incentive to work hard (see *ED*, 579; *LJ*, 185, 191, 453, 523, 526; *WN* I.viii.41, 99; III.ii.9, 387–88; IV.ix.47, 684), but he also acknowledges that a purely financial incentive would not alone be sufficient to bring about an end to slavery because people's natural "love of domination and authority over others" tends to be even stronger than the profit motive (*LJ*, 192; see also 186–87, 452; *WN* III.ii.10, 388). The desire to fulfill one's vanity seems to be, on Smith's account, the only desire strong enough to counter the desire to oppress others.[29] It is only because the desire to gain the esteem of others "is, perhaps, the strongest of all our desires" and because people thus have an "altogether endless" desire for luxuries that their desire to dominate their dependents can be transformed into the comparatively less harmful desire to show off their wealth—that domination can be replaced by ostentation (*TMS* VI.i.3, 212–13; *WN* I.xi.c.7, 181).

In the kind of ironic twist so typical of Smith's writings, then, it seems

---

29. See Lewis, "Persuasion, Domination and Exchange," 286–89.

that people's mistaken view of happiness, which leads them to try to find satisfaction in material goods and in the fulfillment of their vanity, *does* in fact tend to promote their happiness, albeit for very different reasons than they expect. While people will find little true happiness in material goods themselves, their tendency to strive for these goods plays a crucial role in paving the way toward liberty and security and thereby removing the great obstacles to happiness that had so dominated precommercial societies.

4. THE QUESTION OF SMITH ON GOVERNMENT

The main reason Smith advocates commerce and commercial society, we have seen, is that commerce paves the way toward "order and good government, and with them, the liberty and security of individuals" (*WN* III.iv.4, 412). Yet Smith gives surprisingly few specific indications of what form of government he thinks would best protect and promote the liberty and security that constitute his central aim.[30] It is clear that Smith thinks a government should permit free trade, maintain order and stability, and operate under the rule of law, for instance, but he does not put much emphasis on precisely what form such a government ought to take. He offers only a few scattered hints about his political preferences in *The Wealth of Nations* and his *Lectures on Jurisprudence*, so we must try to reconstruct his politics based on these hints in order to fully answer the question raised above, that of what kind of society Smith thinks best promotes people's happiness by providing them with liberty and security.

In one of the most widely cited articles ever written on Smith, Duncan Forbes christens him a "sceptical" Whig, meaning that for Smith "what matters, and the true end of government, is liberty, but liberty in the sense of the Civilians and Grotius, Pufendorf, and the authoritative exponents of natural law: the personal liberty and security of individuals guaranteed by law, equivalent to justice, peace, order, the protection of property, the sanctity of contracts."[31] According to Forbes, Smith's "sceptical" Whiggism stands in contrast to ordinary or "vulgar" Whiggism, which held to "the parochial

---

30. Among the most prominent works that attempt to draw out the character of Smith's politics from the evidence available are Forbes, "Sceptical Whiggism, Commerce, and Liberty," in *Essays on Adam Smith;* Haakonssen, *The Science of a Legislator;* and Winch, *Adam Smith's Politics.*

31. See Forbes, "Sceptical Whiggism, Commerce, and Liberty," 184; see also "'Scientific' Whiggism."

absurdity that absolute monarchies could not be a proper form of government."[32] In other words, Forbes claims that Smith is far less concerned with the form a government takes than that it achieves security under the rule of law; he is to a large degree "indifferent" as to whether it is an absolute monarchy or a mixed or representative government that achieves this security.[33] While we will see that this label is not entirely apt since Smith *does* express a preference—infrequently but unambiguously—for mixed or representative government, it *is* true that he applauds the absolute monarchies that arose throughout Europe on the heels of the feudal age for establishing a "regular government" able to effectively enforce order and administer justice (*WN* III.iv.15, 421). Whereas "the nobility are the greatest opposers and oppressors of liberty that we can imagine," Smith argues in this context, "in an absolute government . . . the greatest part of the nation, who were in the remote parts of the kingdom, had nothing to fear, nor were in any great danger of being oppressed by the sovereign" (*LJ*, 264). Indeed, Smith seems to be referring to these monarchies when he speaks of the "order and good government, and with them, the liberty and security of individuals" that were introduced by the rise of commerce (*WN* III.iv.4, 412).

The fact that Smith praises these governments for providing liberty and security helps controvert the argument, made by a number of prominent scholars, that Smith in truth sees no necessary connection between commerce and the emergence of liberty. Forbes himself contends, for instance, that according to Smith "one cannot have freedom without commerce and manufactures, but opulence without freedom is the norm rather than the exception."[34] Yet this suggestion seems to be belied by the emphasis Smith places on the connection between commerce and liberty—recall yet again his emphatic claim that the introduction of liberty and security is *by far* the most important of *all* of commerce's effects. And the downfall of the feudal lords is not the only instance in which commerce has this kind of effect in Smith's corpus: he tells nearly the identical story regarding the decline of the temporal power of the clergy in medieval Europe and the decline of the nobles' power in Athens and Rome (see *LJ*, 227; *LRBL*, 150; *WN* V.i.g.22–25, 800–804). Indeed, he claims that "such effects must always flow from such causes," meaning that whenever commerce progresses to the point where a great deal of luxuries are introduced, the political power of the

---

32. Forbes, "Sceptical Whiggism, Commerce, and Liberty," 184.
33. Ibid., 198.
34. Ibid., 201; see also 199. A similar argument is made in Winch, *Adam Smith's Politics*, 86.

wealthy will "necessarily" decline, the people will come to be largely independent of them, and the sovereign will have the power to enforce order and the rule of law (*WN* III.iv.8, 416; *LJ*, 264; see also *LJ*, 261, 264, 333, 410, 420; *WN* III.iv.10, 418; V.i.b.7, 712). This outcome had been realized in most of the nations of western Europe, according to Smith, including Britain, France, Spain, and Portugal (see *LJ*, 263–65)—the only large nations that he explicitly dubs "commercial" (see *WN* IV.i.5–6, 431).[35]

It is important here to differentiate the effects that Smith attributes to the downfall of the feudal lords from the subsequent effects that he attributes to a confluence of other circumstances in Britain. Britain *was* something of an atypical case, for Smith: while an absolute monarchy arose there under the Tudors, just as it did in the other countries of western Europe (see *LJ*, 262, 264–65), in Britain the king's power did not remain absolute. Because it was an island and so relatively secure from invasion, especially after the Union between England and Scotland in 1707, no standing army was necessary, so the king's power over the people was not as great as that of the kings on the Continent (see *LJ*, 265–66, 270, 421). An even more idiosyncratic cause of the decline of royal power in Britain was that Queen Elizabeth sold off most of the Crown's lands, in part because she had no direct heirs; for that reason, her Stuart successors were forced to appeal to Parliament to raise taxes. Since the power of the Lords had already declined by this time, the increased importance of taxes naturally gave much greater power to the Commons (see *LJ*, 266–67, 270, 420–21). The absolute monarchy in Britain was thus gradually replaced by a mixed government in which the king, the nobles, and especially the people all had important roles. "In this manner," Smith maintains, "a rational system of liberty has been introduced into Brittain. . . . Here is a happy mixture of all the different forms of government properly restrained and a perfect security to liberty and property" (*LJ*, 421–22).

A similar "system of liberty" had not yet arisen in the other countries of Europe, according to Smith, and while he maintains that the rule of law

35. The one exception Smith noted to the rule described above was Germany, a region that he *does not* call "commercial" and that he indicated was in many ways still in the feudal stage (see *LJ*, 230, 252–53, *WN* III.ii.8, 387). In Germany a number of unusual circumstances—its large territory, its elective rather than hereditary monarchy, and the greatness of the fortunes of the nobility—kept the country from being united under a single authoritative government. Even here, however, Smith contended that commerce had advanced far enough that the sizable dominions of each noble or prince had grown to be nearly independent countries, each with a regular, absolute government of its own (see *LJ*, 263–65, 420).

tends to develop along with extensive commerce (see *LJ*, 16, 205, 213, 313–14), he offers little indication of whether or not commerce will eventually bring mixed or representative government to the Continent (or to the rest of the world, for that matter), or whether he thinks they will remain constitutional monarchies. Yet even if commerce does not always lead to mixed or representative government, on Smith's account, it *does* always lead to the earlier step: the decline in the power of the nobles and the strengthening of the sovereign's capacity to maintain order and stability. As we have seen, Smith argues that this outcome had already occurred in all the commercial societies of his time. And even the absolute monarchies on the Continent and in Britain under the Tudors constituted no small improvement over the feudal age with respect to liberty and security, in his eyes, for the dissipation of the lords' wealth on luxuries led to advances such as a decline in personal dependence, a more effective administration of justice, and the development of the rule of law. The inhabitants of these societies were "really free in our present sense of the word Freedom" (*WN* III.iii.5, 400); *all* commercial societies enjoy a greater degree of liberty and security than precommercial societies did, according to Smith, so there *does* seem to be a necessary connection between commerce and the emergence of liberty.

Just because Smith sees absolute monarchy as a great improvement over the tyranny of the feudal lords, however, does not mean that he endorses this form of government wholeheartedly. Smith sees absolute monarchy as a *legitimate* form of government and as an important historical step forward, but it is fairly clear that he *does not* see it as the best form of government; on the contrary, he consistently shows a preference for the mixed or representative government of Britain over the absolute monarchies that prevailed in Spain, Portugal, and France in his day. He maintains, for instance, that "though the feudal system has been abolished in Spain and Portugal, it has not been succeeded by a much better" (*WN* I.xi.n.1, 256; see also IV.v.b.45, 541; IV.vii.b.6, 567). He holds the French monarchy in slightly higher regard, but still sees it as decidedly inferior to the British government: the French regime, while "legal and free in comparison with those of Spain and Portugal," is "arbitrary and violent in comparison with that of Great Britain" (*WN* IV.vii.b.52, 586; see also V.ii.k.78, 905).

Smith's praise for the liberty and security provided by the British mixed government, on the other hand, is often effusive. He claims, for example, that "the yeomanry of England are . . . as secure, as independent, and as respectable as law can make them" (*WN* III.iv.20, 425), that an "equal and impartial administration of justice . . . renders the rights of the meanest British subject respectable to the greatest" (*WN* IV.vii.c.54, 610; see also IV.v.b.43, 540), and that "the liberty of the subject is . . . as well provided for in Great Britain as in any other country" (*LJ*, 121). Lest anyone think these statements are purely a reflection of parochial bias, Smith puts Britain's government under the Tudors, when *it* was an absolute monarchy, on a par with the other monarchies of Europe and claims that it was only after the House of Commons gained some authority that "liberty was restored" in Britain (*LJ*, 420; see also 262, 264).

Here, then, is the problem with Forbes's "sceptical" Whig label: even if Smith sees absolute monarchy as a legitimate form of government, he plainly prefers the British mixed government to the monarchies found on the Continent in his time, meaning that he is not in any way "indifferent" as to the form a government takes. In his *Lectures on Jurisprudence*, in fact, he devotes several lectures to showing how Britain's government provides numerous "securities for liberty" that are not found in absolute monarchies (see especially *LJ*, 265–87, 420–26). Smith approves of the fact that there is not only a division of authority among the different orders or social classes in Britain—the monarch, the Lords, and the Commons—but also a separation of powers or functions into different branches. The separation of the judicial from the executive power is particularly important to Smith, for "when the judicial is united to the executive power, it is scarce possible that justice should not be frequently sacrificed to, what is vulgarly called, politics" (*WN* V.i.b.25, 722; see also *LRBL*, 176). Hence, Smith argues that judges should be made as independent from the executive as possible, that they should hold their tenure for life (see *LJ*, 271, 422; *WN* V.i.b.25, 723), that they should rule based on a set of standing laws that apply equally to all individuals (see *TMS* VII.iv.36, 340), that cases should be tried before impartial juries (see *LJ*, 283, 425), and that there should be as many protections for accused persons as is feasible, such as an assumption of innocence, the privilege of habeas corpus, and a bail system for all noncapital crimes (see *LJ*, 122, 272, 422, 480).

Smith also contends that representation is a key element of a good political order. He argues, for instance, that in Britain "the frequency of elections is . . . a great security for the liberty of the people, as the representative must be carefull to serve his country, at least his constituents, otherwise he will be in danger of losing his place at the next elections" (*LJ*, 273; see also 422). Whereas the Lords tend to focus mostly on "aggrandizing their families and fortunes . . . the Commons on the other hand must have a respect to the voice of the people and to the good will of their constituents" since "their authority depends on it" (*LJ*, 271). Hence, he notes approvingly that the House of Commons has "by far the greatest and most considerable share" of Parliament's power and that its endorsement is necessary to pass almost any law, to raise taxes, or to go to war (*LJ*, 271; see also 266–67, 421; *WN* IV.vii.b.51, 585). Moreover, Smith applauds England for having less stringent property requirements for voting than Scotland (see *LJ*, 273–74, 323, 435, 524), and he looks favorably on the fact that the American colonial governments were based on an even wider franchise than England and that they had never had a hereditary nobility (see *WN* IV.vii.b.51, 584–85; V.iii.90, 944).

Smith *does* ultimately seem to defend a combination of a representative legislature and a hereditary monarchy rather than a wholly elective government (see *WN* IV.vii.c.78, 625), but most of the (admittedly scarce) hints in his writings regarding his views on government point toward the importance of representation and a widespread franchise. Donald Winch complains of some scholarly works that they look at Smith's writings from such a present-day perspective that "at any moment, one feels, the argument is about to turn into a discussion of universal suffrage—an issue which was not even academic for Smith."[36] Yet there is nothing in Smith's writings that is *incompatible* with widening the franchise indefinitely, and as Griswold writes, "the logic of his system of natural liberty pushes in the direction of a democratic political scheme, if only for a prudential reason—namely, that of controlling the sovereign and minimizing the abuse of power which Smith everywhere predicts."[37]

Before concluding this section on Smith's politics, we should perhaps take a brief look at the range of functions that he argues a government ought to assume. He famously claims that under his "system of natural liberty," the sovereign only has three duties—"three duties of great importance, indeed, but plain and intelligible to common understandings":

> First, the duty of protecting the society from the violence and invasion of other independent societies; secondly, the duty of protecting, as far as possible, every member of the society from the injustice or oppression of every other member of it, or the duty of establishing

36. Winch, *Adam Smith's Politics*, 85.
37. Griswold, *Adam Smith and the Virtues of Enlightenment*, 307.

> an exact administration of justice; and, thirdly, the duty of erecting
> and maintaining certain publick works and certain publick insti-
> tutions, which it can never be for the interest of any individual, or a
> small number of individuals, to erect and maintain. (*WN* IV.ix.51,
> 687–88)

The reader is immediately struck, of course, by the brevity of this list, but
Smith's vision of the role of the state is not quite as limited as this might
seem to suggest. We have seen throughout this chapter how utterly important the first two tasks—defense and the administration of justice—are in
Smith's eyes, and he recognizes that the state must be relatively powerful
in order to carry them out effectively. (He praises the authoritative governments that arose after the fall of the feudal lords for precisely this reason.)
Under the third heading, public works, Smith includes tasks such as the
building and maintenance of infrastructure (highways, bridges, canals, harbors), the coining of money, and the operation of a post office (see *WN*
V.i.d.1–3, 724). The public work that Smith discusses at by far the greatest
length, though, is education—another task whose centrality in Smith's
thought we have already noted.

The extent of the government's duties under Smith's "system of natural
liberty" might seem rather limited even given the great weight he places on
defense, the administration of justice, and education, but this should not
be taken to imply that Smith was rigidly opposed to government in general,
as a common view of him assumes. Rather, as the context of the passage
quoted above makes clear, Smith's limitation of the functions of government was meant to drive home his larger argument against certain types
of government interference in the economic realm under mercantilism—
legal monopolies, bounties, duties, outright trade prohibitions, apprentice-
ship laws, settlement laws, laws of primogeniture and entail, and so on. He
was mainly concerned with limiting *these* kinds of government activities,
not government activity in general.[38] Indeed, Smith devotes the first chapter
of Book V of *The Wealth of Nations*—well over one hundred pages—as well
as substantial sections of his *Lectures on Jurisprudence* to arguing that the
government and its functions must expand as society progresses. (Remember also that Smith himself took a government position as a customs offi-
cer during the last decade of his life.) Fleischacker goes so far as to assert

---

38. See Viner, "Adam Smith and Laissez Faire," in *Adam Smith*, 139.

that Smith's formulation of the government's duty to provide public works "is broad enough to include practically all the tasks that modern welfare liberals, as opposed to libertarians, would put under government purview," including "public housing, health care, unemployment insurance, and much else."[39] This might be a bit of an overstatement, given that Smith does not explicitly advocate any governmental duties even remotely this far-reaching (with the only possible exception being education), but it does help underline the fact that Smith was not the doctrinaire advocate of a minimalist or "night-watchman" state that he is often thought to be. Free trade by no means requires weak government.[40]

In sum, we have seen that, contra Forbes and others who see Smith as to some degree "indifferent" about the form a government takes, Smith endorses a mixed government with a strong representative branch and separation of powers, one that is powerful enough to enforce order and administer justice but that carries out a relatively limited range of functions. He explicitly argues for this form of government because he thinks it affords the greatest protections for people's liberty and security, and we have also seen that he thinks liberty and security are the key prerequisites for promoting people's happiness. On Smith's view, in short, a commercial society with this form of government, while far from faultless, allows people to lead the happiest lives.

CONCLUSION

Smith's decisive argument for commercial society, we have seen, is that it makes possible a better political order. While commerce might not always lead to a mixed or representative government, Smith sees it as a necessary precondition for the emergence of this kind of government. Furthermore, extensive commerce *does* always lead to a greater degree of liberty and security than was available in precommercial societies, on his view, since the dissipation of the political power of the wealthy leads to advances such as a decrease in personal dependence, the development of the rule of law, and a more effective administration of justice. And these improvements are

---

39. Fleischacker, *On Adam Smith's Wealth of Nations*, 234–35. Other recent works that stress the egalitarian, social democratic side of Smith include Kennedy, *Adam Smith's Lost Legacy;* and McLean, *Adam Smith, Radical and Egalitarian.*

40. See also footnote 34 in Chapter 3.

crucial ingredients in promoting people's happiness: while the vast major-ity of human history has been a story of dependence and insecurity, these key obstacles to happiness are finally alleviated in commercial society. Peo-ple in this kind of society are unlikely to be *completely* happy since they *do* tend to undermine their own tranquility by constantly striving to better their condition, but then again this is true of people in *every* society, and the in-habitants of other societies generally face other significant hardships that people in commercial society are able to escape.[41] Scholars often quote the passage in *The Wealth of Nations* to the effect that "commerce and manu-factures gradually introduced order and good government, and with them, the liberty and security of individuals" and that this "is by far the most important of all their effects" (*WN* III.iv.4, 412)—presumably because of its unusually strong phrasing—but very few have given the argument in this passage the central consideration that Smith indicates it deserves. As we have seen, the fact that commerce leads to liberty and security is the ulti-mate solution to the fundamental puzzle of Smith's thought—the ques-tion of why he advocates commercial society despite his sympathy with the many arguments against it.

41. None of this is to say, of course, that Smith thinks there is nothing individuals can do *within* commercial society to increase their chances of attaining happiness. Indeed, James Otteson has argued persuasively that the entire moral system outlined in *The Theory of Moral Sentiments* is designed to show Smith's readers how to do exactly that; because Smith sees warranted approbation as a key component of happiness, Otteson argues, the "meta-argument" of this work "takes the form of a hypothetical imperative: if you wish to obtain a tranquil and happy psychological state, then you should abide by the system of morality that has arisen nat-urally and unintentionally in the way described in TMS." Otteson, *Adam Smith's Marketplace of Life*, 236.

CONCLUSION

The fundamental puzzle in Adam Smith's thought, I have contended, consists of the fact that he simultaneously concedes a good deal of validity to each of Rousseau's rather severe critiques of commercial society and also resolutely defends this kind of society. Smith provides a number of different counterarguments and countermeasures for a number of the problems that Rousseau points to, but the ultimate solution to this puzzle—the key line of reasoning running through most of Smith's arguments—is that while commercial society is far from perfect, all other forms of society are even *less* perfect. Given the enormous economic, moral, and (especially) political drawbacks of *pre*commercial societies, he reasons, it is difficult to see commercial society as anything but a step forward, its very real imperfections notwithstanding. This kind of historical assessment is a—perhaps *the*—central element of Smith's defense of commercial society, for as Charles Griswold writes, "one's affirmation of a particular theory of political economy must be informed by an appreciation of its virtues relative to the competition, and these must be understood at least in part through historical analysis."[1] Rather than simply claiming that commercial society is good or bad, Smith constantly asks, "In comparison to what?"

We have seen throughout this book that the popular caricature of Smith as a crude, dogmatic defender of commercial society is far from adequate; this is not so much because he does not think commercial society is worthy of defending—he does—as because he is rarely dogmatic about *anything*. Contrary to what caricatures of Smith might suggest, his writings tend to shy away from sweeping theories or broad generalizations; as Samuel Fleischacker writes, Smith is "perhaps the most empirical of all the empiricists, pursuing his version of 'the science of man' in a particularly messy,

---

1. Griswold, *Adam Smith and the Virtues of Enlightenment*, 256. For a helpful discussion about how Smith differed from Rousseau with respect to the necessity of relying on historical analysis, see Fleischacker, "On Adam Smith's 'Wealth of Nations': Response," 253–54.

fact-laden rather than theory-laden way."[2] His defense of commercial society rests on a kind of cost–benefit analysis, not an abstract, ideological argument. Smith's most enthusiastic defenders *and* most fervent critics tend to paint him as a kind of free-market ideologue, but actually he is no ideologue of any kind: his defense of commercial society is pragmatic and prudential, not foundationalist or principled (unlike, for instance, Locke's defense of liberalism). This is why he repeatedly acknowledges the downsides of commercial society and insists that it can be improved upon. In misunderstanding the character of Smith's approach, his admirers and critics alike have turned him into the very "man of system" whom he criticizes so severely (*TMS* VI.ii.2.17, 233). Hence, taking a more careful look at the nature of his writings helps cut through some of the partisan uses of his thought.

Smith's thought has been so regularly misunderstood not only because it is often examined with a partisan agenda in mind, but also because it is often put into a false context, a process that Stephen Holmes calls "antonym substitution." Instead of reading the works of seventeenth- and eighteenth-century classical liberal thinkers to see what they were actually arguing against, Holmes points out, opponents of liberalism often contrast liberal ideas with antonyms of their own choosing. Thus, whereas classical liberals like Smith advocated competition over and against monopoly, their critics often denigrate competition by contrasting it instead to brotherly love. Similarly, these critics contrast rights with duties rather than with tyranny and slavery; they contrast private property with charity rather than with princely confiscation; they contrast liberal individualism with public-spiritedness and harmonious community rather than with premodern villages, sects, clans, and tribes, which tended to be parochial, intolerant, and authoritarian; and so on.[3] In so changing the context, these critics make it difficult to imagine how someone like Smith could have defended commercial society; indeed, by portraying him as an enemy of almost any kind of community or goodwill toward others they render his thought virtually unintelligible. A recovery of the context in which Smith actually wrote—an eighteenth-century European world that had only recently escaped the demeaning relations of dependence of the feudal age—can help us make sense of his position and appreciate the purpose of his arguments.

We might go further here and put Smith's response to Rousseau in the

---

2. Fleischacker, *On Adam Smith's Wealth of Nations*, 271.
3. Holmes, *The Anatomy of Antiliberalism*, 253–56.

form of a series of antonym substitutions. Whereas Rousseau contrasts the great economic inequalities of commercial society with the simple uniformity of the state of nature and with the radically democratic society he advocates in *The Social Contract,* Smith contrasts those same inequalities with hunting and gathering societies, where everyone was poor and vulnerable, and with feudal societies, where the serfs were utterly dependent on the caprice of their lords. Whereas Rousseau contrasts the self-interestedness and vanity of most inhabitants of commercial society with the virtuous citizens of *The Social Contract* and with Emile's ingrained honesty and decency, Smith contrasts them instead with the tendencies he sees toward callousness and inhumanity among hunters and gatherers, toward obsequiousness and submissiveness among feudal serfs, and toward domination and arrogance among feudal lords. And whereas Rousseau contrasts people's desire for more and more in commercial society with the idyllic contentment of the state of nature and with his own blissful reveries, Smith contrasts that same desire with the continual fears and anxieties of impoverished hunters and gatherers and with the dependence and misery of oppressed serfs.

Putting Smith's response to Rousseau in this form oversimplifies it, certainly, for Smith does not simply take Rousseau's account of commercial society as given. For instance, he takes issue with the idea that everyone in commercial society will necessarily be the "smiling enemies" Rousseau describes, and he argues that the privations of this kind of society can be alleviated through various countermeasures. But a substantial part of Smith's argument *is* captured in these antonym substitutions: he agrees with Rousseau that commercial society has a number of shortcomings but sees the antonyms Rousseau opposes to them as naive and utterly impracticable—a charge that Rousseau himself largely concedes[4]—and he defends commercial society by pointing instead to some more realistic (and far less attractive) alternatives.

Of course, we do not have to simply accept Smith's historical assessments; we can ask the same question today that he asked in the eighteenth century—"In comparison to what?"—and consider commercial society's record over the past two centuries and more since he lived and wrote, in relation not only to precommercial societies but also to the alternatives to commercial society that were advocated and implemented in the twentieth

---

4. See Chapter 1, Section 6, for a summary of the evidence that Rousseau sees all of the possible "escape routes" from commercial society in his writings—the society of *The Social Contract,* his own life, and Emile's life—as ultimately impracticable in the modern world.

century. A cost–benefit analysis of this kind, I think, largely confirms Smith's claim that commercial society's balance sheet is on the whole preferable to the historical alternatives. Let's briefly revisit each of the main elements of Smith's argument in turn.

With respect to the most famous part of Smith's defense of commercial society—the idea that it creates unprecedented prosperity—the jury has been in for quite a while now: Smith was quite simply right. Today's commercial societies, when compared to their own precommercial past or to other societies around the globe today, enjoy an extraordinary level of affluence. Indeed, the average person in today's commercial societies enjoys a standard of living that is likely beyond even Smith's wildest dreams. In the Europe of his time, most people performed some type of physical labor from sunrise to sunset; education was minimal and most people were illiterate (Scotland was the only exception here); water supplies were unreliable, and severe food shortages occurred around once a generation; meager sanitation measures were incapable of preventing disease, and refuse and smog choked city streets (Edinburgh was known as "Auld Reekie" in Smith's day); long-distance travel and communication were slow, difficult, and unreliable even during the summer, and roads were often impassable during the winter. Perhaps most tellingly of all, life expectancy in late-eighteenth-century Western Europe was less than *one-third* of what it is now due to high infant mortality rates and the general lack of effective medicines (around twenty-five years compared to over seventy-five today).[5] And remember that the standard of living in these emerging commercial societies of eighteenth-century Europe was rightly regarded as a massive *improvement* over the agricultural societies they replaced, not to mention even more primitive societies. The fact that even these difficulties and hardships seem so inconceivable to those of us living in the modern West stands as a tribute to commercial society's continuing ability to produce unparalleled prosperity.

This ability comes as no surprise, however, for even commercial society's critics, like Rousseau and Marx, concede that commercial society tends to produce a great deal of wealth. Just as important and far less often observed by the critics, however, is the fact that the differences in living conditions between the rich and the poor actually shrink in comparison to most earlier societies despite the highly unequal distribution of wealth, for the most

5. See Caton, *The Politics of Progress*, 15; Gay, *The Enlightenment*, vol. 2, 4–5, 20–21; and United Nations Development Programme, *Human Development Report 2005*, 250–53. More generally, see Fogel, *The Escape from Hunger and Premature Death*.

important benefits tend to be extended to the vast majority of the population. *Most* people in today's commercial societies live to a ripe old age and have access to a formal education, safe water, plentiful and varied foods, effective medicines, and relatively quick and easy communication and transportation. The rich might often be the *first* beneficiaries of rising living standards and advances in technology, but these advances are nearly always extended to the vast majority of the people over time. And even if the poor in commercial society do not have the same opportunities as the rich (and they certainly do not), they have much greater freedom to shape their lives—to choose where to live, what occupation to practice, and so on—than the poor do in other societies. Great economic inequalities notwithstanding, then, the differences in lifespan and lifestyle between the rich and the poor in today's commercial societies are probably smaller than in all but the most primitive precommercial societies.

Furthermore, one of Smith's major worries about commercial society—that the division of labor would lead, in the words of Joseph Cropsey, to "the generation of a tremendous industrial mob, deprived of nearly every admirable human quality"[6]—has not, by and large, come to pass. As commercial societies have developed from manufacturing-based economies to service- and information-based economies, the kind of manual, repetitive occupations that so concerned Smith have mostly been supplanted by technological innovations or transferred to developing nations, which use them to develop their own economies in turn. Moreover, the remedy that Smith proposed to help alleviate this problem—universal, government-supported education—has been unanimously adopted by today's commercial societies, and to great effect: these societies almost all have adult literacy rates approaching 100 percent, with the vast majority of people receiving a secondary education and rapidly increasing numbers receiving the equivalent of a college education.[7] All told, there is little question that the average inhabitant of today's commercial societies is better and more broadly educated than all but the most privileged members of most precommercial societies. And while it is doubtful that most of us possess the ruggedness or martial vigor of our early forebears, Smith seems to have been right to claim that the development of military technology and professional armies can more than make up for this limitation when it comes to national defense. The experiences of

6. Cropsey, *Polity and Economy*, 146.
7. See UNDP, *Human Development Report 2005*, 254–61.

the nineteenth century (when the sun never set on the British Empire), the twentieth century (when the nations of the liberal West combined to defeat the forces of fascism and to fend off and outlast the forces of communism), and the early twenty-first century (when the United States has emerged as the world's only superpower) have helped dramatically refute Rousseau's prediction that commercial societies would eventually become too feeble to protect themselves.

Smith's claim that commercial society's moral balance sheet is an improvement over the historical alternatives is a bit harder to assess, for it is difficult to conclusively establish whether the members of today's commercial societies are more or less "moral" than people of the past or of other societies around the globe today. The political and economic arrangements of a society surely do affect (and are surely affected by) the morals, customs, and habits of its inhabitants, however, and there would seem to be at least a measure of truth in Smith's claim that commercial society helps encourage the "prudent" virtues such as reliability, decency, and cooperativeness.[8] The market does seem to have at least *some* restraining or disciplining effects, as nations around the world have learned when they have faced a transition from a traditional or socialist economy toward a market economy. Thomas Friedman has famously noted that these nations have found it necessary to don a "Golden Straitjacket," meaning that in order to prosper in today's global economy they have had to put an end to the endemic corruption, nepotism, cronyism, and instability that characterize many pre-commercial and socialist societies and establish a reasonably level playing field along with greater predictability, transparency, and accountability.[9]

Of course, there are certainly limits to this kind of commercial ethic, for market competition does not require or encourage any kind of universal benevolence, generosity, or goodwill. But to return to our earlier theme of antonym substitutions, Albert Hirschman has shown that the early defenders of commercial society contrasted the ultimately self-interested virtues of this kind of society not with universal benevolence but rather with a number of unruly and destructive passions that flourished in earlier societies, such as the thirst for glory among the military and aristocratic classes, intolerance fueled by religious zealotry, and instinctive hostility toward strangers

8. See, for example, Friedman, *The Moral Consequences of Economic Growth*; Fukuyama, *Trust*; and McCloskey, *The Bourgeois Virtues*.
9. See Friedman, *The Lexus and the Olive Tree*, chap. 6.

caused by group loyalty.[10] And as Jerry Muller notes, while the commercial virtues might seem somewhat lacking when viewed from the moral heights, from a historical perspective "the market's ability to create a self-interested regard for others may be preferable to the more brutal means by which self-interest has been pursued."[11] Of course, one's attitude toward the commercial virtues depends in large part on one's perspective: from an ancient Greek perspective that prizes courage and nobility or a medieval Christian perspective that prizes piety and humility, for example, virtues like reliability and cooperativeness are unlikely to be esteemed terribly highly. (It is as hard to imagine an Achilles or a Francis of Assisi working in a modern office as it is to imagine a Bill Gates or a Donald Trump as an ancient warrior or a Franciscan monk.) But even if these traditional virtues are more exalted from certain points of view, it is hard to deny that they also tend to be more unreliable and dangerous.

A stronger case can be made today for Smith's argument that commercial societies tend to provide a far greater level of liberty and security than other societies. Of course, it is easy enough to dispute Smith's specific account of how the feudal system collapsed, thereby paving the way for liberty and security. Economic historians Douglass North and Robert Thomas, for example, attribute the downfall of the feudal lords not to the dissipation of their wealth on luxuries but rather to a population decline in Western Europe in the fifteenth century (caused by the plague, recurring famines, and a series of military conflicts), which forced the lords to compete with one other to retain tenants and consequently to relax servile obligations.[12] Furthermore, no less figures than Montesquieu and Edmund Burke argued, around the same time Smith wrote, that the key to the emergence of liberty was the *presence* and *strength* of the nobility, not their downfall, for the nobility were the only force capable of checking the king and denying him absolute and arbitrary power.[13] Resolving such disputes is beyond the scope of this book, but we can note that these explanations are not mutually exclusive: it is certainly possible (indeed likely) that there was more than one cause of the decline of the feudal lords' power, and as Guido de Ruggiero

---

10. See Hirschman, *The Passions and the Interests*. For a similar argument, see Holmes, "The Secret History of Self-Interest," in *Passions and Constraint*.

11. Muller, *Adam Smith in His Time and Ours*, 195.

12. See North and Thomas, *The Rise of the Western World*, 79–80.

13. See Burke, *Reflections on the Revolution in France*, 303–4; and Montesquieu, *The Spirit of the Laws*, 18.

argues in his classic history of liberalism, the rise of liberty in Europe should not be attributed to the influence of either the kings or the nobility alone but rather to the conflict between them. He writes that "without the effective resistance of particular privileged classes, the monarchy would have created nothing but a people of slaves; without the levelling effected by royal absolutism, the régime of privilege, however widely extended, would never have bridged the gulf which divides privilege from liberty in the proper sense of the word—that liberty which universalizes privilege to the point of annulling it as such."[14]

Such details aside, however, Smith's larger point about commercial society constituting an improvement with respect to liberty and security is harder to dispute, for a great deal of evidence recently collected by anthropologists and historians essentially confirms the main outlines of Smith's broad historical sketch. First of all, contrary to the popular, romanticized image of early societies as composed of peaceful, noble savages who lived in harmony with nature and with one another, numerous studies have shown that hunter-gatherer bands in fact typically suffered from every bit as much insecurity as Smith suggests. Life was precarious in these societies for many different reasons—lack of nourishment, exposure to harsh weather, and so on—but by far the greatest cause of insecurity was the prevalence of violence and war, which we now know was astoundingly frequent, ruthless, and deadly in these societies. Indeed, when measured as a percentage of the population, casualty rates in hunter-gatherer wars were regularly many times higher than those of the United States and Europe during World Wars I and II.[15] The available evidence suggests, then, that life in these societies was much closer to Smith's account of the hunting stage as poor, nasty, brutish, and short (though, contra Hobbes, not solitary) than to a Rousseauian state of nature in which people are asocial and blissfully free of *amour-propre* and conflict.[16] Moreover, Smith's account of the next stages of society seems to be largely on the mark as well, for anthropological and historical research shows that in most societies now classified as "Big Man" collectivities and chiefdoms—which correspond roughly to the shepherding and early agricultural

---

14. Ruggiero, *The History of European Liberalism*, 3–4.

15. See, for example, Edgerton, *Sick Societies;* Ghiglieri, *The Dark Side of Man;* Keeley, *War before Civilization;* and LeBlanc, *Constant Battles.*

16. For a look at Rousseau's account of the state of nature in light of some of this recent research, see Masters, "Rousseau and the Rediscovery of Human Nature," in *The Legacy of Rousseau.*

stages in Smith's schema—the vast majority of people were almost utterly subordinated to a single "Big Man" or chief. There was generally not quite as much material privation in these societies as in hunter-gatherer bands, but as Smith pointed out and scholars have recently confirmed, the continued prevalence of war and the rise of dependence still left most people in these societies with little liberty and security by today's standards.[17]

In fact, I think we can generalize this point and say that today's commercial societies generally provide a greater combination of liberty and security for a greater percentage of their populations than *any* other form of society consistently has or does. To begin with, the economic liberties that commercial societies by definition afford their inhabitants are an important (and often underappreciated) aspect of liberty more generally; Emma Rothschild has written that "economic life is difficult or impossible to distinguish from the rest of life, and one's freedom to buy or sell or lend or travel or work is difficult to distinguish from the rest of one's freedom."[18] Ensuring that people have access to markets—particularly labor markets—has proven to be a crucial means of freeing them from bondage, as even Marx conceded in his early writings.[19] Moreover, economic liberties tend to go hand in hand with other liberties: throughout the world there is an extremely high correlation between economic freedoms (such as the freedom to compete in labor and product markets and to exchange and contract), political rights (such as the right to vote in free and fair elections and to compete for office), and civil liberties (such as the freedoms of expression, belief, and association).[20] In fact, the nations that today most fully conform to the loose definition of "commercial society" offered in the introduction—the United States, Canada, Australia, New Zealand, Japan, and the twenty-five member states of the European Union—nearly all earned a perfect

17. See, for example, Johnson and Earle, *The Evolution of Human Societies*, parts 2 and 3; Maryanski and Turner, *The Social Cage*, chaps. 5 and 6; Service, *Origins of the State and Civilization*, parts 1 and 2; and Wright, *Nonzero: The Logic of Human Destiny*, part 1. While Smith's leading example of these stages, feudal Europe, is better categorized as a state-level society than as a chiefdom under contemporary classification systems, several scholars have noted that there are numerous similarities between feudalism and typical chiefdoms, especially with regard to personal dependence. See Johnson and Earle, *The Evolution of Human Societies*, 307; Service, *Origins of the State and Civilization*, 80–82; and Wright, *Nonzero*, 141–42.

18. Rothschild, *Economic Sentiments*, 223.

19. See, for example, Marx, "The German Ideology," in *The Marx-Engels Reader*, 169.

20. For the correlation between the Fraser Institute's measure of economic freedom and Freedom House's measure of political rights and civil liberties, see Gwartney and Lawson, *Economic Freedom of the World: 2005 Annual Report*, 26.

Freedom House score in both political rights and civil liberties in 2006.[21] This is not to say that every individual in every commercial society always enjoys perfect liberty and security, of course, for this is obviously untrue. But as Robert Wright points out, our standards in this area are (happily) much higher than they once were: "Now we ask not only that people not be literally enslaved, but that they be paid a decent wage and work under sanitary conditions. Now we ask not only that dissidents not be beheaded en masse, but that they be able to say whatever they want to whomever they want."[22] The extent to which we tend to take liberty and security for granted today is a tribute to commercial society, but not to our sense of history.

Finally, contrary to the multitude of recent studies purporting to show that life in commercial society actually makes people unhappy—or at the very least no *more* happy than they are in other societies[23]—international surveys of what psychologists call "subjective well-being" find that people who live in high-income commercial nations like the ones just listed consistently rate themselves as happier than people who live in low-income nations such as those of Africa and Asia.[24] The correlation is not perfect— for instance, most of the former communist nations score lower than would be expected given their current GDP, and a number of relatively poor Latin American nations score higher than would be expected given their income levels—but taken as a whole, economic prosperity is one of the strongest predictors of national happiness. It is admittedly hard to disentangle the effects of prosperity from those of political and civil liberties and security since all of these things are so closely linked, but this is of course precisely the point: taken together, all of the benefits of commercial society do seem to make people noticeably happier.

The studies that claim that living in commercial society does not add to

21. Of these thirty nations, *all* earned perfect scores in political rights, and the only ones that did not earn a perfect score in civil liberties were Greece and Japan, both of which earned a two on a scale of one to seven (one being the most free, seven being the least free). Freedom House's rankings can be found in *Freedom in the World 2006,* www.freedomhouse.org (see references for a fuller citation).

22. Wright, *Nonzero,* 208, citation omitted.

23. See, for example, Lane, *The Loss of Happiness in Market Democracies;* Layard, *Happiness;* and Scitovsky, *The Joyless Economy.*

24. See, for example, the subjective well-being rankings of nations around the world collected in the *World Database of Happiness,* directed by Ruut Veenhoven of Erasmus University-Rotterdam, www.eur.nl/fsw/research/happiness. See also Diener and Diener, "The Wealth of Nations Revisited"; Diener and Suh, "Money and Happiness"; and Veenhoven, "Freedom and Happiness."

people's happiness base their claims on the fact that the average person in the United States, Western Europe, and Japan does not report being much happier today than in 1946 (when formal surveys of happiness started), despite the rapid economic growth these nations have experienced since that time. These studies maintain that this is because happiness depends on one's social status or *relative* wealth rather than on one's absolute standard of living, which in turn means that happiness is a zero-sum game within any given society and thus that prosperity cannot affect a society's overall level of happiness. If this were true, however, it would be difficult to explain not only why people in wealthy nations tend to be much happier than people in poor ones, but also why people's sense of well-being is more strongly affected by whether they live in a rich or poor country than by whether they are rich or poor themselves.[25]

The reason why many wealthy nations have experienced little or no appreciable gain in happiness over the past sixty years even in the face of tremendous economic growth, it seems, is that the correlation between wealth and reported happiness comes mostly from the bottom part of the income scale; it is only up to a certain threshold—somewhere around $10,000 or $20,000 per capita annual income—that more prosperity tends to produce more happiness, after which returns diminish rather rapidly.[26] But this still means that happiness is *not* a wholly relative matter, for increases in prosperity among poorer nations, at least, *do* yield significant and durable increases in happiness levels; happiness in these nations is mostly a positive-sum game, since increases in prosperity often bring with them increases in liberty and security, as well as easier access to things like adequate food, safe water, and effective health care. If these kinds of happiness surveys are to be believed, then, Smith seems to have been exactly correct in claiming that no society can simply make everyone completely happy but that commercial society does tend to *promote* people's happiness by providing

25. The happiness differences between societies could themselves be a result of relative comparisons, of course, but this is likely only a minor component of these differences: local "reference groups" seem to be much more important determinants of an individual's sense of relative well-being than distant "reference groups." In other words, the well-being of people in the world's poorest nations is likely affected by their standing vis-à-vis their own neighbors much more than by comparisons with wealthier people in the United States or Europe. See Frank, *Choosing the Right Pond*, 30–34.

26. See Easterbrook, *The Progress Paradox*, 170; Layard, *Happiness*, 34; and Wright, "Will Globalization Make You Happy?" 56.

them with liberty, security, and prosperity and thereby removing the greatest causes of *un*happiness.

In short, it seems reasonable to conclude—in the twenty-first century as in Smith's day—that commercial society *is*, on the whole, preferable to the historical alternatives. But this does not, of course, furnish any grounds for complacency in today's world. To begin with, while those of us living in today's commercial societies (which have collectively been dubbed the global "North") enjoy unprecedented levels of prosperity and freedom, billions of people in the global "South"—particularly in Africa and South Asia—remain on the outside looking in. Enormous numbers of people live in dire poverty, as evidenced by the oft-cited and heartbreaking fact that over a billion people live on less than a dollar a day. Smith lamented the living conditions of the poor in China, whose subsistence was so scanty that they were "eager to fish up the nastiest garbage thrown overboard from any European ship" (*WN* I.viii.24, 89–90); sadly, things have not changed much since the eighteenth century for many of the world's poor. And while practices such as slavery, the legal ownership of women, severe repression of minorities, and judicial cruelty have all but been eliminated from today's commercial societies, they are entirely too common in the developing world; as I write these lines in 2006, more than 2.3 billion people (around 36 percent of the world's population) live in nations that Freedom House rates as Not Free.[27] Helping improve the lot of the one-third or more of the earth's inhabitants who suffer from these startling levels of deprivation and oppression is, at least from a global perspective, probably the greatest moral challenge facing today's commercial societies.

The North could and should devote far, far more resources to development assistance than it is currently devoting. As Smith would surely point out, though, one of the biggest steps the North could take to help the South is simply to let their exports in—trade in addition to aid. Today's commercial societies generally preach the doctrine of free trade, but they consistently fail to practice what they preach, to the great detriment of the world's poor: the World Bank estimates that the North's trade barriers (in particular, its protectionist agricultural policies) cost the South at least $100 billion annually in lost exports, which is roughly double what these nations currently receive in aid.[28] Smith argued, as so many proponents of commercial

27. See *Freedom in the World 2006*.
28. See World Bank, *Globalization, Growth, and Poverty*, 53.

society would after him, that commerce could do much to lift nations out of poverty and help them attain liberty and security—in contemporary terms, that trade could spur development. But we should be clear about Smith's priorities here: while development is so often measured today by a nation's GDP or per capita income, we have seen that Smith himself attached at least as much importance to the other side of development, the promotion of liberty and security. Smith's viewpoint on development in today's world, then, would likely be something along the lines of Amartya Sen's conception of development *as* freedom, meaning that development should be seen not simply as economic growth but rather as "a process of expanding the real freedoms that people enjoy," a process that "requires the removal of major sources of unfreedom: poverty as well as tyranny, poor economic opportunities as well as systematic social deprivation, neglect of public facilities as well as intolerance or overactivity of repressive states."[29]

Extending the benefits of commercial society to the noncommercial world is an immensely important and difficult task, but it is far from the only one today's commercial societies face. After all, even if commercial society is preferable, on balance, to the historical alternatives, it is only preferable *on balance;* Smith would be the first to point out that many serious problems remain *within* today's commercial societies. As we have seen throughout this book, Smith himself constantly insisted on the existence and importance of commercial society's shortcomings, from great economic inequalities to the corruption of people's characters, and from the malicious activities of the rich and powerful to people's tendency to toil and strive for ever-more material goods. These problems are all still with us to one degree or another, and new problems have arisen since Smith's time—worries about climate change and the environment, for example. Smith does not offer a prescription for passivity or quietism in the face of such problems: he was a *reformer,* not a facile champion of existing society. His writings cannot offer specific policy prescriptions for our very different world, of course,[30] but I think his most enthusiastic admirers and most strident critics alike could learn something from the pragmatic character of his approach.

Let's take the problem of combating poverty as an illustration. We saw in Chapter 3 that providing for the poor was one of Smith's deepest and most enduring concerns, and his main (though not only) policy proposal on this

29. Sen, *Development as Freedom,* 3.
30. On the difficulties of establishing where Smith might stand on contemporary political issues, see Fleischacker, *On Adam Smith's Wealth of Nations,* chap. 12.

score was the elimination of the restrictive mercantilist policies of the eighteenth century that gave privileges to the wealthy. Such a proposal, of course, is now rather dated: very few people in today's commercial societies believe that merely instituting free enterprise is sufficient to ensure that the poor are adequately provided for. But the fact that Smith thought this was the appropriate course of action in his time does *not* mean that it is also what he would propose in the twenty-first century; in his eyes this was the first step that needed to be taken, but there is absolutely no indication in his writings that he thought the elimination of the worst mercantilist policies was the *only* measure that would ever be needed to combat the problem of poverty. Indeed, it is hard to imagine, given the high priority he placed on improving the lot of the poor, that he would not advocate taking further steps toward this goal today, especially in our era of astonishing opulence. It is impossible to say exactly *what* measures Smith would advocate taking to combat poverty today, but the pragmatic character of his approach suggests that he would be open to almost any possibility, including redistribution, social welfare measures, "living wage" laws, and so on.

It might be protested that such measures smack of the kind of "government intervention" that Smith so heavily opposed, but we saw in Chapter 4 that he only opposed *certain kinds* of government intervention and did not take any kind of principled stand against government in general. As Jerry Muller writes, "Smith's many comments on the evil and folly of politicians and legislators were no more a condemnation of government than his many criticisms of merchants were a condemnation of commerce."[31] The government interventions to which Smith objected most strongly were the laws of his time that were designed by and intended to help the rich and powerful; it is far from clear that he would also object to twenty-first century interventions designed to curb their influence and aid the very poor. Smith believed that free markets were generally both an effective means of promoting growth and a valuable component of freedom itself, but he was not dogmatic about this belief. For instance, if poverty causes a greater degree of unfreedom among the poor than restricting markets in some way would for the population as a whole—an entirely plausible scenario—then Smith's stated priorities (that liberty and security are by far the most important of commerce's effects) indicate that he would likely favor aiding the poor even at the cost of hampering free trade to some degree. Of course, he would want

---

31. Muller, *Adam Smith in His Time and Ours*, 203.

to aid the poor in the most effective and efficient way possible and would likely want to *minimize* the degree to which free trade is hampered, but to suggest that he would rigidly adhere to a doctrine of free trade even at the cost of condemning the poor to a life of dependence and insecurity is to radically misunderstand the nature of his thought. Those who think of themselves as Smith's heirs, then, ought to put the problem of combating poverty high on their priority list (as they so often do not).

The fact that Smith strenuously advocated repealing the mercantilist policies of his time that privileged the wealthy but that he did not look too far beyond this first step or put forward any kind of theoretical or comprehensive program for combating poverty helps highlight another aspect of his pragmatic approach, which we might call his gradualism or meliorism. Smith was certainly no simple defender of the status quo or opponent of political change, we have seen, but he did argue that change should generally proceed incrementally; the steps toward reform do not even necessarily have to be small ones—recall yet again his claim that *The Wealth of Nations* was a "very violent attack . . . upon the whole commercial system of Great Britain" (CAS, 251)—but they should be taken one at a time, on his view. While Smith himself argued for significant reforms, he forcefully criticized the "spirit of system" that leads people to try to design entirely new institutions on the basis of abstract principles: "to insist upon establishing, and upon establishing all at once, and in spite of all opposition, every thing which [a systematical idea of the perfection of policy and law] may seem to require, must often be the highest degree of arrogance" (TMS VI.ii.2.18, 234). Improvements can and should be made to ameliorate commercial society's problems, according to Smith, but policy makers should begin with existing institutions and proceed piecemeal, carefully weighing the available options and continually taking changing historical circumstances into account. The nature of human beings and of society places limits on what can be accomplished through social reform, and an awareness of the often rather repellant record of precommercial societies should provide a crucial check on aspirations toward a perfect world.

Smith's pragmatic, gradualist approach can be contrasted with the approach taken by Rousseau and many of his successors. Rousseau's writings push in two different–even opposite—directions, both of which differ sharply from the one advocated by Smith. On the one hand, Rousseau's radical critique of virtually every aspect of the European world of his time seems to be a revolutionary call to arms; his famous assertion that "man is born free, and everywhere he is in chains" (*SC* I-1, 131) has often been read—perhaps against Rousseau's own intentions—as an invitation to rise up, break the chains, and institute something wholly new and different.[32] This was, of course, the side of his thought that inspired the French Revolutionaries. On the other hand, Rousseau's writings often take on something of the character of a jeremiad, lamenting the nearly irresistible spread and triumph of a form of society that he thinks will bring little but gross injustice, moral decay, and misery. This pessimistic side of his thought occasionally led him to advocate a reactionary political solution, as in his *Plan for a Constitution for Corsica,* where he counseled the Corsicans to try to doggedly preserve the kind of egalitarian, autarkic, agrarian societies that were quickly disappearing in eighteenth-century Europe. In his even more pessimistic moments, Rousseau cast aside politics altogether and recommended individual withdrawal from society's corrupting influences as the only feasible alternative to the ills of commercial society—the route he claims to have taken in *The Reveries of a Solitary Walker.* While Smith agreed with Rousseau that commercial society entails numerous problems, he advocated pragmatic action rather than revolution (which he saw as dangerous), reactionary conservatism (which he saw as futile and undesirable in any case), or solitary withdrawal (which he probably would have seen as selfish).

Smith's prudent yet constructive approach is, I have argued, largely a result of his realism about the historical alternatives to commercial society. This kind of historical realism is also, I think, one of the most valuable lessons to be taken from Smith's writings for today's critics of commercial society on both ends of the political spectrum: too seldom, when we lament the downfalls of our society, do we ask the Smithian question, "In comparison to what?" Given the predominance of commercial society in the modern West, it is easy for us to lose sight of this question in a way that it was not for Smith and his contemporaries, for whom commercial society was something essentially new and different. Hence, Smith helps call our attention to the fact that in most precommercial societies—the vast majority of human history—problems such as famine, disease, violence, and servitude

---

32. Marx, interestingly, fell on both sides of this dichotomy: he accepted Smith's contention that commercial society constituted a major improvement over the societies that had come before it, but he was also nothing if not a supporter of revolution. This seeming contradiction was of course a result of Marx's historicist perspective—itself derived from Rousseau, via Kant and Hegel—which led him to believe that the upward trend of history could continue until virtually all problems were solved. Needless to say, the history of communism since his time has cast some doubt on this possibility.

were the rule rather than the exception. Nostalgic and romantic longings not-withstanding, I suspect that few people today would want to return to the Middle Ages—or even ancient Greece at its peak, for that matter—in full awareness of all that such a return would entail. And our appreciation for the benefits of commercial society can of course only be heightened when we further compare it to the fascist and communist societies of the twen-tieth century. When commercial society's virtues and vices are considered relative to the historical alternatives, it becomes difficult to take entirely seri-ously the kind of sweeping denouncements of this form of society that Rous-seau and some of his successors have put forth. Those of us living in today's commercial societies perhaps ought to think twice, then, before demanding radical change, especially when such change would be based on abstract, ahistorical principles or visions of an ideal society.

Yet neither, needless to say, should we ignore the downsides of commer-cial society. Because Smith was continually, soberly aware of the potential drawbacks of this kind of society and the critical importance of addressing them, his writings offer some useful reminders to today's champions of commercial society, who tend to excuse its faults in the name of more growth and greater affluence. Too many of today's self-proclaimed "Smithians" choose to remember the Smith who argued against many forms of govern-ment intervention in the economy; too many forget the Smith who railed against poverty and the selfish greed of the rich and powerful and who con-stantly emphasized the need for things like a strong central government to enforce rules of fair play and state-supported education to remedy the divi-sion of labor's potential stultifying effects. When today's defenders of com-mercial society simply overlook these and other problems, they are not being true to Smith's thought, nor are they being true friends of commercial soci-ety. It is precisely because commercial society is (to adapt Winston Chur-chill's famous line about democracy) the worst form of society except for all the others that have been tried that we need to pragmatically address its shortcomings even as we defend it against utopian aspirations for a perfect world. As Smith's writings remind us, only once we ameliorate the prob-lems of commercial society will we be able to redeem its real promise.

REFERENCES

Annas, Julia. *The Morality of Happiness*. Oxford: Oxford University Press, 1993.
Aristotle. *Nichomachean Ethics*. 2nd ed. Trans. Terence Irwin. Indianapolis: Hackett Publishing, 1999.
————. *The Politics*. Trans. Carnes Lord. Chicago: University of Chicago Press, 1984.
Bagehot, Walter. "Adam Smith as a Person." In *Biographical Studies*. London: Longmans, Green, 1895.
Barry, Norman. "Hume, Smith, and Rousseau on Freedom." In *Rousseau and Liberty*. Ed. Robert Wokler. Manchester: Manchester University Press, 1995.
Baugh, Daniel. "Poverty, Protestantism, and Political Economy: English Attitudes Toward the Poor, 1660–1800." In *England's Rise to Greatness*. Ed. Stephen B. Baxter. Berkeley and Los Angeles: University of California Press, 1983.
Berlin, Isaiah. *Freedom and Its Betrayal: Six Enemies of Human Liberty*. Princeton: Princeton University Press, 2002.
Berry, Christopher J. "Adam Smith: Commerce, Liberty, and Modernity." In *Philosophers of the Enlightenment*. Ed. Peter Gilmour. Totowa: Barnes and Noble Books, 1990.
————. *Social Theory of the Scottish Enlightenment*. Edinburgh: Edinburgh University Press, 1997.
Bloom, Allan. "Introduction." In Jean-Jacques Rousseau. *Emile, or On Education*. Trans. Allan Bloom. New York: Basic Books, 1979.
————. "Rousseau's Critique of Liberal Constitutionalism." In *The Legacy of Rousseau*. Ed. Clifford Orwin and Nathan Tarcov. Chicago: University of Chicago Press, 1997.
Blum, Carol. *Rousseau and the Republic of Virtue: The Language of Politics in the French Revolution*. Ithaca: Cornell University Press, 1986.
Bonar, James. *A Catalogue of the Library of Adam Smith*. 2nd ed. New York: A. M. Kelley, 1966.
Burgelin, Pierre. *La philosophie de l'existence de Jean-Jacques Rousseau*. Paris: Presses Universitaires de France, 1952.
Burke, Edmund. *Reflections on the Revolution in France*. Stanford: Stanford University Press, 2001.
Campbell, T. D. *Adam Smith's Science of Morals*. London: George Allen and Unwin, 1971.
Caton, Hiram. *The Politics of Progress: The Origins and Development of the Commercial Republic, 1600–1835*. Gainesville: University of Florida Press, 1988.
————. "The Preindustrial Economics of Adam Smith." *Journal of Economic History* 45 (1985): 833–53.

Coats, A. W. "Adam Smith and the Mercantile System." In *Essays on Adam Smith*. Ed. Andrew S. Skinner and Thomas Wilson. Oxford: Clarendon Press, 1975.

Colletti, Lucio. *From Rousseau to Lenin: Studies in Ideology and Society*. New York: Monthly Review Press, 1972.

Cohler, Anne M. *Rousseau and Nationalism*. New York: Basic Books, 1970.

Cooper, Laurence D. *Rousseau, Nature, and the Problem of the Good Life*. University Park: Pennsylvania State University Press, 1999.

Cranston, Maurice. *Jean-Jacques: The Early Life and Works of Jean-Jacques Rousseau, 1712–1754*. Chicago: University of Chicago Press, 1982.

———. *The Noble Savage: Jean-Jacques Rousseau, 1754–1762*. Chicago: University of Chicago Press, 1991.

———. *The Solitary Self: Jean-Jacques Rousseau in Exile and Adversity*. Chicago: University of Chicago Press, 1997.

Crocker, Lester G. *Rousseau's Social Contract: An Interpretive Essay*. Cleveland: Case Western Reserve University Press, 1968.

Cropsey, Joseph. *Polity and Economy: With Further Thoughts on the Principles of Adam Smith*. South Bend: St. Augustine's Press, 2001.

Darwall, Stephen. "Equal Dignity in Adam Smith." *Adam Smith Review* 1 (2004): 129–34.

———. "Sympathetic Liberalism: Recent Work on Adam Smith." *Philosophy and Public Affairs* 28 (1999): 139–64.

Dawson, Deidre. "Is Sympathy So Surprising? Adam Smith and French Fictions of Sympathy." *Eighteenth-Century Life* 15 (1991): 147–62.

De Marchi, Neil, and Jonathan A. Greene. "Adam Smith and Private Provision of the Arts." *History of Political Economy* 37 (2005): 431–54.

Den Uyl, Douglas J. *The Virtue of Prudence*. New York: Peter Lang, 1991.

Descartes, René. *The Philosophical Writings of Descartes*. 2 vols. Trans. John Cottingham, Robert Stoothoff, and Dugald Murdoch. Cambridge: Cambridge University Press, 1985.

Diener, Ed, and Carol Diener. "The Wealth of Nations Revisited: Income and the Quality of Life." *Social Indicators Research* 36 (1995): 275–86.

Diener, Ed, and Shigehiro Suh. "Money and Happiness: Income and Subjective Well-Being Across Nations." In *Culture and Subjective Well-Being*. Ed. Ed Diener and Eunkook M. Suh. Cambridge, Mass.: MIT Press, 2003.

Easterbrook, Gregg. *The Progress Paradox: How Life Gets Better While People Feel Worse*. New York: Random House, 2003.

Edgerton, Robert B. *Sick Societies: Challenging the Myth of Primitive Harmony*. New York: Free Press, 1992.

Edmonds, David, and John Eidinow. *Rousseau's Dog: Two Great Thinkers at War in the Age of Enlightenment*. New York: HarperCollins, 2006.

Encyclopedia: Selections. Trans. Nelly S. Hoyt and Thomas Cassirer. Indianapolis: Bobbs-Merrill, 1965.

Fleischacker, Samuel. *On Adam Smith's Wealth of Nations: A Philosophical Companion*. Princeton: Princeton University Press, 2004.

———. "On Adam Smith's 'Wealth of Nations': Response." *Adam Smith Review* 2 (2006): 246–58.

———. "Philosophy in Moral Practice: Kant and Adam Smith." *Kant-Studien* 82 (1991): 249–69.

———. Review of Charles Griswold, *Adam Smith and the Virtues of Enlightenment*. In *Mind* 109 (2000): 16–23.

———. "Smith und der Kulturrelativismus." In *Adam Smith als Moralphilosoph*. Ed. Christel Fricke and Hans-Peter Schütt. Berlin: Walter de Gruyter, 2005.

———. *A Third Concept of Liberty: Judgment and Freedom in Kant and Adam Smith*. Princeton: Princeton University Press, 1999.

Fogel, Robert William. *The Escape from Hunger and Premature Death, 1700–2100: Europe, America, and the Third World*. Cambridge: Cambridge University Press, 2004.

Forbes, Duncan. "Sceptical Whiggism, Commerce, and Liberty." In *Essays on Adam Smith*. Ed. Andrew S. Skinner and Thomas Wilson. Oxford: Clarendon Press, 1975.

———. "'Scientific' Whiggism: Adam Smith and John Millar." *Cambridge Journal* 7 (1954): 643–70.

Force, Pierre. *Self-Interest Before Adam Smith: A Genealogy of Economic Science*. Cambridge: Cambridge University Press, 2003.

———. "Self-Love, Identification, and the Origin of Political Economy." *Yale French Studies* 92 (1997): 46–64.

Frank, Robert H. *Choosing the Right Pond: Human Behavior and the Quest for Status*. Oxford: Oxford University Press, 1985.

Freedom House. *Freedom in the World 2006*. www.freedomhouse.org/template.cfm?page=15&year=2006.

Fridén, Bertil. *Rousseau's Economic Philosophy: Beyond the Market of Innocents*. Dordrecht: Kluwer Academic Publishers, 1998.

Friedman, Benjamin M. *The Moral Consequences of Economic Growth*. New York: Alfred A. Knopf, 2005.

Friedman, Thomas L. *The Lexus and the Olive Tree*. New York: Anchor Books, 2000.

Fukuyama, Francis. *The End of History and the Last Man*. New York: Free Press, 1992.

———. *The End of History and the Last Man*. Reprint ed. New York: Free Press, 2006.

———. *Trust: The Social Virtues and the Creation of Prosperity*. New York: Simon and Schuster, 1995.

Furet, François. "Rousseau and the French Revolution." In *The Legacy of Rousseau*. Ed. Clifford Orwin and Nathan Tarcov. Chicago: University of Chicago Press, 1997.

Garrard, Graeme. *Rousseau's Counter-Enlightenment: A Republican Critique of the Philosophes*. Albany: SUNY Press, 2003.

Gay, Peter. *The Enlightenment: An Interpretation, Vol. 1: The Rise of Modern Paganism*. New York: W. W. Norton, 1966.

———. *The Enlightenment: An Interpretation, Vol. 2: The Science of Freedom*. New York: W. W. Norton, 1969.

———. *The Party of Humanity: Essays in the French Enlightenment*. New York: Alfred A. Knopf, 1964.

Ghiglieri, Michael P. *The Dark Side of Man: Tracing the Origins of Male Violence*. Reading: Perseus Books, 1999.

Gourevitch, Victor. "Rousseau's Pure State of Nature." *Interpretation* 16 (1988): 23–59.

Grant, Ruth W. *Hypocrisy and Integrity: Machiavelli, Rousseau, and the Ethics of Politics*. Chicago: University of Chicago Press, 1997.

Grimsley, Ronald. "Rousseau and the Problem of Happiness." In *Hobbes and Rousseau:*

A Collection of Critical Essays. Ed. Maurice Cranston and Richard S. Peters. Garden City: Doubleday, 1972.

Griswold, Charles L., Jr. *Adam Smith and the Virtues of Enlightenment*. Cambridge: Cambridge University Press, 1999.

Gwartney, James, and Robert Lawson, eds. *Economic Freedom of the World: 2005 Annual Report*. Vancouver: Fraser Institute, 2005.

Haakonssen, Knud. "Adam Smith." In *The Routledge Encyclopedia of Philosophy*. Vol. 8. Ed. Edward Craig. London: Routledge, 1998.

———. *The Science of a Legislator: The Natural Jurisprudence of David Hume and Adam Smith*. Cambridge: Cambridge University Press, 1981.

Hamowy, Ronald. *The Scottish Enlightenment and the Theory of Spontaneous Order*. Carbondale: Southern Illinois University Press, 1987.

Hanley, Ryan. "From Geneva to Glasgow: Rousseau and Adam Smith on the Theatre and Commercial Society." *Studies in Eighteenth-Century Culture* 35 (2006): 177–202.

———. "Commerce and Corruption: Rousseau's Diagnosis and Adam Smith's Cure." Forthcoming in *European Journal of Political Theory*, 2008.

Hartwell, R. M. "Comment." In *The Market and the State*. Ed. Thomas Wilson and Andrew S. Skinner. Oxford: Oxford University Press, 1976.

Heilbroner, Robert L. "The Paradox of Progress: Decline and Decay in *The Wealth of Nations*." In *Essays on Adam Smith*. Ed. Andrew S. Skinner and Thomas Wilson. Oxford: Clarendon Press, 1975.

———. *The Worldly Philosophers: The Lives, Times, and Ideas of the Great Economic Thinkers*. 7th ed. New York: Simon and Schuster, 1999.

Herman, Arthur. *How the Scots Invented the Modern World*. New York: Three Rivers Press, 2001.

Himmelfarb, Gertrude. *The Idea of Poverty: England in the Early Industrial Age*. New York: Alfred A. Knopf, 1984.

Hirsch, Fred. *The Social Limits to Growth*. Cambridge, Mass.: Harvard University Press, 1976.

Hirschman, Albert O. *The Passions and the Interests: Political Arguments for Capitalism Before Its Triumph*. Princeton: Princeton University Press, 1997.

Hobbes, Thomas. *Leviathan*. Ed. Edwin Curley. Indianapolis: Hackett, 1994.

Hollander, Samuel. *The Economics of Adam Smith*. Toronto: University of Toronto Press, 1973.

Holmes, Stephen. *The Anatomy of Antiliberalism*. Cambridge, Mass.: Harvard University Press, 1993.

———. "The Secret History of Self-Interest." In *Passions and Constraint: On the Theory of Liberal Democracy*. Chicago: University of Chicago Press, 1995.

Hont, Istvan. "The Language of Sociability and Commerce: Samuel Pufendorf and the Theoretical Foundations of the Four Stages Theory." In *The Languages of Political Theory in Early Modern Europe*. Ed. Anthony Pagden. Cambridge: Cambridge University Press, 1987.

———. "The 'Rich Country–Poor Country' Debate in Scottish Classical Political Economy." In *Wealth and Virtue: The Shaping of Political Economy in the Scottish Enlightenment*. Ed. Istvan Hont and Michael Ignatieff. Cambridge: Cambridge University Press, 1983.

Hont, Istvan, and Michael Ignatieff. "Needs and Justice in the *Wealth of Nations*."

In *Wealth and Virtue: The Shaping of Political Economy in the Scottish Enlightenment.* Ed. Istvan Hont and Michael Ignatieff. Cambridge: Cambridge University Press, 1983.

Hopfl, H. M. "From Savage to Scotsman: Conjectural History in the Scottish Enlightenment." *Journal of British Studies* 17 (1978): 19–40.

Hulliung, Mark. *The Autocritique of Enlightenment: Rousseau and the Philosophes.* Cambridge, Mass.: Harvard University Press, 1994.

Hume, David. *Essays: Moral, Political, and Literary.* Ed. Eugene F. Miller. Indianapolis: Liberty Fund, 1987.

———. *The History of England.* 6 vols. Indianapolis: Liberty Fund, 1983.

———. *The Letters of David Hume.* Ed. J. Y. T. Greig. 2 vols. Oxford: Clarendon Press, 1932.

———. *A Treatise of Human Nature.* 2nd ed. Ed. L. A. Selby-Bigge and P. H. Nidditch. Oxford: Clarendon Press, 1978.

Hundert, E. G. *The Enlightenment's Fable: Bernard Mandeville and the Discovery of Society.* Cambridge: Cambridge University Press, 1994.

———. "The Thread of Language and the Web of Dominion: Mandeville to Rousseau and Back." *Eighteenth-Century Studies* 21 (1987–88): 169–91.

Hurtado Prieto, Jimena. "Bernard Mandeville's Heir: Adam Smith or Jean Jacques Rousseau on the Possibility of Economic Analysts." *European Journal of the History of Economic Thought* 11 (2004): 1–31.

Ignatieff, Michael. "Smith, Rousseau, and the Republic of Needs." In *Scotland and Europe, 1200–1850.* Ed. T. C. Smout. Edinburgh: John Donald, 1986.

Jack, Malcolm. *Corruption and Progress: The Eighteenth-Century Debate.* New York: AMS Press, 1989.

———. "One State of Nature: Mandeville and Rousseau." *Journal of the History of Ideas* 39 (1978): 119–24.

Johnson, Allen W., and Timothy Earle. *The Evolution of Human Societies: From Foraging Group to Agrarian State.* 2nd ed. Stanford: Stanford University Press, 2000.

Jouvenel, Betrand de. "Rousseau's Theory of the Forms of Government." In *Hobbes and Rousseau: A Collection of Critical Essays.* Ed. Maurice Cranston and Richard S. Peters. Garden City: Doubleday, 1972.

Keeley, Lawrence H. *War Before Civilization: The Myth of the Peaceful Savage.* Oxford: Oxford University Press, 1996.

Kelly, Christopher. *Rousseau's Exemplary Life: The Confessions as Political Philosophy.* Ithaca: Cornell University Press, 1987.

Kelly, Christopher, and Roger D. Masters. "Rousseau's Prediction of the European Revolution." In *Jean-Jacques Rousseau et la Révolution, Pensée Libre 3.* Ottawa: North American Association for the Study of Jean-Jacques Rousseau, 1991.

Kennedy, Gavin. *Adam Smith's Lost Legacy.* New York: Palgrave Macmillan, 2005.

Kindleberger, C. P. "The Historical Background: Adam Smith and the Industrial Revolution." In *The Market and the State.* Ed. Thomas Wilson and Andrew S. Skinner. Oxford: Oxford University Press, 1976.

Lane, Robert E. *The Loss of Happiness in Market Democracies.* New Haven: Yale University Press, 2000.

Layard, Richard. *Happiness: Lessons from a New Science.* New York: Penguin Books, 2005.

LeBlanc, Steven A. *Constant Battles: The Myth of the Noble Savage and a Peaceful Past*. New York: St. Martin's Press, 2003.

Leigh, R. A. "Liberté et autorité dans le *Contrat social*." In *Jean-Jacques Rousseau et son oeuvre*. Paris: Librarie C. Klincksieck, 1964.

———. "Rousseau and the Scottish Enlightenment." *Contributions to Political Economy* 5 (1986): 1–21.

Lewis, Thomas J. "Persuasion, Domination, and Exchange: Adam Smith on the Political Consequences of Markets." *Canadian Journal of Political Science* 33 (2000): 273–89.

Locke, John. *Two Treatises of Government*. Ed. Peter Laslett. Cambridge: Cambridge University Press, 1988.

Lomonaco, Jeffrey. "Adam Smith's 'Letter to the Authors of the *Edinburgh Review*.'" *Journal of the History of Ideas* 63 (2002): 659–76.

Macfie, A. L. "Adam Smith's Moral Sentiments as Foundation for His Wealth of Nations." *Oxford Economic Papers* 11 (1959): 209–28.

———. *The Individual in Society: Papers on Adam Smith*. London: George Allen and Unwin, 1967.

Maine, Henry Sumner. *Ancient Law: Its Connection with the Early History of Society and Its Relation to Modern Ideas*. Boston: Beacon Press, 1963.

Malthus, Thomas. *The Works of Robert Thomas Malthus*. 8 vols. Ed. Edward A. Wrigley and David Souden. London: Pickering and Chatto, 1986.

Mandeville, Bernard. *The Fable of the Bees: or Private Vices, Publick Benefits*. 2 vols. Ed. F. B. Kaye. Indianapolis: Liberty Fund, 1988.

Marshall, Monty G., and Robert Gurr. *Peace and Conflict 2005*. College Park, Md.: Center for International Development and Conflict Management, 2005.

Marx, Karl. *The Marx–Engels Reader*. 2nd ed. Ed. Robert C. Tucker. New York: W. W. Norton, 1978.

Maryanski, Alexandra, and Jonathan H. Turner. *The Social Cage: Human Nature and the Evolution of Society*. Stanford: Stanford University Press, 1992.

Masters, Roger D. *The Political Philosophy of Rousseau*. Princeton: Princeton University Press, 1968.

———. "Rousseau and the Rediscovery of Human Nature." In *The Legacy of Rousseau*. Ed. Clifford Orwin and Nathan Tarcov. Chicago: University of Chicago Press, 1997.

McCloskey, Deirdre N. *The Bourgeois Virtues: Ethics for an Age of Commerce*. Chicago: University of Chicago Press, 2006.

McLean, Iain. *Adam Smith, Radical and Egalitarian: An Interpretation for the 21st Century*. Edinburgh: Edinburgh University Press, 2006.

McMahon, Darrin M. *Enemies of the Enlightenment: The French Counter-Enlightenment and the Making of Modernity*. Oxford: Oxford University Press, 2001.

Meek, Ronald L. "The Scottish Contribution to Marxist Sociology." In *Economics and Ideology and Other Essays: Studies in the Development of Economic Thought*. London: Chapman and Hall, 1967.

———. *Smith, Marx, and After: Ten Essays in the Development of Economic Thought*. London: Chapman and Hall, 1977.

———. *Social Science and the Ignoble Savage*. Cambridge: Cambridge University Press, 1976.

Meek, Ronald L., and Andrew S. Skinner. "The Development of Adam Smith's Ideas on the Division of Labor." *Economic Journal* 83 (1973): 1094–116.

Melzer, Arthur. *The Natural Goodness of Man: On the System of Rousseau's Thought.* Chicago: University of Chicago Press, 1990.

———. "The Origin of the Counter-Enlightenment: Rousseau and the New Religion of Sincerity." *American Political Science Review* 90 (1996): 344–60.

———. "Rousseau and the Modern Cult of Sincerity." In *The Legacy of Rousseau.* Ed. Clifford Orwin and Nathan Tarcov. Chicago: University of Chicago Press, 1997.

Millar, John. *An Historical View of the English Government.* In William C. Lehman. *John Millar of Glasgow.* Cambridge: Cambridge University Press, 1960.

———. *The Origin of the Distinction of Ranks.* In William C. Lehman. *John Millar of Glasgow.* Cambridge: Cambridge University Press, 1960.

Miller, James. *Rousseau: Dreamer of Democracy.* New Haven: Yale University Press, 1984.

Minowitz, Peter. *Profits, Priests, and Princes: Adam Smith's Emancipation of Economics from Politics and Religion.* Stanford: Stanford University Press, 1993.

Mizuta, Hiroshi, ed. *Adam Smith's Library: A Catalogue.* Oxford: Clarendon Press, 2000.

Montes, Leonidas. *Adam Smith in Context: A Critical Reassessment of Some Central Components of His Thought.* New York: Palgrave Macmillan, 2004.

Montesquieu, Charles de Secondat, baron de. *The Spirit of the Laws.* Trans. Anne M. Cohler, Basia C. Miller, and Harold S. Stone. Cambridge: Cambridge University Press, 1989.

Morrow, Glenn R. *Ethical and Economic Theories of Adam Smith.* New York: Longmans, Green, 1923.

Mossner, Ernest Campbell. *The Life of David Hume.* 2nd ed. Oxford: Clarendon Press, 1980.

Mueller, John. *The Remnants of War.* Ithaca: Cornell University Press, 2004.

———. *Retreat from Doomsday: The Obsolescence of Major War.* New York: Basic Books, 1989.

Muller, Jerry Z. *Adam Smith in His Time and Ours.* Princeton: Princeton University Press, 1993.

Neuhouser, Frederick. "*Wealth of Nations* and Social Science." *Adam Smith Review* 2 (2006): 233–38.

North, Douglass C., and Robert Paul Thomas. *The Rise of the Western World: A New Economic History.* Cambridge: Cambridge University Press, 1973.

Orwin, Clifford, and Nathan Tarcov. "Introduction." In *The Legacy of Rousseau.* Ed. Clifford Orwin and Nathan Tarcov. Chicago: University of Chicago Press, 1997.

Otteson, James R. *Adam Smith's Marketplace of Life.* Cambridge: Cambridge University Press, 2002.

Pack, Spencer J. *Capitalism as a Moral System: Adam Smith's Critique of the Free Market Economy.* Aldershot: Edward Elgar, 1991.

———. "The Rousseau–Smith Connection: Towards an Understanding of Professor West's 'Splenetic Smith.'" *History of Economic Ideas* 8 (2000): 35–62.

Palmer, Michael. "The Citizen Philosopher: Rousseau's Dedicatory Letter to the *Discourse on Inequality.*" *Interpretation* 17 (1989): 19–39.

Pascal, Roy. "Property and Society: The Scottish Contribution of the Eighteenth Century." *Modern Quarterly* 1 (1938): 167–79.

Peled, Yoav. "Rousseau's Inhibited Radicalism: An Analysis of His Political Thought in Light of His Economic Ideas." *American Political Science Review* 74 (1980): 1034–45.

Plamenatz, John. "Ce qui ne signifie autre chose sinon qu'on le forcera d'être libre." In *Hobbes and Rousseau: A Collection of Critical Essays*. Ed. Maurice Cranston and Richard S. Peters. Garden City: Doubleday, 1972.

Plato. *The Republic*. Trans. Allan Bloom. New York: Basic Books, 1968.

Plattner, Marc. *Rousseau's State of Nature: An Interpretation of the* Discourse on Inequality. Dekalb: Northern Illinois University Press, 1979.

Plutarch. *Lives of the Noble Grecians and Romans*. Trans. John Dryden. New York: Modern Library, 2001.

Pocock, J. G. A. *Barbarism and Religion, Vol. 2: Narratives of Civil Government*. Cambridge: Cambridge University Press, 1999.

Rae, John. *Life of Adam Smith*. With introductory guide by Jacob Viner. New York: Augustus M. Kelley, 1965.

Raphael, D. D. *Adam Smith*. Oxford: Oxford University Press, 1985.

Reisert, Joseph R. *Jean-Jacques Rousseau: A Friend of Virtue*. Ithaca: Cornell University Press, 2003.

Robinson, John P., and Geoffrey Godbey. *Time for Life*. 2nd ed. University Park: Pennsylvania State University Press, 1999.

Roddier, Henri. *J.-J. Rousseau en Angleterre au XVIIIe siècle*. Paris: Boivin & Cie., 1950.

Rosenberg, Nathan. "Adam Smith and Laissez-Faire Revisited." In *Adam Smith and Modern Political Economy: Bicentennial Essays on The Wealth of Nations*. Ed. Gerald P. O'Driscoll Jr. Ames: Iowa State University Press, 1979.

———. "Adam Smith and the Stock of Moral Capital." *History of Political Economy* 22 (1990): 1–17.

———. "Adam Smith on Profits—Paradox Lost and Regained." In *Essays on Adam Smith*. Ed. Andrew S. Skinner and Thomas Wilson. Oxford: Clarendon Press, 1975.

———. "Adam Smith on the Division of Labor: Two Views or One?" *Economica* 32 (1965): 127–39.

———. "Some Institutional Aspects of the Wealth of Nations." *Journal of Political Economy* 68 (1960): 557–70.

Rosenblatt, Helena. *Rousseau and Geneva: From the First Discourse to the Social Contract, 1749–1762*. Cambridge: Cambridge University Press, 1997.

Ross, Ian Simpson. *The Life of Adam Smith*. Oxford: Clarendon Press, 1995.

Rothschild, Emma. *Economic Sentiments: Adam Smith, Condorcet, and the Enlightenment*. Cambridge, Mass.: Harvard University Press, 2001.

Ruggiero, Guido de. *The History of European Liberalism*. Trans. R. G. Collingwood. Oxford: Oxford University Press, 1927.

Saint Fond, B. Faujas de. *A Journey Through England and Scotland to the Hebrides in 1784*. Trans. Sir Archibald Geikie. 2 vols. Glasgow: Hugh Hopkins, 1907.

Salkever, Stephen G. "Rousseau and the Concept of Happiness." *Politics* 11 (1978): 27–45.

Schliesser, Eric. "Adam Smith's Benevolent and Self-Interested Conception of Philosophy." In *New Voices on Adam Smith*. Ed. Leonidas Montes and Eric Schliesser. New York: Routledge, 2006.

Schumpeter, Joseph. *A History of Economic Analysis*. New York: Oxford University Press, 1954.

Scitovsky, Tibor. *The Joyless Economy: The Psychology of Human Satisfaction*. Oxford: Oxford University Press, 1992.

Scott, John T., and Robert Zaretsky. *So Great a Noise: Jean-Jacques Rousseau, David Hume, and the End of Enlightenment*. New Haven: Yale University Press, forthcoming.

Scott, W. R. *Adam Smith as Student and Professor*. Glasgow: Jackson, Son and Company, 1937.

———. "Studies Relating to Adam Smith During the Last Fifty Years." In *Proceedings of the British Academy*. Ed. A. L. Macfie. London: British Academy, 1940.

Sen, Amartya. *Development as Freedom*. New York: Anchor Books, 1999.

Service, Elman R. *Origins of the State and Civilization: The Process of Cultural Evolution*. New York: W. W. Norton, 1975.

Sewall, Richard B. "Rousseau's Second Discourse in England from 1755 to 1762." *Philological Quarterly* 17 (1938): 97–114.

Sher, Richard B. "Adam Ferguson, Adam Smith, and the Problem of National Defense." *Journal of Modern History* 61 (1989): 240–68.

Shklar, Judith. *Men and Citizens: A Study of Rousseau's Social Theory*. Cambridge: Cambridge University Press, 1969.

———. *Political Thought and Political Thinkers*. Chicago: University of Chicago Press, 1998.

Skinner, Andrew S. "Adam Smith: An Economic Interpretation of History." In *Essays on Adam Smith*. Ed. Andrew S. Skinner and Thomas Wilson. Oxford: Clarendon Press, 1975.

———. *A System of Social Science: Papers Relating to Adam Smith*. 2nd ed. Oxford: Clarendon Press, 1996.

Smout, T. C. *A History of the Scottish People, 1560–1830*. New York: Charles Scribner's Sons, 1969.

Starobinski, Jean. *Jean-Jacques Rousseau: Transparency and Obstruction*. Trans. Arthur Goldhammer. Chicago: University of Chicago Press, 1988.

Stewart, Dugald. "Account of the Life and Writings of Adam Smith, LL.D." In Adam Smith, *Essays in Philosophical Subjects*. Ed. W. P. D. Wightman and J. C. Bryce. Indianapolis: Liberty Fund, 1982.

Talmon, Jacob. *The Origins of Totalitarian Democracy*. New York: Praeger, 1960.

Teichgraeber, Richard F. *"Free Trade" and Moral Philosophy: Rethinking the Sources of Adam Smith's Wealth of Nations*. Durham: Duke University Press, 1986.

———. "Rethinking Das Adam Smith Problem." *Journal of British Studies* 20 (1981): 106–23.

Tocqueville, Alexis de. *Democracy in America*. Trans. Harvey C. Mansfield and Delba Winthrop. Chicago: University of Chicago Press, 2000.

Todorov, Tzvetan. "Living Alone Together." *New Literary History* 27 (1996): 1–14.

United Nations Development Programme. *Human Development Report 2005*. Oxford: Oxford University Press, 2005.

Veenhoven, Ruut. "Freedom and Happiness: A Comparative Study in Forty-Four Nations in the Early 1990s." In *Culture and Subjective Well-Being*. Ed. Ed Diener and Eunkook M. Suh. Cambridge, Mass.: MIT Press, 2003.

Viner, Jacob. "Adam Smith and Laissez Faire." In *Adam Smith, 1776–1926*. Chicago: University of Chicago Press, 1928.

Vivenza, Gloria. *Adam Smith and the Classics: The Classical Heritage in Adam Smith's Thought*. Oxford: Oxford University Press, 2001.

Voltaire. *Philosophical Letters*. Trans. Ernest Dilworth. Indianapolis: Bobbs-Merrill, 1961.

Waszek, Norbert. "Two Concepts of Morality: A Distinction of Adam Smith's Ethics and Its Stoic Origin." *Journal of the History of Ideas* 45 (1984): 591–606.

Werhane, Patricia. *Adam Smith and His Legacy for Modern Capitalism*. Oxford: Oxford University Press, 1991.

West, E. G. "Adam Smith and Alienation: Wealth Increases, Men Decay?" In *Essays on Adam Smith*. Ed. Andrew S. Skinner and Thomas Wilson. Oxford: Clarendon Press, 1975.

———. "Adam Smith and Rousseau's *Discourse on Inequality*: Inspiration or Provocation?" *Journal of Economic Issues* 5 (1971): 56–70.

———. "Adam Smith on the Cultural Effects of Specialization: Splenetics Versus Economics." *History of Political Economy* 28 (1996): 83–105.

Winch, Donald. "Adam Smith: Scottish Moral Philosopher as Political Economist." *Historical Journal* 35 (1992): 91–113.

———. "Adam Smith's 'Enduring Particular Result': A Political and Cosmopolitan Perspective." In *Wealth and Virtue: The Shaping of Political Economy in the Scottish Enlightenment*. Ed. Istvan Hont and Michael Ignatieff. Cambridge: Cambridge University Press, 1983.

———. *Adam Smith's Politics: An Essay in Historiographic Revision*. Cambridge: Cambridge University Press, 1978.

———. *Riches and Poverty: An Intellectual History of Political Economy in Britain, 1750–1834*. Cambridge: Cambridge University Press, 1996.

Wokler, Robert. *Rousseau*. Oxford: Oxford University Press, 1995.

———. "Rousseau and His Critics on the Fanciful Liberties We Have Lost." In *Rousseau and Liberty*. Ed. Robert Wokler. Manchester: Manchester University Press, 1995.

———. "Todorov's Otherness." *New Literary History* 27 (1996): 43–55.

World Bank. *Globalization, Growth, and Poverty: Building an Inclusive World Economy*. Washington, D.C.: World Bank, 2002.

Wright, Robert. *Nonzero: The Logic of Human Destiny*. New York: Vintage Books, 2001.

———. "Will Globalization Make You Happy?" *Foreign Policy* 120 (2000): 55–64.

Yack, Bernard. *The Longing for Total Revolution: Philosophic Sources of Social Discontent from Rousseau to Marx and Nietzsche*. Berkeley and Los Angeles: University of California Press, 1992.

INDEX

CPSIA information can be obtained
at www.ICGtesting.com
Printed in the USA
LVHW11s0114220918
590994LV00001B/46/P